Healthcare Research Ethics and Law

The book explores and explains the relationship between law and ethics in the context of medically related research in order to provide a practical guide to understanding for members of research ethics committees (RECs), professionals involved with medical research, and those with an academic interest in the subject.

The law will be set out as it relates to the functions of RECs within the context of the process of ethical review so that it is accessible and readily understood by REC members. Each chapter begins by locating the material within the practical context of ethical review, and goes on to provide a more theoretical and analytical discussion detailing how the theory and practice fit together. The key legal issues of confidentiality, consent and negligence are addressed in detail, as well as a discussion of how and when liability may be incurred in these areas. Alongside this the practical and legal implications of the implementation of European Directive 2001/20/EC are considered together with a discussion of its socio-political background and relevance for medical research in the United Kingdom.

Healthcare Research Ethics and Law will be of great interest to members of RECs, students, academics and professionals involved in all aspects of research ethics.

Professor Hazel Biggs is Professor of Medical Law at the University of Southampton, UK.

Biomedical Law and Ethics Library

Series Editor: Sheila A.M. McLean

Scientific and clinical advances, social and political developments and the impact of healthcare on our lives raise profound ethical and legal questions. Medical law and ethics have become central to our understanding of these problems, and are important tools for the analysis and resolution of problems – real or imagined.

In this series, scholars at the forefront of biomedical law and ethics contribute to the debates in this area, with accessible, thought-provoking, and sometimes controversial ideas. Each book in the series develops an independent hypothesis and argues cogently for a particular position. One of the major contributions of this series is the extent to which both law and ethics are utilised in the content of the books, and the shape of the series itself.

The books in this series are analytical, with a key target audience of lawyers, doctors, nurses, and the intelligent lay public.

Available titles:

Human Fertilisation and Embryology (2006)
Reproducing Regulation
Kirsty Horsey & Hazel Biggs

Intention and Causation in Medical Non-Killing (2006)
The Impact of Criminal Law Concepts on Euthanasia and Assisted Suicide
Glenys Williams

Impairment and Disability (2007)
Law and Ethics at the Beginning and End of Life
Sheila A.M. McLean & Laura Williamson

Bioethics and the Humanities (2007)
Attitudes and Perceptions
Robin Downie & Jane Macnaughton

Defending the Genetic Supermarket (2007)
The Law and Ethics of Selecting the Next Generation
Colin Gavaghan

The Harm Paradox (2007)
Tort Law and the Unwanted Child in an Era of Choice
Nicolette Priaulx

Assisted Dying (2007)
Reflections on the need for law reform
Sheila A.M. McLean

Medicine, Malpractice and Misapprehensions (2007)
Vivienne Harpwood

Euthanasia, Ethics and the Law (2007)
From Conflict to Compromise
Richard Huxtable

Best Interests of the Child in Healthcare (2007)
Sarah Elliston

Values in Medicine (2008)
The realities of clinical practice
Donald Evans

Autonomy, Consent and the Law (2009)
Sheila A.M. McLean

Forthcoming titles include:

Medicine, Law and the Public Interest (2010)
Communitarian Perspectives on Medical Law
J Kenyon Mason and Graeme Laurie

About the Series Editor

Professor Sheila A.M. McLean is International Bar Association Professor of Law and Ethics in Medicine and Director of the Institute of Law and Ethics in Medicine at the University of Glasgow.

Healthcare Research Ethics and Law

Regulation, Review and Responsibility

Hazel Biggs

 Routledge·Cavendish
Taylor & Francis Group
LONDON AND NEW YORK

First published 2010
by Routledge-Cavendish
2 Park Square, Milton Park, Abingdon, Oxon, OX14 4RN

Simultaneously published in the USA and Canada
by Routledge-Cavendish
711 Third Avenue, New York, NY 10017

*Routledge-Cavendish is an imprint of the Taylor & Francis Group,
an informa business*

Transferred to Digital Printing 2011

© 2010 Hazel Biggs

Typeset in Times New Roman by Keyword Group Ltd

British Library Cataloguing in Publication Data
A catalogue record for this book is available from the British Library

Library of Congress Cataloging in Publication Data
A Catalogue record for this book has been requested

ISBN10: 1-904385-48-6 (hbk)
ISBN13: 978-1-904385-48-6 (hbk)

ISBN10: 0-415-42917-X (pbk)
ISBN13: 978-0-415-42917-7 (pbk)

ISBN10: 0-203-94040-7 (ebk)
ISBN13: 978-0-203-94040-2 (ebk)

. . . divorced from ethics, leadership is reduced to management and politics to mere technique

James MacGregor Burns

Contents

Acknowledgements

I owe very many people a debt of gratitude in relation to this work. Jane Barrett, Jenny Billings and José Miola all read and commented on draft chapters, and their contribution has been invaluable in making this book what it is. Barbara Mauthe was always willing to listen and helped enormously when my limited understanding of some public law concepts needed bolstering. Sara Fovargue and Suzanne Ost showed understanding and empathy, which helped immeasurably and will always be remembered. Added to that, the tolerance and understanding shown by Southampton Law School has been immense. My gratitude is equally large, and I now hope to demonstrate that I will not always be an absent colleague.

Last, and by no means least, the unwavering support shown by Stuart Brittle and especially David Thackeray has been humbling. Stuart, you were right that 'a girl needs to eat', but hopefully time away from the computer will now redress the effects of the sustenance provided. And David, your encouragement, sound advice and compassion has been the greatest comfort throughout and cannot be repaid. I take credit for my own mistakes, but thank one and all for everything else.

Preface

Healthcare research is a vital component of good healthcare. It is essential that good research is carried out if advances in healthcare are to be discovered or invented, and the achievement of this relies upon the participation of human beings. In the past many people have been included in research projects without their agreement, sometimes even without their knowledge, but this is no longer generally regarded as ethically acceptable. Today it is widely believed that individuals have the right to decide whether or not to be involved in research, and to do so voluntarily and on the basis of full understanding. There are some legitimate exceptions, but the basic premise holds true.

The research ethics committees (RECs) that are the subject of this book are charged with the difficult task of deciding whether proposed research projects involving human participants are sufficiently ethical that they should proceed. In this there are no obvious right or wrong answers, but their ultimate aim is to protect the interests of those people who may eventually agree to participate in the research. They do so by referring to a myriad of authoritative guidance, and against the backdrop of a legal framework that touches upon their areas of concern but is not explicitly applicable. This is not an easy task. The vast majority of REC members are not professional ethicists. Neither are they lawyers. Most are ordinary people who bring either lay or professional experience to their role as REC members. These are the people who have inspired this book.

In recent years the landscape of research ethics has changed enormously. RECs have operated in the NHS since the 1960s, but the last decade has witnessed a proliferation of RECs outside the NHS, in universities, social care organisations and research-funding bodies, amongst others. It is, however, the NHS RECs that form the main focus of this book. This is because healthcare research is the central theme, and the NHS model tends to inform most other RECs working in this area. In addition, there have been immeasurable changes to the governance of RECs in the recent past, due to several transformations in their governing body and the simultaneous introduction of a new legal framework. With the introduction of European legislation aimed primarily at drug development, but introducing a regime that has subsequently been applied to all forms of health research within the NHS, the law has assumed a new prominence.

Aside from the law, the work of NHS RECs is informed by a vast array of information and guidance, which operates according to established theoretical frameworks. Much of this is provided by bodies such as the World Health Organisation, the National Research Ethics Service, the General Medical Council and a range of others. It is, however, informative, but not definitive, and it can be difficult to gain an overview. This book attempts to provide such an overview. To this end it seeks to describe the central features of the process of ethical review, whilst also setting out the responsibilities of those involved in the research process and the process of ethical review. It does so by exploring the legal and ethical frameworks under which RECs currently operate. In the process it examines central aspects of the work of RECs, such as consent, confidentiality and the protection of the vulnerable, from the perspectives of both law and ethics. Through this it reveals that there are genuine tensions between the two, and tries to suggest ways in which these might be navigated. It does not, however, explicitly direct the reader in any particular direction; there are no right and wrong answers when it comes to ethics. Instead, it attempts to explain how the law and ethics interrelate in specific contexts, and introduces some controversies that exemplify the theoretical, procedural and practical animosity that often exists. Some of these are contentious, and the readers are invited to form their own opinions. After all, as is acknowledged in Chapter 3, it is a necessary feature of committee ethics that the members will hold differing views.

A central aim of the book is to provide a work that will be accessible to members of RECs, both NHS and others. Though it might be described as a law book, it is not aimed solely at lawyers, and it is hoped that its discursive style will make it intelligible not just to non-lawyers but also to lay members of RECs. Its key themes arise out of concerns expressed by REC members attending training courses about the way that law and ethics fit together in the context of ethical review, the intricacies of relatively new legislative changes, and members' own potential liability. Within that it tries to pull together some of the regulatory and academic guidance in one location, and underpin it with some theoretical discussion to contextualise the surrounding arguments and debates. It does not aim to be comprehensive. Rather, it seeks to point out some issues of interest and concern in relation to each area focussed upon in an attempt to contextualise what can otherwise be a very dry and technical account.

This book has been a long time in the writing and gone through many incarnations in the process. In part, this has been the result of the extensive regulatory and legal changes that have had a profound impact on the work and operation of RECs in the NHS and beyond. For example, the European Clinical Trials Directive, the Mental Capacity Act 2005 and the Human Tissue Act 2004 have all changed the parameters within which RECs work. The legal and regulatory landscape has been dynamic, and will no doubt continue to change. Given the fast pace of change in the context of the law, and, more particularly, the regulation associated with research ethics, I anticipate that some of the detail included here will be out of date before this book even reaches the bookshop shelves. However, the focus on principle will, I hope, mean that its content remains relevant. To the best of my knowledge the law and regulation stated here should be correct as of the end of April 2009. I take full responsibility for all inaccuracies.

Hazel Biggs
May 2009

Case list

Statute list

List of abbreviations

BMA	British Medical Association
CIOMS	Council for International Organisations of Medical Sciences
COREC	Central Office for Research Ethics Committees
CTIMPs	clinical trials of investigational medicinal products
DoH	Department of Health
DPA 1998	Data Protection Act 1998
ESRC	Economic and Social Research Council
FOI Act	Freedom of Information Act
GAfREC	*Governance Arrangements for Research Ethics Committees*
GCP	good clinical practice
GMC	General Medical Council
HTA 2004	Human Tissue Act 2004
ICH	International Conference on Harmonisation
IEC	independent ethics committee
IRAS	Integrated Research Application System
IVF	in vitro fertilisation
MCA	Medicines Control Agency
MCA 2005	Mental Capacity Act 2005
MHRA	Medicines and Healthcare Regulatory Agency
MRC	Medical Research Council
NHS	National Health Service
NIGB	National Information Governance Board for Health and Social Care
NPSA	National Patient Safety Agency
NRES	National Research Ethics Service
OREC	Office of Research Ethics Committees
PIAG	Patient Information Advisory Group
RCT	randomised controlled trial
REC	research ethics committee
SCREC	Social Care Research Ethics Committee
UKAEA	United Kingdom Atomic Energy Authority
UKECA	United Kingdom Ethics Committee Authority
WMA	World Medical Association

Chapter 1

Research ethics and law in context

Introduction

When new healthcare interventions, including pharmaceutical products, are being investigated for their potential use in human applications it is inevitable that they will need to be tested on human beings. This book concerns the regulation of research involving human participants, human tissues and data pertaining to the health, welfare and social care of individuals. It will assess the ethics and law that govern the conduct of healthcare research, taking account of biomedical and pharmaceutical research, as well as studies that are more concerned with social and practical issues associated with the provision of care. The central focus of the work will be the role and responsibilities of research ethics committees (RECs) in relation to the process of the ethical review of research involving human participants. It will therefore be relevant to RECs operating in the NHS, social care organisations and universities, as well as some private sector organisations. A close examination of the operation of RECs will be conducted to assess the legal and regulatory mechanisms that confront them in the practical conduct of their work. Through this, the extent of the potential legal liability of RECs and their members will be investigated and placed in context. In so doing the book aims to join up the dots and make connections between the theoretical philosophical and ethical principles that underpin the review process and the relevant law, regulation and guidance that pertain in practice.

The relationship between research, ethics and law has a rather fraught history. Researchers have often complained that they are prevented from the exploits of what they regard as beneficial research by restrictive and overly bureaucratic laws (Brazier, 2005). More recently, controversy has been sparked by suggestions that RECs do and should bear greater responsibility than has hitherto been acknowledged (Roy-Toole, 2008). This book aims to explain how law and ethics operate in the context of the review of healthcare research. To do this it will explore the background, form and operation of the law and regulation that applies to medical research in the United Kingdom and locate it within the context of the philosophies and ethical guidelines that underpin the process of ethical review.

This introductory chapter will briefly outline the background against which RECs operate. It will do so by first defining what is meant by research and how it differs from experimentation and innovative treatment, before giving an overview of the process of drug development. Pharmaceutical research takes place within a highly formalised regulatory environment which places constraints on researchers and RECs. This, in turn, has been influential in shaping the organisational approach to the ethical review of healthcare research in the United Kingdom, and also has implications for the regulation and ethical review of social care and university-based research.

Since the early 1960s, a number of prominent professional bodies in the United Kingdom have developed guidance on the ethical conduct of research involving human participants. Notable amongst these was a document formulated by the Medical Research Council (MRC) in 1963 which located the necessity to obtain informed consent from the participant at the centre of any research proposal (MRC, 1967). In 1967 this was followed by a call from the Royal College of Physicians for the establishment of formal RECs to oversee the conduct of medical research (Rosenheim, 1967). After that a system for the ethical review of healthcare research developed in an ad hoc way until the Department of Health (DoH) eventually recommended the formation of properly constituted local RECs in 1991 (DoH, 1991). The fact that these RECs were locally based and locally administered was at once their strength and their weakness, however. Their local knowledge made them ideally placed to assess locally based applications from local researchers, but where investigators sought to conduct studies in a number of centres across many geographical boundaries, the level of bureaucracy involved in the process and inconsistency of outcomes between committees often resulted in delays and discontent (Lewis *et al*, 2001).

These problems were partially resolved in 1997 by the establishment of multi-centre NHS RECs, which were authorised to conduct a single ethical review of research to be conducted in more than four NHS sites (DoH, 1997). Shortly after this, in 2000, the Central Office for Research Ethics Committees (COREC), which subsequently became the National Research Ethics Service (NRES), was established, and quickly took over responsibility for the governance of all NHS RECs. It published *Governance Arrangements for Research Ethics Committees* (DoH, 2001) (GAfREC), and embarked on an extensive programme of training and education for REC members, as well as introducing formal processes for member recruitment and standardised researcher applications.

In 2002, following a series of scandals involving poor research practices (the details of which will be discussed in Chapter 2), the DoH published the *Research Governance Framework for Health and Social Care* (DoH, 2002) ('Research Governance Framework'), which was revised and updated in 2005. Research ethics is just one aspect of this framework, which also lays down detailed arrangements for maintaining and monitoring standards in health and social care research. Its central aim is to protect the interests of research participants by imposing a chain of responsibility and accountability between researcher and the NHS so that any risks can be identified and managed. Since the introduction of this strict regulatory approach to human research in the health service, there has been a gradual proliferation of formal processes to scrutinise the ethical aspects of all forms of research involving human participants. It is now the case, for example, that universities' research-funding bodies, like the Economic and Social Research Council (ESRC) (ESRC, 2007), and many private research organisations, compel researchers to submit their research proposals to an ethical review procedure before they can begin their research. Whilst ethical review and research governance may be regarded as providing greater protection for human research participants, its ability to safeguard those participants and the bureaucratic processes that accompany it are not without controversy (Hammersley, 2009).

Some of the reasons behind the increasing formalisation of research ethics will be investigated in Chapter 2, which briefly traces the history of research ethics, including examples of research misconduct in recent history that have resulted in the ethical guidance and regulatory frameworks that now govern healthcare research. Through an exposition of some of the high-profile scandals that have characterised healthcare research in the past, this chapter will demonstrate how we got to where we are today, and try to explain and contextualise the current emphasis on precautionary regulation as a mechanism to safeguard the interests of future research participants.

From there the discussion will continue in Chapter 3 with an overview of the ethical and philosophical frameworks within which research ethics operate in practice. It will consider the philosophical theories that underpin the process of ethical review, such as the interaction between consequentialism and deontology, and the relationship with applied biomedical ethics in this context. Chapter 3 will also investigate the legal status of numerous guidelines relating to the conduct of research involving humans, setting the scene for a more detailed discussion in Chapter 4 of the legal responsibilities of those who undertake the ethical review of research. The aspects of this discussion that relate to the EU Clinical Trials Directive (2001/20/EC), and the Regulations that transpose it into domestic law (the Medicines for Human Use (Clinical Trials) Regulations 2004, SI 2004/1031 ('Clinical Trials Regulations')), will relate specifically to the legal status of both NHS RECs themselves and their individual members. However, the common law implications of conducting ethical review and the application of guidance issued by non-statutory bodies will also be of relevance to ethics committees outside the NHS.

Some features of the ethics and law of research involving human participants, such as the need to protect their dignity and well-being, ensuring that they have given consent and that their confidentiality and privacy are assured, are common to all types of research involving human participants. These aspects, amongst others, are central to the work of NHS RECs and will therefore be discussed at length in Chapters 5 and 6 respectively. From there, Chapter 7 will conduct an in-depth analysis of issues relating to the recruitment of members of particularly vulnerable groups as research participants. Particular emphasis will be placed on research involving children, and adults who lack mental capacity. The impact of the Mental Capacity Act 2005 and its interaction with the Clinical Trials Regulations will be assessed at length, to explain the responsibilities of RECs and researchers in this regard. Chapter 8 will consider the significance of the Human Tissue Act 2004 in relation to research involving human tissue and organs, as well as biobanks and tissue databases. Finally, once the reader is familiar with the central features of the law attached to these areas of healthcare research, Chapter 9 will conclude by drawing together some of the threads and themes apparent throughout the book and introducing some concerns around the issue of research fraud and misconduct.

Research involving the participation of human beings may range from simple surveys or questionnaires, through laboratory research on human tissues and cells, to the study of the effects of new surgical procedures or novel pharmaceutical compounds on healthy volunteers. It is also important to recognise that the researchers themselves are also participants in the research process, and that sometimes their own involvement, for example in some kinds of participatory research methods, or where they are conducting their research in remote locations, may in itself raise ethical concerns. In addition, different regulatory mechanisms exist for different types of research; hence it is sometimes necessary to review these separately in order to generate an understanding of the differences and similarities between them. Pharmaceutical research, for example, is today governed by rigid definitions, regulations and guidelines that pertain only in that context and relate particularly to product licensing. By contrast, much social care research is conducted against a backdrop of ethical guidelines developed by professional bodies and local institutions such as universities. However, international instruments like the World Health Organisation's Declaration of Helsinki 2008, and the Council for International Organisations of Medical Sciences (CIOMS), *International Ethical Guidelines for Biomedical Research Involving Human Subjects* (2002), apply generally to research involving human beings, though their legal status may be ambiguous.

Much of the legislation recently introduced in the United Kingdom and Europe applies specifically to the regulation of research involving clinical trials of investigational medicinal products (CTIMPs) and medical devices. Therefore, after outlining some of the methodological techniques associated with healthcare research more generally, this introductory chapter will briefly describe the various stages of drug development in order to outline the broad scientific and regulatory context within which RECs charged with reviewing clinical research involving drugs operate. This will provide some insight into the background against which law and ethics interact in the context of research. The impact of other recent legal changes will be assessed in dedicated chapters on vulnerable groups and the Human Tissue Act 2004. However, before embarking on this process it is important to first introduce and define the concept of research so that the associated ethics and regulatory processes are clearly located within their practical context.

What is research?

Research can be difficult to define, particularly in the healthcare setting where there are a number of practices allied to research, such as audit, service development and project evaluation, which are peripheral to research and can generate confusion (Smith, 1992; Wade, 2005). Ordinarily, this can be overcome by referring to the stated aims of audit and service evaluation, which involve measuring an existing form of care or an established service against predetermined standards. Such techniques never assign patients to specific groups to generate new data or study outcomes, and they rarely involve anything more than the administration of a brief questionnaire. As a result there is generally no need for systematic ethical review of audit or service evaluation. By contrast, research involving human subjects, which has the potential to expose the participant to some risks, however minimal, ought properly to be subjected to a thorough ethical review prior to commencement. So great has been the uncertainty about the distinctions between research, audit and service evaluation amongst RECs, however, that they have become the subject of specific guidance from the NRES (NRES, 2007(a)).

The controversy over the potential overlap between these procedures is hardly surprising since there are some clear examples of projects that would not ordinarily be categorised as research that have led to valuable and generalisable results. The long-term institutional confidential inquiries into maternal or peri-operative deaths are described by the Royal College of Physicians as a clear example of this kind of phenomenon (Royal College of Physicians, 2007: 17). It is also not unknown for audit, or service evaluation, to raise ethical issues, although this is rare. As a result, whilst it is broadly accepted that their primary aims take them out of the realms of formal research, some grey areas remain. It is therefore important that researchers are prepared to consider whether projects described as audit pose ethical risks, and, if so, whether those risks are proportional to the prospective benefits of the project concerned. In general, concerns about the overlap between service evaluation, audit, and research in the NHS and social care can be resolved by recourse to appropriate guidance and experienced managers under the Research Governance Framework. Similarly, in the university sector, research managers and RECs will usually be able to assess whether a research proposal requires full ethical scrutiny.

Many authors have attempted to produce a precise form of words to describe research, and as part of this endeavour the British Medical Association provides a helpful working definition:

> 'Research' can be defined as the attempt to derive generalisable new knowledge by addressing clearly defined questions using systematic and rigorous methods. All research must meet certain minimum standards. It must, for example, have a well designed protocol, constitute a well conducted project, involve statistically appropriate participant numbers, not necessarily duplicate previous research, and be subject to external review

and continuing surveillance. In addition, research involving people who are somehow dependent or vulnerable must also take special account of their interests and priorities.

(BMA, 2004: 490)

From this it is apparent that where the aim of research is to generate new knowledge and understanding, it will not usually be expected to benefit the individual participants. Occasionally there will be an incidental benefit to the individual, but in general the beneficiaries of healthcare research will be future patients. Any definition of healthcare research should also recognise that an assortment of practices, ranging from simple observation to more intrusive pharmaceutical or physical interventions, may be included under its auspices. In practice, deciding what counts as simple observation and what amounts to a minimal intervention is often problematic. Merely observing patients, for example, can sometimes require taking measurements and recording changes using intrusive methods such as electrocardiograms or blood tests, for which ethical approval would be required.

Research should also be distinguished from experimentation (Dickens, 1975), which implies a more 'speculative, ad hoc, approach to an individual subject' or patient (Mason and Laurie, 2006: 651), and from innovative therapy, which aims to treat a specific patient, often where there is no alternative treatment available. In practice it is clear that there may be some overlap between experimentation and innovative treatment since an experiment is quite likely to involve the application of a novel therapeutic approach. However, whilst research involving medicinal products, drugs and the testing of medical devices is highly regulated and requires ethical scrutiny, the regulation of new surgical or physical diagnostic procedures have not traditionally been monitored to the same degree. The controversy surrounding the somewhat unorthodox approaches to children's heart surgery adopted at the Royal Bristol Infirmary is illustrative of some of the problems inherent in using untested techniques without formal scientific or ethical review. This example led to calls for greater scrutiny of new invasive techniques (Kennedy, 2001).

Aside from the overlap between ad hoc experimentation and innovation, similarities are also evident between research and experimentation, especially where the initial results from an experiment on an individual subject are later tested systematically in a formal research protocol. Some of the issues are revealed in the authoritative case of *Simms v Simms* (2003), which involved a young man who had fallen victim to variant Creutzfeldt-Jakob disease (vCJD). Here the patient was not competent to give a valid consent and the court was called upon to decide on the legality of using a new treatment known as PPS. The treatment was untried in humans, but early tests in Japan indicated that it had beneficial effects in mice with similar symptoms. Authorising the treatment of Jonathan Simms, Dame Elizabeth Butler-Sloss explained that 'although this cannot be a research project, there would be an opportunity to learn, for the first time, the possible effect of PPS on patients with vCJD and to have the opportunity to compare it with the treatment about to be given in Japan'. Whilst the prospect of improvement in this case was described as 'slight but not non-existent', the judgment took account of the extreme nature of the condition and the surrounding circumstances to permit the intervention. Dame Butler-Sloss regarded this as justifiable because 'a patient who is not able to consent to pioneering treatment ought not to be deprived of the chance in circumstances where he would be likely to consent if he had been competent'.

This case also raises a further issue of debate, that concerning the relationship between therapeutic and non-therapeutic research. The issue in *Simms* was not simply a question of whether or not the patient could consent, but also concerned how best to balance the potential for benefit against the possibility of harm to the individual concerned. This will be a recurring theme throughout this book. Its legal significance will be examined in more detail in the context of best interests in Chapter 7. However, for the present discussion, the case also highlights some controversies surrounding the ways in which potential harm and benefit might be assessed in the context of therapeutic research. Some commentators have argued that research designed to improve patient care might properly be described as therapeutic (BMA, 2004: 490), so that innovative treatment, which could also be of benefit to the subject, should be regarded as a form of therapeutic research. Others, however, maintain that a more accurate definition of therapeutic research encompasses research interventions that have a potential to benefit the specific subject.

The distinction between therapeutic and non-therapeutic research first became controversial in the World Medical Association's Declaration of Helsinki in 1964. In clause 6 of this highly influential document, it was stated that where medical judgment suggested that it would be helpful, a doctor 'must be free to use a new diagnostic or therapeutic measure', which seemed to imply that therapeutic research would receive more limited scrutiny than research that had no direct therapeutic intent. Contemporary thinking, however, insists that this distinction between therapeutic and non-therapeutic research is outdated, and even potentially dangerous, because it fails to acknowledge the reality that therapeutic research frequently involves greater risks than non-therapeutic research (Royal College of Psychiatrists, 2001). Furthermore, present-day ethical values raise concerns regarding the quality of any consent that might be obtained from a participant involved in therapeutic research, especially where there is no proven treatment. These issues will be revisited later in the book in relation to consent and concerns about vulnerability, but for now it is important to appreciate that where the treatment is only available as part of a research protocol, extra care must be taken to ensure that the full implications are understood, and that participation is entirely voluntary.

Different, but related issues are raised by the practice known as sham surgery. Here, the object of the exercise is to assess the effect of a new surgical technique by comparing it to a mock procedure, where the subjects who experience the surgery do not know whether they have received the full surgical intervention or just a minimal procedure involving little more than an incision. Perhaps the closest comparison that can be made with this type of research is the placebo-controlled drugs trial, where some participants receive the intervention to be tested and others get a dummy application. The use of placebo remains controversial but, where there is no established treatment for a given condition, and it is not known whether a proposed therapy will be more beneficial than nothing at all – that is to say, there is genuine equipoise – its use is ethically unproblematic (Kennedy, 1988: 219; London, 2001). In such a case, the subjects may or may not benefit from the intervention, but those in the placebo arm of the study will be no worse off than they would have been if they had not been entered into the study. This is not the position with sham surgery. In that situation all those who take part in the study are exposed to risks associated with surgery. Even if it is only minor surgery the risks will include pain, infection, trauma and other possible complications of recovery, at a minimum. In addition, if the procedure requires general anaesthesia the risks are magnified concomitant with the risks of the anaesthetic. Given this, it is questionable whether the potential benefit to the wider population can ever outweigh the potential, and inevitable, harm to the individual research subject (Clark, 2002).

In the past it has been customary practice for new surgical techniques to be developed and introduced into clinical practice without formal testing. Instead, new methods have tended to be developed through ad hoc improvisation without stringent appraisal of their efficacy. Ultimately, this can lead to many patients being exposed to ineffective new surgical interventions that are eventually abandoned (Albin, 2002). From this perspective it is arguable that it is ethically preferable to expose fully consenting research subjects to the risks of sham surgery in order to obtain sound results from a properly designed research study, rather than to subject the patient population to an uncontrolled experiment. In terms of utilitarian theory this is certainly a viable argument. More specifically, as long as sham surgery is the only way to generate the data, the research patients are fully aware of the procedures involved and the risks are kept to an absolute minimum, it is acceptable practice (Albin, 2002). The ethics of this kind of research require very careful consideration before they can be sanctioned, as do the practicalities.

Sham surgery, however, is a relatively new and still rare problem for most RECs. By comparison, the more traditional forms of research, such as those involving quantitative methodologies like the randomised controlled trial (RCT), often described as the 'gold standard', still make up a large proportion of the work of RECs (Jackson, 2006: 463). Quantitative research methods involve the analysis of numerical data generated objectively and seek to produce generalisable results. They tend to be deductive, often moving towards making causal explanations or predictive assumptions and, as such, they are concerned with identifying and measuring variables and ensuring that sample sizes and populations are statistically appropriate and representative.

Of these, the RCT is exactly what its name suggests – a trial, often of a new pharmaceutical product, in which some of the participants are selected at random to receive either the new drug or other intervention. The effects of the new therapy will then be assessed against the performance of either the best available existing treatment or a placebo, which is administered to those in the control group.

In this context a placebo is a dummy preparation which outwardly appears to be the same as the intervention to be tested but contains no active ingredient. Ethically, this can raise concerns as to the efficacy of the participants' consent; specifically, does agreeing to participate in a process that involves being kept unaware of the details of the intervention constitute a proper consent? In addition, healthcare research of this type potentially raises issues of legal liability for the medical professionals who are involved with it. For example, if an established treatment would ordinarily be regarded as the optimal therapy for a given patient, then the clinician's duty would usually be to offer that treatment. If, instead, the doctor or therapist recruits the patient into an RCT, she or he could be in breach of that duty of care to the patient, and potentially liable in negligence. The nature of this type of legal duty will be explored further in Chapter 4, but at this point it is sufficient to explain that such a procedure will be legitimate if there is genuine equipoise.

Increasingly, RECs are also called upon to assess the ethical implications of research that employs qualitative methods, such as interviews, focus groups, narrative analysis and questionnaires. Used predominantly by social science researchers, these methods tend to raise different kinds of issues and therefore call for a different type of assessment. For example, whereas the researcher is required to be detached and objective in quantitative research, here the aim is to study things within their natural setting, and often to assess associated subjective experiences. Consequently, the researcher is frequently called upon to empathise with the subject and may even be an active participant; as such, objectivity is frequently absent. Numerical analysis is rare when using qualitative research methods (Greenhalgh and Taylor, 1997), the variables can be complex, and the results are contextual, interpretive and descriptive. Some commentators believe that qualitative and quantitative approaches are therefore not compatible (Lincoln and Guba, 1985), and some have been openly hostile to qualitative methods, regarding them as unscientific (Pope and Mays, 1993). Other interpretations, however, suggest that both qualitative and quantitative methods have merit and indeed can usefully be combined to give a holistic view of a particular phenomenon or experience (Patton, 1990). Often, in fact, qualitative methods are necessary at the early stages of a research project to establish the parameters required to conduct more formal quantitative research.

It is important that REC members have a good grasp of research methodologies and their implications so that they can assess the potential risks, burdens and benefits of a research proposal. REC members have an obligation to ensure that research participants are not exposed to unethical research. To do so, it may be necessary to ascertain that the research has the required rigour to achieve its stated aims and produce the results sought, otherwise the participants may be needlessly exposed to the risk of suffering harm. Consequently, determining that research is properly designed so as to be scientifically valid as well as ethically sound is regarded by many as a central part of the process of ethical review, although this remains controversial (Royal College of Physicians, 2007: 10). Indeed, with regard to clinical trials of medicinal products, reg 15(5) of the Clinical Trials Regulations, requires, *inter alia*, that the REC must be satisfied with the scientific aspects of the study under consideration:

> . . . the committee shall consider, in particular, the following matters (a) the relevance of the clinical trial and its design; (b) whether the evaluation of the anticipated benefits and risks as required under paragraph 2 of Part 2 of Schedule 1 is satisfactory and whether the conclusions are justified; (c) the protocol; . . . (e) the investigator's brochure . . .

Failure to discharge that obligation may mean that the REC is negligent in the performance of its responsibilities, as will be seen in Chapter 4.

However, the Research Governance Framework insists that the onus is on research sponsors to ensure the quality of research to be performed under their auspices, which brings with it a requirement of peer and scientific review. RECs may therefore be entitled to claim that their responsibility in this regard has been discharged so long as they are satisfied that adequate peer review has been undertaken. More particularly, the detailed guidance in GAfREC insists (at para 9.8) that scientific review is not part of the RECs' remit, and that '[T]he Research Governance Framework makes it clear that the sponsor is responsible for ensuring the quality of the science'. Yet it is difficult to reconcile this approach with the remit of the REC. In order to ascertain that research complies with ethical standards, including the requirement outlined in para 9.9 of GAfREC that it 'should satisfy itself that the review already undertaken is adequate for the nature of the proposal under consideration', the REC needs to be cognisant not only of the existence of a scientific review, but also of its substance, which may be problematic in practice.

Similarly, where a peer review has been conducted and recommends alterations to the research design or protocol, the REC may need to be able to ascertain whether or not the researcher has responded appropriately before giving a favourable opinion. That will inevitably require RECs to engage with the scientific aspects of the study under consideration. One obvious example concerns the continuing controversy over the use of placebo in clinical research where a proven treatment exists. If RECs were to refrain from engaging with any assessment of the scientific validity of a study the validity of the use of placebo would not even arise as an issue, yet it is often a major consideration in the determination of whether a specific research design is regarded as ethical. Further controversial issues will be considered in Chapter 4, which looks at the legal responsibilities of RECs and their members, and in Chapter 9.

The broad categories of research described above are just one aspect of defining research. Alongside these are some more formal, practical and regulatory definitions which relate specifically to the process of drug development in the pharmaceutical industry. Under this umbrella there is even a strict legal definition of what amounts to a clinical trial. Regulation 2 of the Clinical Trials Regulations specifies that a clinical trial is:

any investigation in human subjects . . . intended (a) to discover or verify the clinical, pharmacological or other pharmacodynamic effects of one or more medicinal products, (b) to identify any adverse reactions to one or more such products, or (c) to study absorption, distribution, metabolism and excretion of one or more such products, with the object of ascertaining the safety or efficacy of those products.

In practice, a number of different stages of product development fall within this definition.

A 'Phase I study' is defined in reg 2 as one which aims 'to study the pharmacology of an investigational medicinal product when administered to humans, where the sponsor and investigator have no knowledge of any evidence that the product has effects likely to be beneficial to the subjects of the trial'. These studies are conducted after *in vitro* laboratory studies and animal studies have established baseline data about novel preparations. They aim initially to assess the toxicity and delivery of these products in their first use in human beings, and later to evaluate safety by ascertaining whether dose-related reactions occur. By definition it is usual for very little to be known about the behaviour of the drug in the human body prior to its first administration in humans. Generally, Phase I trials involve healthy volunteers, but occasionally novel pharmaceutical substances will be tested in therapeutic trials on patients rather than volunteers, for example where highly toxic new chemotherapy drugs are involved. More usually, however, small numbers of healthy volunteers, usually male, will be recruited to these trials, so that the potential risks to individual subjects can be minimised when balanced against the potential benefits to a wider patient population. Participants in these trials are closely monitored in minute detail, often in purpose-designed clinical units.

Overall, the Phase I testing of each new substance will usually last about one year. Often testing will take place in the private sector, where volunteer participants are recruited through public advertising in the community local to the research unit. In common with all other research involving human participants, Phase I research conducted in this way always requires prior ethical approval from a properly constituted REC. Usually, such RECs will be independent, appointed by the Appointing Authority for Phase I Committees, and recognised by the United Kingdom Ethics Committee Authority (UKECA). However, there remains some uncertainty concerning the ethical review of healthcare research conducted in the private sector that does not involve CTIMPs. Whilst the EU Directive and the associated UK Regulations make it clear that all CTIMPs must be subjected to proper ethical review, other kinds of healthcare research conducted in the private sector appears to be governed by GAfREC, para 7.22, which simply encourages researchers to approach 'an NHS REC for advice'. It is of course probable that GAfREC II, which was about to be opened up for public consultation as this book went to print, will address this issue.

The uncertain nature of Phase I trials requires that participants must be very closely monitored throughout the research process, and Chapter 9 will touch briefly upon some of the issues raised following the TGN1412 incident at Northwick Park Hospital in March 2006. Ideally, participants in Phase I trials should be dosed sequentially, so that any adverse reactions or events can be rapidly identified and managed appropriately. Here, as with all CTIMPs, the terms 'adverse reaction' and 'adverse event' have carefully defined regulatory meanings. An adverse reaction is defined in the 2004 Regulations as one that represents an 'untoward and unintended response in a subject to an investigational medicinal product which is related to the dose administered'. An adverse event, however, is more widely construed to include all untoward medical occurrences in subjects who have received a medicinal product, 'including occurrences which are not necessarily caused by or related to that product'. Researchers, regulators and members of RECs are also concerned about serious eventualities which may cause a participant to require hospitalisation, or result in life-threatening or permanent injury, or even death. These are variously described as 'serious adverse events', 'serious adverse reactions' or 'unexpected serious adverse reactions'. Clearly, such events can occur at any stage in the research, and in any of the phases of the drug-development process, but they always have implications for the determination of whether it is ethical for the trial to continue.

Phase II clinical trials normally represent the first use of a new compound in patients, and the trial period will tend to last around two years. A maximum of a few hundred participants (but more usually around 50) will be recruited to these studies. They will be patients who suffer from the disease or condition in which the drug is expected to be useful, but are otherwise healthy. The object of Phase II trials is to further assess the safety and efficacy of the drug in the disease, and to give an indication of therapeutic dose ranges. Following the Phase II trials, a decision will usually be made as to whether or not the drug is suitable to go into production for widespread use.

Phase III of drug development is a longer process than either Phase I or Phase II, typically lasting three to four years. Those recruited will be patients requiring treatment who are representative of the general patient population that is expected to benefit from using the drug. As such, these patients may also have other medical conditions and may be using other prescribed medications, which introduces the possibility for drug interactions to occur. Potentially thousands of patients will participate in the Phase III trials of any particular product. Dosage levels will be confirmed at this stage of testing in order to assess the long-term safety of the drug, and the drug or product will also be tested against any existing therapies for the same condition, to further assess its specific benefits. Once the Phase III trials are completed the data required for registration of the product will have been obtained.

Phase IV studies relate to the post-registration period when the product has been marketed for general use. At this stage further comparisons with other drugs used in the same application may be made, and long-term safety data will be collected. In addition, post-marketing surveillance, including the reporting of adverse events, will be conducted. In the United Kingdom this involves the so-called 'yellow card scheme', administered by the Medicines and Healthcare Regulatory Agency (MHRA). This invites doctors and members of the public to report suspected adverse drug reactions, and has been in operation since 1964, when it was introduced in the wake of the thalidomide tragedy. Recent alterations have been introduced to ensure that confidentiality is maintained, and the scheme is regarded as a central plank of post-marketing surveillance, and as such is fundamental to the protection of public health.

In 2005 the House of Commons Select Committee on Health, *Fourth Report* (2005), concluded (at para 160) that approximately 90 per cent of clinical trials of medicinal products (as defined above) are conducted by, or on behalf of, the pharmaceutical industry. Consequently, much of the regulation of medical research and the ethical guidelines attached to them have been developed with the requirements of drug development and the needs of the pharmaceutical industry in mind, a fact that some commentators have found problematic (Cave and Holm, 2002). As might be expected, in these circumstances there is a raft of legislation and regulation attached to the development and licensing of new medicines which operates alongside the Research Governance Framework and the process of ethical review. Key to this aspect of regulation is the role of the MHRA.

The MHRA came into existence in April 2003 following the merger of the Medicines Control Agency (MCA), which was initially set up under the Medicines Act 1968, with the Medical Devices Agency. Under the EU Directive and associated UK Regulations, the MHRA is the designated competent authority with responsibility for the authorisation of all clinical trials of medicinal products and medical devices. It is also responsible for monitoring all research trials. As such, it describes itself as 'an executive agency of the Department of Health . . . whose principal aim is to safeguard the public's health. It does this by making sure that medicines and medical devices – from painkillers to pacemakers – work properly and are acceptable safe' (MHRA, 2008: 2). It operates within the public domain and undertakes not only to protect the interests of the public with regard to the safety of medicines and devices, but also to ensure that the public has confidence in the systems involved in their development. Accordingly, its web pages make the claim that 'Underpinning all our work lie robust and fact-based judgements to ensure that the benefits to patients and the public justify the risks'.

The main function of the MHRA is to issue licences, or marketing authorisations, for new medicinal products and devices, and its work is central to their development and use. Within this, the definition of 'medicinal products' is broad, encompassing vaccines and biological medicines as well as pharmaceutical products, and the MHRA claims that 'no product is risk free'. Medical devices, by contrast, include all products other than medicines used for diagnostic treatment and monitoring purposes. Everything from X-ray equipment and prosthetics, to surgical dressings, needles and syringes and wheelchairs, is included, from which it will be apparent that as well as ensuring that they work properly, the regulator is also concerned with the consequences of possible operational malfunctions (Feigal, 2003).

Under the Medical Devices Regulations 2002, SI 2002/618, which implements three separate EU Directives (the Medical Devices Directive (93/42/EEC), the Active Implantable Medical Devices Directive (90/385/EEC) and the In Vitro Diagnostic Medical Devices Directive (98/79/EC)), manufacturers of clinical devices are required by law to provide information and full details of investigations of clinical devices to be carried out in the United Kingdom to the UK's competent authority, the MHRA. NHS RECs are responsible for the review of research involving devices in the same way as they are for pharmaceuticals and other interventions, and such research is relatively common. However, to reflect the fact that this is a specialist area that can raise particular ethical issues, especially where devices and pharmaceuticals are combined, the NRES has designated a small number of specialist committees to review these protocols. These special arrangements were announced in March 2006 and definitive guidance was issued in 2008 (NRES, 2008).

Although clinical trials of medicinal products and devices is highly regulated by law, the majority of the work conducted by RECs does not involve research on industry-developed products. Instead, the vast majority of the work of RECs focuses on areas of healthcare research conducted by nurses and social science researchers, which tends to involve surveys, questionnaires and other, non-clinical interventions. The ethical guidelines and principles that inform this type of research also form the basis of much of the legislation and regulation that governs clinical trials of medicinal products and devices. However, the nature of law making dictates that it is influenced by political and economic considerations that may be rejected by ethical principles. Consequently, the discussion of the ethics and law that follows will highlight a number of tensions and contradictions between ethics and law, which can have an impact upon the work of RECs reviewing health-related human participant research.

Conclusions

Research ethics is highly topical and rarely far from the public consciousness. Awareness has been raised in a number of ways, with obvious recent examples being the film *The Constant Gardener* (le Carre, 2001) and publicity over the tragic events at the Northwick Park Hospital Phase I unit. The continuing revelations about the mistreatment of military volunteers at Porton Down (Evans, 2008; Sample, 2009) also demonstrate the ways in which historical instances of research abuses can come to the fore long after the events actually occurred. Furthermore, the case of Dr Tonmoy Sharma (Dyer, 2008) illustrates not only the lengths to which some unscrupulous researchers will go to secure a personal advantage from exploitation of the research environment, but also the need for ethical scrutiny and vigilance in the research governance process. These, and other infamous examples, will be discussed in detail in Chapter 2 to outline the context for the rest of the book and the environment within which the law and ethics of research involving human participants operates.

The regulation of human participant research, of which research ethics is just one aspect, aims primarily at protecting the interests of research subjects and preventing abuses by ensuring that research proposals are scrutinised and research is monitored. This book will use anecdotal and hypothetical examples alongside documented evidence of historical abuses to illustrate the practical consequences of failing adequately to regulate research involving human participants. It will also consider a number of recent legislative changes that impact upon the process of ethical review, specifically the Mental Capacity Act 2005 in the context of consent and the Human Tissue Act 2004 with regard to the use of human tissues and body parts in research.

In general it is notable that legislation serves only to give legal force to ethical principles that RECs have hitherto upheld as a matter of good practice. However, recent legislative changes may also have implications for the operation of RECs, and raise the possibility of liability for REC members. These possibilities will be explored and assessed throughout this text alongside the ramifications of established legal actions to determine their affect on the process of ethical review, and the legal responsibility imposed on researchers and members of RECs.

Part I

Universal themes

Chapter 2

How did we get here?

A brief history of research ethics

> In their zeal to extend the frontiers of medical knowledge, many clinicians appear to have lost sight of the fact that the subjects of their experiments are in all cases individuals with common rights and in most cases sick people hoping to be cured.
>
> (Pappworth, 1967)

The importance of the regulation of healthcare research and the central role of research ethics and research ethics committees (RECs) is best explained when located against the backdrop of the chequered history of research involving human participants. This history includes a number of controversial incidents across a range of jurisdictions, such as the Nazi atrocities during the Second World War, the Tuskegee Syphilis study (Shamoo and Resnik, 2003: 181–186), and the now infamous Porton Down experiments (Evans, 2008). Such scandals have led to law reform aimed at ensuring that ethical imperatives are properly adhered to. The result is the development of a number of legal and regulatory measures based on ethical principles and guidelines and designed to protect the interests of human research participants. For example, in the United States it was not until after the public hearings on the thalidomide disaster that the pharmaceutical industry was legally required to publicly demonstrate the scientific efficacy and safety of new drugs for human use. The outcome on this occasion was the enactment of the 1962 Kefauver-Harris amendments to the Food, Drug and Cosmetics Act 1938 (Rothmann, 1987), which enhanced the control of the US Food and Drugs Administration (FDA) over research involving human participants. European legislatures later followed, leading to the introduction of legislative frameworks for the development of pharmaceutical products (Santoro, 2005: 12), which has culminated in the EU Clinical Trials Directive (2001/20/EC) and the UK Medicines for Human Use (Clinical Trials) Regulations 2004, SI 2004/1031 ('Clinical Trials Regulations'). Many of these legislative instruments contain detailed requirements for the conduct of research involving human beings and the process of ethical review that should be undertaken prior to the research commencing. Consequently, many of the functions of NHS RECs in the

United Kingdom are now prescribed by law, and predicated on ethical principles and guidelines that resulted from the controversies of the past. It is therefore of more than purely academic interest to trace the history of research ethics in order to explain the background to the current legal position.

Experiment and exploitation

The Nuremberg war crime trials, which condemned the atrocities conducted by Nazi medical scientists during the Second World War, ensured that research ethics and the law became forever closely associated in the public consciousness. The war crimes trials revealed that tens of thousands of prisoners held in concentration camps had been forced to become the involuntary subjects of callous and inhumane experiments. Probably the most notorious of these were the research projects undertaken by Joseph Mengele which, amongst other things, involved the psychosocial and sexual abuse of identical twins, non-consensual surgical interventions and subjecting prisoners to extreme levels of radiation or electric shock. Nazi scientists also conducted research into hypothermia by plunging naked people into freezing water to assess their tolerance to extreme cold, whilst other experiments involved deliberate physical wounding. Some prisoners, for instance, were deliberately wounded by being shot or impaled in order to study the healing process, apparently with a view to improving the treatment of battlefield casualties. Large numbers of these research subjects died or were permanently injured or disabled as a result of the experimentation, some were even deliberately killed. None of them participated voluntarily.

Nothing can condone the extreme abuse to which the Nazis subjected their victims. However, there is evidence to show that the atrocities they perpetrated were, at least to some extent, modelled upon eugenic practices prevalent in many states prior to the Second World War, and were far from unique. From the beginning of the twentieth century in the United States, for example, compulsory sterilisation was commonplace for people with mental illness, psychopathic personality disorders and those defined as criminally insane. The practice was so customary and routine that some states passed legislation supporting and enforcing the policy of sterilisation of the 'feeble-minded' (Proctor, 1988). Although not strictly medical research, these sterilisations might be seen as an experiment in social engineering, and one which would be regarded as unethical today.

In an environment where such abuses have become habitual it is not difficult to anticipate that experimentation on vulnerable groups within society might also come to be regarded as unproblematic. The large number of exploitative medical studies carried out on disadvantaged groups such as prisoners, children, the terminally ill and a range of other minority populations in the early twentieth century provides clear evidence of this phenomenon (Lederer, 1995). It is true to say, therefore, that these examples, including the brutality of the Nazi scientists, reveal underlying discriminatory tendencies that devalued the lives of some people within the societies that practised them. Taken together, they graphically demonstrate what can happen when the vulnerable, or those who are simply different, are treated without equal respect, leading to the normalisation of their mistreatment.

The Nuremberg Code of 1947 (Nuremberg Principles, 1996) was produced after the atrocities perpetrated by the Nazis were disclosed during the war crimes trials, and today most of the ethical principles governing research on human participants are still based broadly on those outlined in the Code. It set out 10 clear standards to which all medical researchers should adhere, including, centrally, the necessity for voluntary consent, the avoidance of unnecessary physical or mental suffering and adequate protection against them, even if that means terminating the experiment. The requirement that research subjects should be able to withdraw from the research at any time was also included. Yet even in 1947 the fundamental ethical principles outlined in the Nuremberg Code were not new or groundbreaking. An early example of a written consent form for medical research can be traced to a study on yellow fever conducted by the US army in 1900. The participants were provided with written information about the trial and how much they would be paid, and invited to sign to indicate their consent. The language used in the document might today properly be regarded as somewhat coercive however, and participants were not informed of the known, or unknown, risks to which they might be exposed, which makes the validity of any consent given highly questionable.

Even in pre-war Germany the importance of voluntary participation and informed consent in medical research had long been recognised (Vollmann and Winau, 1996), the historical background of which is littered with documented examples of unethical medical research (Schmidt, 2002). However, the graphic revelations of Nuremberg, depicting scientific excess coupled with medical malevolence, highlighted the need for stringent regulation and generated a climate within which research on human subjects would thereafter be expected to comply with acceptable ethical standards. Nevertheless, some, now notorious, examples of abuse still continued.

Notorious examples

The Tuskegee syphilis study in the United States is a case in point. The study took place in Tuskegee, Alabama, between 1932 and 1972 and was sponsored by the US Government. The study involved a total of 600 African-American men and was designed to trace the natural progression of untreated syphilis until the death of the subject. Two-thirds of the men were known to have been infected with syphilis, but the subjects were kept unaware of their medical condition throughout the study. Instead, they were told only that they suffered from 'bad blood' for which they were provided with free medical care, hot lunches and free burials when they died. During the course of the study the subjects were denied penicillin, despite the fact that its effectiveness as a cheap and reliable treatment for syphilis was well established by the early 1950s. Some patients died untreated during the study, some 40 wives became infected and 19 children were born with congenital syphilis. In some cases the researchers even intervened to prevent treatment when syphilis was independently diagnosed by clinicians outside of the study. The subjects were deceived as to the purpose of the study and the nature of their own medical condition, and denied therapy that could have cured them and saved lives, all in the name of research.

Eventually, in 1966, the true nature of the study was exposed in an influential article published by Henry Beecher (Beecher, 1966). However, the US Department of Health, Education and Welfare still failed to stop the experiment. It was not until clinicians objected to it on ethical grounds and public awareness was raised by press reports in 1972, that the Tuskegee study was finally halted (Jones, 1993). President Bill Clinton finally publicly apologised for the abuses perpetrated in the Tuskegee study 25 years later, in 1997.

Alongside the Tuskegee project, Beecher's article also described numerous other examples of minority and vulnerable groups being exploited in medical experiments. One such incident occurred in the United States between 1956 and 1980 and involved children with learning difficulties who were living at the Willowbrook State School in New York. Viral hepatitis was known to be so prevalent amongst the children resident in the school that the majority of them had contracted the illness within six months of their admission. The research team sought to study the transmission and progression of the disease as well as the efficacy of gamma globulin in its treatment. In order to do so the children were deliberately infected with hepatitis. Some children were given the virus orally through the ingestion of contaminated food, whilst others were exposed to it by injection. Their response, and the progression of the disease, was monitored over time.

At the time, the researchers obtained approval to conduct the study from the Willowbrook State School, the New York State Department of Mental Hygiene and the Human Experimentation Committee of New York University School of Medicine, as they were required to do (Munson, 1992). As such, it is arguable that the study was legitimate and performed in accordance with the ethical standards of the day. Approval was given by the bodies responsible for the school and the institution within which the researchers worked, and the parents of the children gave consent for their inclusion. There is, however, evidence to suggest that the full implications of the study were not properly explained to the parents, who therefore could not have fully understood the consequences before giving their consent (Shamoo and Resnik, 2003: 188). Furthermore, it is difficult to justify the deliberate exposure of children to the harmful long-term consequences of hepatitis for the sake of an experiment. With the benefit of hindsight, therefore, the legitimacy of the study is highly questionable. Even if the standards of the day were lower than those expected of contemporary research, it is difficult to envisage how circumstances such as this could be regarded as ethically acceptable in the post-Nuremberg era.

Similar revelations were made about the involvement of UK researchers in unethical research practices after the Advisory Committee on Human Radiation

Experiments (ACHRE), set up by President Clinton in 1994, published its report in 1996 (ACHRE, 1996). The Committee investigated and published evidence on a series of global research studies conducted under the name 'Project Sunshine', which commenced in 1944 and continued until 1974.

Scientists from around the world, including the United Kingdom, were involved throughout the various stages of the study. Initially, the experiments involved the intentional release of radiation into the environment as part of weapons testing, followed by an assessment of the effects of radiation exposure on the environment. Then, after the detonation of many nuclear bombs under controlled conditions in the deserts of New Mexico, concerns were raised about the possible effects of the resultant polluting radiation on human health. In particular, it was known that the nuclear tests could potentially result in exposure to strontium-90, a radioactive isotope that can be absorbed by human bone and eventually result in cancer. More specifically, it was feared that the toxic strontium-90 would travel around the world through air currents and then be washed to earth in rain, where it would be absorbed by the vegetation and consumed by large numbers of people. It seemed inevitable that, ultimately, the strontium-90 would find its way into the food chain, resulting in the exposure of large numbers of the public, especially through milk. Infants were thought to be at an especially high level of risk of exposure because they consume relatively high quantities of milk at a time when their bones are developing rapidly. Speaking of the extent of the concern at the time, one scientist, Professor Gavin Arneil, was quoted as stating that 'every tin of dried milk and every drop of breast milk was ticking and we needed answers' (Edwards, 2001).

As a result, specific research was carried out to try to ascertain the extent of any contamination and its effects. In the United Kingdom this involved a group of scientists based across England and Scotland working under the direction of the UK Atomic Energy Authority (UKAEA). Some of the research involved the teams conducting experiments themselves, whilst other aspects of the project required children's bodies and body parts to be exported to the United States for testing (Goncalves, 2001). Most of the samples were taken from young children and stillborn infants whose parents were unaware of the research or its implications because they were not consulted or informed. It has been suggested that, despite the fact that many parents probably would have consented to the inclusion of their offspring, informed consent was considered 'too sensitive to obtain, or even irrelevant' in the cold war culture that prevailed at the time (Rabbitt-Roff, 1999). The authorities and scientists who participated in this research were rightly and appropriately concerned about the possible effects of radiation exposure on the population. Research was necessary to ascertain the extent of any contamination and its possible implications for human health, but the failure to seek the consent of the parents cannot be condoned. Regardless of whether or not this neglect of the parents' rights was well-intentioned and based on a utilitarian imperative, it is reminiscent of the recent scandals at Alder Hey (Redfern, 2001) and Bristol (Kennedy, 2001), and would today be regarded as more akin to abuse than negligence.

Similar issues arose in relation to post-war research in the United States, known as the Jewish chronic disease case study (Fadan and Beauchamp, 1996). The study took place in 1963 and was designed to investigate the process of tissue rejection in relation to cancer cells and transplantation. Earlier research had suggested that the response of the body's immune system might be different in patients with cancer than it is in healthy subjects, so the study aimed to further assess the body's immuno-physiological responses to cancer cells. Twenty-two patients were involved and all were injected with live cancer cells without their knowledge. None of them had cancer. Consent was apparently obtained verbally, but the patients were not informed that they would be given live cancer cells and no documentary evidence of consent was recorded, although some commentators claim that some fraudulent consent forms were later produced. Because information that was crucial to the efficacy of the consent process was withheld the researchers denied the participants the opportunity to exercise their autonomy in deciding whether or not to be involved in the study. The researchers exposed the participants to the potential of great physical harm of which the participants were unaware, and may even have actively deceived them. As a result, the patients were put at great risk in relation to their physical health and treated with extreme disrespect, and the basic tenets of the Nuremberg Code and several other ethical codes were completely neglected.

Controversy in social science

Aside from what might be described as pure healthcare or medical research, RECs are today frequently called upon to review research that draws on methodology used in the field of social science. Here, also, is a history littered with unethical research practices, perhaps the most iniquitous of which are known as the Milgram experiments conducted at Yale University in the early 1960s. This series of studies involved multiple deceptions of the participants, together with emotional discomfort, manipulation and coercion, in varying degrees. Those involved as research subjects were told that the experiment involved an investigation of the effects of punishment on memory and learning, whereas in reality the researcher was interested in learning about obedience to authority. The subjects were recruited through newspaper advertisements and offered the inducement of a small sum of money if they agreed to participate. They were instructed that they would work in pairs with other participants, who were actually actors or stooges. Through a simulated randomisation process in which all participants were asked to select a slip of paper designating which role they would play, the actual subjects were assigned to play the part of teacher. In fact, the word 'teacher' was written on all of the notes but the actors were primed to ignore that and take the role of learners. During the experiment the learners were to be given the task of memorising certain information about which the teachers had to ask predetermined questions in order to test their recall.

The details of the tests varied depending on the specific experiment, but a typical example began with the teachers witnessing the learners being taken into an adjoining room and strapped into a chair that appeared to be connected to electrodes. In their separate room, from which they could hear but not see the learners, they were then required to ask the designated questions and activate a mechanism that allegedly administered an electric shock to the learner every time an incorrect answer was given. At the beginning of the experiment the teachers were instructed how to use the equipment and given a demonstration of the electric shock process. They were told that the voltage, and thus the severity of the shock, would increase with every incorrect answer up to potentially fatal levels, and the equipment was labelled with warnings that reflected the severity of the shock administered. As the shocks were apparently received the stooges playing the role of learners would simulate discomfort by shouting or pleading for the process to be stopped. Whenever the teachers seemed reluctant to continue, the supervisors of the research would calmly encourage them to continue with the experiment.

The participants were made aware throughout the process that they would be paid regardless of whether or not they completed the task, and most, generally around 65 per cent, responded to the gentle persuasion of the research team. Some participants questioned who would be responsible for any harm that resulted from the experiment and were assured that the researcher would take full responsibility. As a result some participants continued administering shocks even after they had reached the potentially fatal level and their learner had fallen silent. The results have been influential in developing theories about obedience to authority and have been used to try to explain why people might be prepared to commit atrocities against other human beings, particularly in war time. However, it is questionable whether the knowledge obtained can be justified by the means.

The Milgram experiments have become synonymous with unethical research practices because of the deception involved and the distress caused to the research participants. However, unlike many of the unethical clinical trials on record, some degree of deception was probably essential to this study. (For example, in the 1969 San Antonio Contraceptive study involving 70 Mexican-American women of low socioeconomic status, half were given a contraceptive and half a placebo, but they were not informed of this and none consented.) Nevertheless, the degree of harm caused to the participant in the Milgram study could probably have been mitigated. For example, the experiment was recently replicated in the United States and screened by *ABC News Primetime* in November 2007 using more ethical methodology. On this occasion Milgram's results were confirmed but the fake electric shocks were administered only up to 150 volts, rather than the allegedly fatal 450 volts in the original experiment. In addition, the participants were extensively counselled immediately after the experiment when the objectives of the exercise were explained to them and the fact that their partner stooges were safe and unharmed was confirmed. A 60-minute video of the event can be viewed at: http://thesituationist.wordpress.com/2007/12/22/the-milgram-experiment-today/

(last accessed August 2008). Approval for this replica study was given by the Institutional Review Board, which was reassured by the amendments to the original study, and the researcher, Professor Jerry Burger of Santa Clara University, claims that none of the participants has subsequently reported any ill-effects. It must be stated, however, that it was only possible to confirm the results from the 1960s because Milgram's original data demonstrated that those participants who were prepared to administer shocks past the 150-volt mark – the point at which the stooges first complained that they had had enough – were likely to continue to the top of the range, making it unnecessary for the replica study to proceed past this point. Had Milgram's results not existed, equivalent data probably could not have been generated under modern-day ethical constraints.

Modern day ethical constraints?

When the Nuremberg Code was introduced in 1947 following the Nazi war crimes trials, it took a broad human rights approach to research involving human participants. It introduced 10 basic guiding principles to be followed when conducting research involving human participants:

- Voluntary consent is essential.
- The research should be expected to generate fruitful results.
- The research design should be based on the results of animal experimentation or natural history, the results of which provide justification for human experimentation.
- All unnecessary physical and mental suffering should be avoided.
- No research should be conducted if it is expected that death or injury will be caused.
- The risks involved should never exceed the importance of the problem to be solved.
- Adequate facilities and preparations should be provided to protect the subject.
- Only properly qualified persons should conduct the research.
- The participant should have a right to terminate the research/experiment.
- The researcher must end the research if it seems probable that death, injury or disease will occur.

The Code was laudable in making informed consent the central requirement; however, it was silent on key issues like confidentiality and the need, as far as practicable, to distribute the benefits and burdens of research across the wider society. It also failed to provide guidance on whether and when ethical research might be conducted involving participants who are unable to give consent. Moreover, even though it was effectively an instrument of international legal regulation, the Code was largely ignored by medical professionals, despite public concerns that healthcare research should be conducted to high ethical standards. Consequently, in 1964 the World Medical Association (WMA) published the Declaration of

Helsinki (Mason and Laurie, 2006: 745; WMA, 2008). This encapsulated the main principles of the Nuremberg Code, addressed areas not covered by it and was endorsed by the medical profession as a mechanism through which the principles contained in the Code could be upheld.

The Declaration of Helsinki provides a more comprehensive code that sets out in its introduction detailed guidance on ethically acceptable rationale for research involving human participants. It goes on to outline (at paras 10–27) the basic principles that apply to the conduct of all medical research, including that which is combined with medical care (included at paras 28–32). The fundamental principles of research ethics, such as the need to ensure that the subjects are 'volunteers and informed participants in the research' (para 20), and that 'Medical research involving human subjects should only be conducted if the importance of the objective outweighs the inherent risks and burdens to the subject' (para 18) are also clearly articulated. Alongside these basic provisions it is also made clear that there are circumstances, albeit limited, within which it may be permissible for those who cannot give consent to participate in research. The situations within which this may occur and the mechanisms involved to protect the interests of such participants are carefully detailed at paras 24–26 of the Declaration.

Since 1964 the Declaration of Helsinki has been revised several times, most recently in Edinburgh in 2000 and Seoul in 2008. The 2000 revision was introduced after concerns were raised about the ethical implications of some pharmaceutical research, specifically placebo-controlled trials involving HIV/AIDs medication in developing countries. That revision was followed by the addition of two notes of clarification, one by the WMA General Assembly in Washington in 2002, relating to para 29, and one by the WMA General Assembly in Tokyo in 2004, relating to para 30. These addenda provided further detail on when placebo-controlled trials are ethically acceptable, and on making provision for participants to gain access to best acceptable post-trial treatment methods in the study design. In essence, according to the clarification note on para 29 of the 2000 revision, placebo-controlled trials should only be used 'in the absence of existing proven therapy'. However, even where there is an established treatment, they may be regarded as ethically acceptable where the trial is investigating a minor condition and 'patients who receive placebo will not be subject to any additional risk of serious or irreversible harm'. Consultation is currently underway regarding further revisions of the Declaration.

A number of other international codes and guidelines have been implemented since the Declaration of Helsinki was formulated. For instance, the Council for International Organisations of Medical Sciences (CIOMS) published its *International Ethical Guidelines for Biomedical Research Involving Human Subjects* in 1982, and these were revised in 1993 and 2002. They offer extensive guidance on all aspects of research involving human participants, ranging from the ethical justification and scientific validity of research, through the process of ethical review, to informed consent. The Guidelines provide a useful introduction to general ethical principles and include detailed sections on vulnerability, equity and compensation for injury alongside the more predictable aspects of the research process, such as consent and confidentiality. Commentary and discussion is integrated throughout the Guidelines, which flesh out the basic principles so that they can be readily applied to practical situations. Particularly interesting here is the approach to vulnerability, which is described as:

> . . . a substantial incapacity to protect one's own interests owing to such impediments as lack of capacity to give informed consent, lack of alternative means of obtaining medical care or other expensive necessities, or being a junior or subordinate member of a hierarchical group . . .
>
> (CIOMS, 2002: 10)

In general, the CIOMS Guidelines provide an excellent resource for anybody concerned with the ethics of research, not least researchers and members of RECs.

In 1996 the International Conference on Harmonisation of Technical Requirements for Registration of Pharmaceuticals for Human Use ('ICH') published a set of guidelines designed specifically to govern clinical trials of medicinal products. These are known as its Good Clinical Practice (GCP) Guidelines on the performance of clinical trials, and their origins are firmly rooted in the principles of the Declaration of Helsinki, insisting that clinical trials should be conducted in accordance with these principles. They have been adopted by the pharmaceutical industry in order to provide a unified standard across the European Union, the United States and Japan and to establish common practices. If strictly adhered to the technical requirements associated with drug development and testing in the various jurisdictions will be met and thus the need for duplication of testing and documentation during the product registration process will be avoided. In addition, the GCP Guidelines form the basis of the EU Clinical Trials Directive and the Clinical Trials Regulations, which govern clinical trials in the United Kingdom. Therefore, the ICH GCP Guidelines serve to streamline the process of pharmaceutical product development and registration whilst advocating sound ethical practices. The Additional Protocol to the Convention on Human Rights and Biomedicine Concerning Biomedical Research has been also influential in setting standards, but the United Kingdom is not currently a signatory to it.

In the United Kingdom, research ethics have been championed by a number of influential organisations led by the Medical Research Council (MRC), which actually published its first set of guidelines, *Responsibility in Investigations on Human Subjects* (MRC, 1962), prior to the Declaration of Helsinki. Guidance on research ethics has also been produced by numerous bodies of medical professionals such as the General Medical Council and the Royal College of Physicians. Most of these ethical codes of conduct are informed by the international codes previously described, which have also been inculcated into the legislative measures recently introduced in the European Union and United Kingdom. More specifically, clinical trials research in the United Kingdom is now the subject of EU legislation in the form of the Clinical Trials Directive and the Clinical Trials

Regulations 2004, which transposed the Directive into domestic law. These measures were largely responsible for shaping the process of the ethical review of healthcare research in the United Kingdom, and provide a model for social care and social science research.

Contemporary misdemeanours

Given the fact that the examples of unethical research discussed earlier in this chapter focused largely on incidents from the middle of the twentieth century, one might be forgiven for thinking that the closer levels of ethical scrutiny and research regulation described above have done away with unethical research practices. That would be a mistake. The late twentieth century and early twenty-first century provide many controversial cases of similar or greater gravity. Space forbids a comprehensive review, so only those examples that resulted in public concern or changes in regulatory practice will be included.

One such example is the case of Mrs Thomas, who underwent a mastectomy for breast cancer in the 1980s (Nicholson, 1992). After the surgery she observed that other patients who had had the same treatment for the same condition received post-operative counselling, but she did not. After four years of investigation, Mrs Thomas discovered that she had unwittingly been part of a research study assessing the impact of post-operative counselling on breast cancer patients. The study compared the outcomes of women who had been counselled with those who had not across 58 different healthcare institutions and over 2,300 patients. The women were not informed that they were part of a research project, nor were they asked to consent. It transpired that the ethics committee had allowed the study to proceed without the usual requirement for consent because the healthcare researchers involved had found it distressing to have to explain the full details of the study to the patients. It is tempting to conjecture here that the research team may have had concerns that revealing the full facts could have led to a failure to recruit so many 'volunteers'. Ethical review always involves a balancing act between the interests of the potential subject and those of science and society, but the balance should not tip to the detriment of the participant.

Perhaps the most notorious recent examples of research abuses in the United Kingdom occurred at around the turn of the twentieth century and had far-reaching effects with regard to the regulation of healthcare research. Of significance here is an incident that has become known as the Staffordshire Babies Case (Bowsley, 2000), which took place between 1989 and 1993 and was instrumental in the formulation and implementation of the *Research Governance Framework for Health and Social Care* (DoH, 2002) ('Research Governance Framework') in 2001. The case involved the trialling of a kind of ventilator that had the potential to replace the conventional incubators used in the care of very young babies with breathing difficulties. The device was similar to the 'iron lungs' used to treat polio in the 1950s and was called the continuous negative extrathoracic pressure, or CNEP, machine. It was described to parents as a 'kinder, gentler treatment'.

Of the 122 babies entered into the study, 15 suffered brain damage and 28 died. However, this figure is not regarded as statistically significant when compared with conventional treatment, as 32 babies in the control group also died. Despite the protocol being subjected to the required ethical review, it was later alleged that many babies were entered into the study without proper consent from their parents. Clearly, great care would need to be taken to explain the implications of a study such as this to parents whose newborn infants were so gravely ill that they required a ventilator for life support. In fact, many were never told what was involved, and others subsequently claimed that they did not understand the implications of what they were told. In addition, evidence later came to light that some consent forms appeared to have been forged. The exposure of these obvious failures to adhere to sound ethical principles in the Staffordshire Babies Case combined with other revelations about unethical practices to prompt a complete overhaul of the regulation of healthcare research in the United Kingdom, and led directly to the introduction of the Research Governance Framework. In addition, the publicity around the retention of children's bodies and tissues at Liverpool's Alder Hey hospital (Redfern, 2001), the poor practices at the Bristol Royal Infirmary (Kennedy, 2001) and the contents of the Isaacs Report (HM Inspector of Anatomy, 2003) concerning the retention of Mr Isaacs' brain for research purposes despite his express prohibition, also resulted in the introduction of the Human Tissue Act 2004, which now governs the procurement, storage and use of human tissue.

It is interesting to note that despite the rigid regulatory and ethical frameworks within which healthcare and social science research now operates, and the introduction of ethical guidance and formal ethical review processes since Nuremberg, research on the development and use of new therapies has continued to court controversy. The majority of the publicity has centred upon the safety of drugs such as Prozac and Vioxx once they have gone through the trials phases and reached the market, but research into other types of healthcare interventions has also made headlines and called the conduct of research into question.

The reasons why?

The reasons behind the kinds of research abuses described throughout this chapter are many and complex. It would be easy, and perhaps trite, to argue that the examples from the early twentieth century were due to lack of regulation and poor understanding of research ethics; however, that would be misinterpreting the issue. Reasons for the attitudes of some medical researchers have already been suggested in the early part of this chapter, but it is interesting to question why similar research misconduct has continued even after Nuremberg, Helsinki and the myriad of guidance and regulatory documents now available. With specific reference to Nuremberg, Claire Foster suggests that it is possible that some clinicians 'thought that the Code was only for badly behaved doctors like those tried at Nuremberg' (Foster, 2001: 141). In addition, because the Code applied only to non-therapeutic research, doctors themselves were the only arbiters of what constituted ethical practice in research directly involving clinical care in a climate where 'the doctors would regard themselves as professionals bound by strict ethical principles, and their patients would simply do as they were told' (Foster, 2001: 141). Attitudes such as this may be regarded as outdated and irrelevant in today's climate of strict professional regulation, but the recent testimony of Dr Andrew Wakefield at the General Medical Council (GMC) might suggest otherwise.

In 1998 Dr Wakefield and colleagues published an article in *The Lancet*, the content of which was subsequently renounced by the journal, but which at the time suggested a link between autism and the Measles Mumps and Rubella (MMR) vaccine. This was controversial in itself but it was the details of Dr Wakefield's research practice that saw him before the GMC in 2008. At the hearing it was admitted that as part of his research Dr Wakefield had, *inter alia*, 'treated' children despite not being qualified in paediatrics, and drawn blood from children at his son's birthday party in return for payments of £5 without ethical approval. In his defence Dr Wakefield admitted to believing that parental consent alone was sufficient to authorise taking the blood samples, and to having a poor understanding of research ethics (BBC, 2008), which seems difficult to believe given the well-publicised history of research ethics outlined in this chapter. Why, then, do examples of exploitation in healthcare research continue to surface despite the proliferation of national and international regulatory instruments?

It is arguable that in some circumstances the regulation associated with research and research ethics is itself responsible for researchers flouting ethical codes and guidelines due to inflexible governance arrangements resulting in delays and overly burdensome administration. Whilst it is essential that proper scientific and ethical reviews are conducted in the process of drug development and other healthcare interventions, it is also imperative that avoidable delays that can have the effect of stifling or limiting the research enterprise do not become institutionalised. If researchers ignore the formalities or seek out ways to avoid the review process the effect is counter-productive and detrimental to the protection of research participants. More specifically, inappropriate delays in the ethical review of proposed healthcare research might ultimately result in patients being denied interventions that could improve their health and quality of life for longer than is necessary. It may also result in the continuation of outdated or outmoded practices that will subsequently be reassessed and found wanting in the light of research data. Safe and efficient systems of ethical review are crucial to ensure that research is conducted according to acceptable standards and the resulting health services and treatments have been reliably tested, but care should be taken to ensure that the bureaucracy associated with the process of ethical review does not in itself promote misconduct by researchers who try to avoid engaging with the system.

Conclusions – implications flowing from this history

This chapter has explored recent, and not so recent, examples of abusive research practices in order to locate the development of the ethics and regulation of research involving human participants within its historical context. The examples given here, and others available in the extensive literature on this topic, clearly demonstrate the consequences that can flow from treating research participants merely as a means to an end, and the dangers that are inherent in prioritising research and its aims over respect for the needs of the participants involved (LaFleur *et al*, 2007). Research ethics have their origins in the basic principles of medical ethics which apply to the delivery of healthcare generally as well as to the conduct of research (Chalmers, 2006: 83). However, whereas the aim of healthcare is to benefit the individual patient, research usually aims to provide knowledge and understanding that will benefit science or a particular patient population, rather than the individual research participant. For this reason, amongst others, the ethical imperative to protect the interests and rights of the research participant, alongside her physical and emotional well-being, dictate that research should be the subject of more stringent regulation and guidance than ordinary healthcare.

It is evident from this discussion that the regulatory frameworks developed to govern healthcare research represent a precautionary response to the exploitative practices witnessed throughout the history of medical research. This type of precautionary principle is generally applied to prevent unacceptable harm to individuals or groups, and is frequently used in generating government policy, especially with regard to health and the environment in situations of scientific uncertainty. It has been described as 'a culturally framed concept that takes its cue from changing social conceptions about the appropriate roles for science, economics, ethics, politics, and the law in pro-active environmental and management' (O'Riordan and Cameron, 1994: 12), a description which clearly encompasses the regulation and ethical guidance associated with healthcare research. As such, the ethical guidelines and regulatory mechanisms that govern research on humans are designed primarily to help to minimise the risk of harm resulting from participation in research. However, it must be noted that this often happens in circumstances where the risk of harm occurring is uncertain, as is the possible magnitude of any harm that might result. The role of the REC is to try, as far as is possible, to work within the guidance available to anticipate the kinds of harms that might occur, and advise the researcher of ways in which they might be avoided. However, it must be accepted that a researcher who is intent on deliberately flouting the ethical rules is unlikely to be deterred by the regulation or the advice of an REC. Chapter 9 will therefore introduce some examples and implications of contemporary fraud and misconduct in research.

One thing that is certain is that 'Public trust is a precondition to the success of health research' (Chalmers, 2006: 100), and the unethical behaviour of clinicians and researchers involved in practices such as those described above has had far-reaching effects. Not only has it been responsible for the strict governance arrangements that now attach to health and social care and social science research, it has also had an impact on public attitudes to research. For example, it has been noted that in some geographic areas the adverse publicity surrounding scandalous research practices has resulted in the extreme reluctance of some groups to participate in healthcare research (Burroughs, 2005). This is particularly known to be the case amongst members of the African-American community in the United States, who have been on the receiving end of numerous research abuses. It has been claimed that this is especially important in clinical research on medicinal products, where diverse population groups should be included because 'pharmacogenetic research shows that drug effectiveness and toxicity can vary substantially among racial and ethnic groups' (Burroughs, 2005). Burroughs explains this further, reporting that:

> Genetic variations, or polymorphisms, are naturally occurring variants in the structure of genes and the products they encode. These genetic polymorphisms change gradually in prevalence across continents and do not separate populations into clearly demarcated groups that correspond to popular ideas of race. The most obvious manifestations of racial differences – skin color, cranial features, and so forth – are superficial characteristics that have little relevance to drug responses or the progression of complex diseases such as diabetes mellitus and coronary heart disease.
>
> (Burroughs, 2005: 81)

If the result of research misconduct is that it becomes impossible to recruit cohorts of research participants representing a broad cross-section of the population, the effects could be very damaging. At a minimum the failure to include participants from a cross-section of society could lead to the research findings not being readily generalisable, and in extreme situations the ability to research at all may be inhibited if public support is lost. The destructive effects that bad research practice can have on the research enterprise are therefore easy to see.

Furthermore, the failure to adhere to established guidelines and codes can lead to successful legal action relating to negligence, crime or breach of specific statutory provisions. In addition, research can be curtailed or funding withdrawn or withheld in the future, through non-compliance with ethical standards. Chapters 3 and 4 will discuss the regulation of research in relation to ethical codes and guidelines, and outline their legal status in more detail. For now, however, it is sufficient to note that many codes and guidelines hold merely advisory status and are not in themselves legally binding. It is also evident that in most, if not all, jurisdictions, the work of RECs is not supported by mechanisms for legal enforcement. Despite this, most researchers do observe sound ethical principles simply because it is the right thing to.

Chapter 3

Ethics in theory and practice

Introduction

Chapters 1 and 2 introduced the fundamentals of research ethics review and briefly outlined the chequered history of research involving human participants. It now falls to this chapter to provide an overview of the ethical and philosophical frameworks within which research ethics committees (RECs) operate in practice. The chapter will open with an overview of the role and remit of RECs as a central part of research practice, in order to identify and explain some of the practicalities associated with the process of ethical review. A consideration of the philosophical and bioethical theories that underpin the process of ethical review, as conducted by RECs, will follow on from that to explore the relationship between theory and practice in the work of RECs. It will become clear in this process that there is no single guiding theory of research ethics. Instead, the ethical review of human participant research relies upon the interaction between the various theories that apply so that in practice the response is often both pragmatic and subjective.

The role of the REC – within and outside the NHS

The primary role of an NHS REC is to advise its appointing authority on how far a research proposal complies with established ethical standards. Alongside this it is charged with protecting the dignity, safety, rights and welfare of actual or potential subjects, whilst taking account of the needs and safety of researchers undertaking research of good quality. RECs outside the NHS will do this according to their own remit which will, in turn, depend on the constitution and standard operating procedures associated with the relevant governing or appointing body. Thus, university RECs, for example, tend to operate to a remit designed and approved by the university itself, but which will generally be informed by principles established by general ethical guidance, such as the Declaration of Helsinki. The principles enshrined in other codes and guidelines, such as those recognised by professional bodies like the General Medical Council, British Psychological Society, and the research funding councils that finance much of the research conducted in the university sector, will usually also be incorporated. In addition, university and other institutional ethical review committees will often consider the wider implications of research that may be conducted under their auspices. Should they, for example, permit research that might inform the arms race, or accept funding from controversial sources such as cigarette manufacturers? These concerns are beyond the remit of NHS RECs and others that focus solely upon the implications of research for human participants. They will therefore not be discussed in this work.

An NHS REC is required to provide an independent, competent and timely review. Independence is generally assured by maintaining constitutional autonomy from the appointing body, and at an individual member level, through the appointments process and the requirement for potential conflicts of interest to be disclosed. Education and training on research ethics, the process of ethical review and relevant contemporary issues are designed to ensure that committee members are competent for the job. Regulatory time constraints operate to ensure that researchers are not unduly delayed in the commencement of their research or unfairly discriminated against. These provisions are enshrined in the *Standard Operating Procedures for Research Ethics Committees* (NRES, April 2009), described in *Governance Arrangements for Research Ethics Committees* (DoH, 2001) (GAfREC) and, in relation to clinical trials, they are upheld by law in the EU Clinical Trials Directive (2001/20/EC) and the Medicines for Human Use (Clinical Trials) Regulations 2004, SI 2004/1031 ('Clinical Trials Regulations').

In addition, a central part of the role of an NHS REC is that regard should be had for the requirements of relevant regulatory agencies and applicable laws. In general this means that the REC must be aware of the law as it applies to each proposed research project, and require researchers to agree to comply with it. For example, RECs need to be aware of the implications of the Human Tissue Act 2004 (HTA 2004) and the Mental Capacity Act 2005 (MCA 2005), as well as the common law of consent and negligence as they relate to the research context. Negligence and other common law responsibilities will be considered in Chapter 4, consent in Chapter 5, and the specialist concerns relating to the MCA 2005 and the HTA 2004 will be addressed in Chapters 7 and 8 respectively. Alongside these specifically legal concerns, each REC will primarily be concerned with maximising the autonomy of potential research participants and upholding the ethical principle of justice as it tries to assess the potential benefits and burdens of the research and how these may be distributed across society.

This is the point where it becomes necessary to consider the essence of what an REC actually does, and how it performs its role in practice. There are two aspects to this, which may be termed 'the practical' and 'the intellectual'. The practical aspects are related to the physical process of ethical review, such as the constitution of the committee, including the number of members and their qualifications for membership, alongside the administration of the meetings and the decision-making process. The reasoning behind the ultimate decision arrived at may be regarded as the intellectual part of the process and is based upon philosophical theories and bioethical guidelines and principles. Each of these areas will be discussed in turn.

The practicalities of the review process

There are a number of models that could be adopted by an organisation in order to facilitate the ethical review of research proposals involving human participants. It could, for example, develop a system of committees, each of which has a fixed number of members, meets on a regular basis and follows a prescribed decision-making method – as is the case with NHS RECs. Alternative approaches might involve the appointment of a single individual or small group of personnel to consider ethical issues related to research, or the implementation of a virtual committee that conducts its decision-making in cyber-space (by email for example) and never physically meets. In some situations, depending on the need for the review process, it is also possible to construct a tick box approach to ethical review where an individual or group assesses research protocols by reference to predetermined questions. NHS RECs are, however, constituted according to strict rules concerning the composition of the committee, qualifications of members, the regularity of meetings and the kinds of research protocols that ought to be reviewed. Their role and remit are strictly defined by the Clinical Trials Regulations, the Department of Health in GAfREC, and in continually updated standard operating procedures, which dictate the structure and practice of NHS RECs in detail. These governance arrangements will be the main focus of this section.

Governance of NHS RECs

In the NHS the ethical review of research proposals forms a vital part of the *Research Governance Framework for Health and Social Care* (DoH, 2005a: 7), and properly constituted RECs are a fundamental part of the governance and regulation of research in the NHS. According to the National Research Ethics Service (NRES) web pages there were 155 NHS RECs in the United Kingdom as of January 2008, all of which were categorised as either recognised or authorised RECs. Three types of recognised RECs exist and are designated as either Type 1, 2 or 3. These committees are all recognised by the United Kingdom Ethics Committee Authority (UKECA) for the purpose of reviewing clinical trials of investigational medicinal products (CTIMPs). Schedule 2, para 5(1) to the Clinical Trials Regulations defines the members of the UKECA as the Secretary of State for Health, the National Assembly for Wales, the Scottish Ministers and the Department for Health, Social Services and Public Safety for Northern Ireland. These are essentially the appointing authorities for RECs.

Type 1 RECs only review Phase I CTIMPs, which involve healthy volunteers rather than patients. It should be noted that because of the requirement in the Clinical Trials Regulations that adults who lack the capacity to consent for themselves should only participate in trials where there are grounds to expect that some benefit to the participant will result, Type 1 RECs cannot be flagged to review research involving incapacitated adults. They are, however, the only RECs permitted to review clinical trials involving healthy volunteers and, unlike the other types of recognised RECs, some of these committees operate outside the NHS. As such, they may be described as independent, or non-NHS, ethics committees (IECs).

Type 2 RECs are empowered to review CTIMPs other than those involving healthy volunteers, but only where these will take place in a single NHS domain, which in England is defined as a single strategic health authority. In Wales, a domain is defined as a regional office of the NHS, in Scotland it is defined as a health board, and the whole of Northern Ireland is designated as one domain. By comparison with Types 1 and 2 RECs, a Type 3 REC may review all multi-site or multi-domain research anywhere in the United Kingdom, including CTIMPs, except where they involve healthy volunteers. Authorised committees are distinct from those recognised for these purposes and are authorised to review proposals to conduct all kinds of health-related research in the NHS other than CTIMPs.

In terms of governance, the UKECA has ultimate responsibility for the RECs that review research involving clinical trials of investigational medicinal products, whether they are NHS or independent RECs. The specific operational role of NHS RECs and their relationship to researchers and research participants is the subject of extensive guidance developed by the Department of Health and the NRES. Formerly known as the Central Office for Research Ethics Committees (COREC), this body sets out measures governing the operation and accountability of RECs. More formally, these responsibilities are outlined in GAfREC. Alongside this the Clinical Trials Directive and the Clinical Trials Regulations provide the statutory framework within which NHS RECs are constituted, including requirements about appropriate membership and operating procedures. Theoretically, these do not apply to authorised committees, or to the review of non-clinical trials research. However, guidance from the NRES makes it clear that the same arrangements should be followed for all research involving human participants within the NHS (NRES, May 2008: 9).

The Clinical Trials Directive and the Clinical Trials Regulations provide specific details of who is eligible to be a member of a recognised NHS REC and in what capacity. In this regard Sch 2 of the Regulations stipulates that each REC should have a maximum of 18 members, one-third of whom should be lay members. A lay member is defined primarily as a person who does not qualify as an expert member (see below). Former, non-medical healthcare professionals such as nurses, physiotherapists and the like, may sit as lay members, but only if they are not registered to practise in that professional capacity at the time of their membership. Similarly, those who have previously been involved in conducting clinical research are permitted to become lay members, but are not eligible to sit as lay plus members. Schedule 2 does not specifically define what is meant by the term 'person involved in the conduct of clinical research other than as a research subject', but it should be construed as including persons such as scientists, monitors and data collectors, as well as those performing monitoring and management tasks.

Lay membership of an REC tends to consist largely of people with expertise in philosophy, ethics, bioethics, law and theology. Frequently, they also have a professional interest in research ethics, perhaps as academics or practitioners, but they are not regarded as expert members within the NHS context. Interestingly, those who are, or have in the past acted as, a chairman, member or director of any body responsible for the provision of healthcare are also eligible to sit on an REC as a lay member, but previously registered doctors or dentists will never be eligible as such.

At least half of the lay members on each REC must also meet further criteria, which will qualify them as lay plus (lay+) members. These individuals must never have had prior experience in the healthcare professions or any involvement in clinical research other than as a subject. They must never have been a chairman, member or director of a body involved in providing healthcare. In addition, people who have previously been involved in research involving human data or tissue are also excluded from this lay+ category. The role of lay+ members is specifically to be the voice of the lay person, 'the person on the London Underground', to provide an entirely independent perspective on the ethical implications of the proposed research. They are regarded as uniquely qualified to do this because they have no experience of working in the health services or in clinical research. RECs outside the NHS, such as those in the university sector, tend also to make use of lay members, who will usually be drawn from populations independent of the institution concerned.

As well as the patients and members of the public who are typical lay members, a majority of REC members will be expert or professional members, drawn from disciplines including medicine, nursing, statistics, pharmaceuticals and a range of academic specialities. Ideally, included amongst these members will be people with an interest in both hospital and community medicine, a practicing nurse or midwife, a pharmacist, and at least one person who is registered by the Health Professions Council. Others groups of people who might qualify as expert members include academic scientists, data monitors and statisticians. All NHS REC members are accountable to their appointing authority, which will be a strategic health authority in England and their equivalents in Scotland and Wales. In Northern Ireland, RECs are appointed by the Central Service Agency supporting health and personal social services.

It is notable that under the current definitions certain people, despite the fact that they are not and never have been qualified as healthcare professionals, clinical researchers or former doctors or dentists, are not be eligible for membership of an NHS REC. This very limited category includes persons such as hospital or nursing home managers. These are personnel who can be regarded as providing medical, dental or nursing care in the course of their business, which would exclude them from falling under the definitions for both lay and expert membership.

All members are appointed for a fixed term set by their appointing authority. Generally, this will not exceed five years. Under Sch 2, para 5 of the Regulations, an REC should have a chairman, vice-chairman and alternate vice-chairman. These key members will be appointed by the appointing authority for a defined period 'not exceeding the remainder of his term as a member' (Sch 2, para 5(2)).

It is the primary role of the vice-chairman to step in whenever the chairman is unavailable to perform her duties, and in practice she or he will also tend to chair sub-committees and take on other tasks as designated by the chair.

In recent years the number of NHS RECs has been adjusted to try to ensure that the workload is distributed relatively equally amongst them, and that each committee reviews sufficient numbers of applications for its members to maintain an appropriate level of expertise and competence. Generally, these committees meet once a month, and review approximately eight new research proposals at each meeting. Their work is overseen by the NRES, which is part of the NHS National Patient Safety Agency (NPSA). Like many departments within the NHS, these organisations have been the subject of extensive reorganisation and restructuring in recent years, and the delivery of their operation seems to be in an almost permanent state of flux.

Regardless of changes to the management of NHS RECs, however, the basic remit and role of the committees remains fairly constant. They are required to review research protocols that will involve patients and users of the NHS, including those recruited by virtue of being in receipt of treatment either at present or in the past, and those treated under contracts with private sector institutions (GAfREC, para 3.1). In addition, research that will involve carers and relatives of NHS patients must also be subjected to the review process. These groups can provide valuable insights and information about healthcare and the experiences of being a patient or a carer, but in the past they fell outside the remit of NHS RECs. As a result some researchers were able to involve them in research without being required to undertake an ethical review, and potentially without affording them the kinds of protections that ought properly to be extended to research participants. This situation was rectified with the publication of GAfREC.

Healthcare research that involves only NHS staff who will be recruited by virtue of this fact must also be subjected to scrutiny by an REC (GAfREC, para 3.1b). Ethical review is considered necessary here in order to protect staff from potential exploitation, and to ensure that they will not be unduly distracted from their workplace obligations. Imagine, for example, the situation where a senior staff member wishes to enlist colleagues to participate in a study that involves them donating blood every day for a month. Not only would this raise concerns about the ability for individual members of staff to decline to participate, especially if there is a power imbalance in the relationship between the colleagues, but it might also result in staff being absent from their work stations and possibly unavailable to provide patient care, both of which are important ethical issues.

Beyond this, and under an agreement between HM Prison Service and the Department of Health, the remit of NHS RECs extends also to the review of research involving prisoners who are inmates of the prison service in England and Wales, Scotland or Northern Ireland. This includes those who have been convicted as well as those held on remand or temporarily imprisoned for other reasons, but excludes patients detained at special hospitals or other psychiatric secure units under mental health legislation, and juvenile offenders detained in local authority secure accommodation or secure training centres. Research involving only prison staff does not require ethical review by an NHS REC, but is likely to fall within the remit of other RECs, such as university human participant RECs.

Clearly, conducting research involving groups such as these raises a myriad of ethical issues around privacy and dignity, as well as the freedom to consent or refuse to participate. It may also introduce concerns around researcher security and safety, all of which are entirely valid in terms of the need for ethical review. However, although it is abundantly clear that the interests of this, literally captive, population need to be protected, it is less apparent why research involving prisoners should fall within the remit of NHS RECs. One can only speculate that this may be because, as evidenced by the examples discussed in Chapter 2, prisoners have frequently been the victims of abusive health research practices. That being the case it is perhaps less surprising that as host to the longest established formal system of ethical review in the United Kingdom it should fall to the NHS to provide this service. It must be acknowledged, however, that whilst NHS RECs have a wealth of experience and expertise in ethical review generally, the specific issues associated with conducting research in prison populations may require particular skills and understanding. With that in mind only a limited number of specialist NHS RECs are authorised to conduct this type of specialist review and their focus is on issues around the potential vulnerability of prisoner participants.

Ethical review is also required where researchers do not need direct contact with patients or other human participants, but seek instead to make use of data related to patient care, or to tissues, organs or other bodily material. Specific issues related to healthcare data and human tissue will be considered in detail in Chapters 6 and 8 respectively. In addition, ethical review by an NHS REC is required where the research proposes only to make use of NHS premises or facilities. Included here are all types of equipment, such as X-ray machines, heart monitors or the like, and physical space, including operating theatres or consulting rooms, whose use for research might deprive patients of access to them. Similarly, it is important that the ethics associated with the potential benefits and burdens of research are assessed if there might be cost implications related to the use of health service resources.

Where research is designed to involve in vitro fertilisation (IVF) on NHS patients or fetal material, it too will require ethical review by an NHS REC, as will any projects pertaining to the recently dead in NHS premises. Requiring these types of research to be subjected to NHS ethical review is today largely uncontroversial; however, for some researchers great controversy arises in relation to the ethical review of social care research. The *Research Governance Framework for Health and Social Care* applies to both health and social care research but a great deal of research involving social care clients concerns aspects of their care other than areas related specifically to their health and health-related needs. Where research has no health implications, the complex NHS REC applications process has been regarded by many as too cumbersome for projects which involve, as they see it, minimal potential for harm. Consequently, a separate ethical review process has been introduced with its own committees and distinct applications procedure. Unfortunately, for those researchers whose work spans both health and social care, the result can be an additional layer of bureaucracy whereby the ethical review process is duplicated and different operational approaches must be navigated. However, in some areas improved communication and joint planning between NHS research governance offices and health and social care organisations is now helping to reduce the bureaucratic burden.

The NRES has actively striven to reduce the amount of red tape involved in research governance, for instance through the development and introduction of the Integrated Research Application System (IRAS) in 2008. More particularly, the NRES has been empowered by the Department of Health to develop national standard operating procedures that apply to all RECs under its purview. These apply across the whole of the United Kingdom even though Scotland has adopted its own, slightly different, version of GAfREC (DoH, October 2001). The standard operating procedures are published and regularly updated by the NRES and are designed to establish uniform operating practices across RECs so that researchers can expect to receive consistent treatment. As well as detailed guidance on the role, remit and operation of RECs, they also cover all matters relating to the administration of applications made to NHS RECs and the organisation of REC meetings. Within this they contain information and advice about matters such as the minimum number of members that must be present at a meeting to ensure that it is quorate, the establishment and functions of sub-committees, and the form of decisions that RECs can reach. For example, on completion of the review process, an REC is entitled to give either a favourable or unfavourable opinion of the proposal. In the interim it can also give a provisional opinion with a request for further information, or it can decide to formally record 'no opinion' if it is felt that the views of an external referee need to be sought (NRES, April 2009: 75).

The standard operating procedures also include details of the statutory and regulatory requirements surrounding research involving human tissue and research involving adults who are unable to consent (NRES, April 2009: ss 11 and 12). Issues relating to these areas will be discussed in detail in Chapters 8 and 7 respectively. Extensive guidance is provided within these sections, but in general RECs are not required to become experts in the law as it applies to these specialist areas. Instead, they are expected only to have sufficient understanding to be able to ascertain that researchers are sufficiently cognisant of their obligations when conducting research in these areas (Roy-Toole, 2008). Although the NHS standard operating procedures are comprehensive, it is also legitimate for an NHS REC to establish its own standard operating procedures independent of the NRES, but these would have to be specifically approved by the UKECA as being compliant with the Clinical Trials Directive and other regulatory requirements.

The introduction of inclusive standard operating procedures to govern the operation of the ethical review process is clearly beneficial to RECs and their members. They draw upon a wealth of experience as well as setting out the legal and regulatory environment within which NHS RECs must operate. However, they also help to define the legal responsibilities of RECs by setting out standards to which they are expected to adhere. The legal implications of this will be considered in detail in Chapter 4, after an examination of the intellectual aspects of the review process.

Intellectual aspects of the process of ethical review

The work of human participant RECs may be broadly construed as balancing the potential for scientific progress against the safety and well-being of those who may take part in the experimental process. In healthcare this can be a complex process, hence the development of ethical codes such as the Declaration of Helsinki referred to in Chapter 2, and the legal and regulatory measures that will be discussed in Chapter 4. The basic tenets of research ethics are, however, outlined and clearly stated in the various codes of conduct. For example, the Declaration of Helsinki states at para 18 that:

> Medical research involving humans should only be conducted if the importance of the objective outweighs the inherent risks and burdens to the subject.

Paragraph 19 states:

> Medical research is only justified if there is a reasonable likelihood that the populations in which the research is carried out stand to benefit from the results of the research.

The review process therefore always involves weighing the risk of potential harm to the welfare of the research participant against the possible benefits to society more broadly.

Balancing competing moral interests is an imprecise calculation, particularly in situations where the potential harm is great or the potential benefit speculative. Hence, in deciding whether or not a research project is ethical these issues can cause division between researchers and RECs, and amongst REC members. Added to this, some types of experiment or intervention will always cause moral divisions within society. Outside of the arena of healthcare research, for instance, one only needs to observe the discord surrounding techniques like the genetic modification of agricultural plants, human cloning and the use of pre-implantation genetic diagnosis to select the sex of embryos, to appreciate the significance of strong moral views in such deliberations. Not everyone holds the same moral view, and some situations will provoke more dissent than others. It should be no surprise therefore that RECs will occasionally struggle to reach a consensus decision about a proposed piece of research.

In such circumstances, where a committee's deliberations lead to disagreement or dissent and a consensus of opinion is difficult to achieve, the ability to assess a research protocol by reference to philosophical theory, or by going back to first principles, can be invaluable. Recourse to philosophical and bioethical theories will not only provide a conceptual foundation against which committee members can analyse the problem at hand, but can also offer a basis upon which to justify the decision ultimately reached.

A number of theoretical, philosophical and bioethical theories based broadly on duty or deontological reasoning, and consequentialist or teleological approaches, underpin the type of ethical review conducted by RECs. Other influences, such as religion, rights and feminism, also have a part to play in the review process, since these tend to inform the moral reasoning of individual REC members. In practice, however, these theoretical perspectives are rarely overtly discussed or explicitly considered. Instead, the deliberations of an approvals committee tend to implicitly adhere to the underlying ethical principles by referring to the issues and concerns routinely addressed, such as consent and confidentiality. Despite this, the importance of theoretical perspectives like consequentialism, deontology and rights, amongst others, cannot be over stated. Therefore, beginning with utilitarianism, the main theoretical approaches relevant to ethical review will be briefly described below to examine how they might assist RECs in reaching decisions about whether or not to advise that a piece of research meets established ethical standards.

Consequentialism – the utilitarian principle

The moral theory of utilitarianism is generally believed to represent an alternative to the Christian religious ethics that preceded it. It was championed in the late eighteenth and nineteenth centuries by philosophers such as Jeremy Bentham (1789), who is regarded by some as its founding father in the modern era, and John Stuart Mill (1859), who further developed the theory. In essence, utilitarianism looks to the consequences of any given action to determine its moral correctness, or otherwise. It rests on the premise that actions are morally right if they maximise pleasure or happiness amongst those who are affected by them, and vice versa. Generally, therefore, the outcome of a consequentialist or utilitarian analysis of a particular situation depends on whether the interests or well-being (welfare) of those involved will be maximised, which is often defined as achieving 'the greatest good for the greatest number'. Since the aim of utilitarianism is to ensure maximum happiness, or good, it may therefore be termed a goal-based philosophy, which makes it a particularly apt approach to adopt in REC decision-making.

Conducting a utilitarian analysis of a research protocol will require an REC to determine the maximum net benefit that can be achieved from the proposal. Put simply, the pros and cons of any proposal will be assessed to weigh the potential harm, or disbenefit, to the participant, against the potential benefit, or good, that may result. For Bentham this could, in theory, be calculated numerically by assessing how many people would experience pain, and how many pleasure, as a result of a single action. Additionally, the qualities of the displeasure, such as its intensity and duration, could also be measured as a part of the calculation. Of course in many ways this approach is too simplistic, as it offers no indication of what is meant by either happiness or pain. It also allows the possibility for morally objectionable actions to be countenanced even if they might otherwise be considered intrinsically wrong, as long as their consequences can be regarded as maximising happiness.

Identifying what is a good or a negative outcome will inevitably divide people where strongly held moral opinions exist. In these circumstances it is evident that prioritising one course of action to achieve what is believed by some to be a positive outcome might involve disregarding other ethical principles (Gillon, 1985: 25). Consider, for instance, a research study that has the potential to revolutionise an aspect of healthcare practice but can only be successfully conducted by ensuring the participants are unaware of their participation in the research. Permitting the study to go ahead in this way would mean flouting the established ethical principles of honesty and autonomy, but can the outcome justify the means? Emily Jackson discusses the issue through the pertinent example of whether or not we should keep the promises we make (Jackson, 2006). Where promises can have good or bad consequences, her argument suggests that if the good consequences of a promise surpass the bad then it should be kept, but that the promise may be broken if the bad consequences will outweigh the good. However, this takes no account of the intrinsic value attached to keeping promises. It seems clear, therefore, that consequences alone cannot always be relied upon to generate ethical outcomes, or to produce a consensus decision in an REC.

Some commentators believe that in situations where strict adherence to moral principles such as honesty would undermine overall welfare by limiting potentially very good consequences, the more intuitive principles can be combined with utilitarianism by a process described as 'critical reasoning'. Instinctively, this seems to prioritise outcomes that might be more generally regarded as desirable (Hare, 1981). Similarly, some approaches, such as rule consequentialism, advocate that the consequences may be weighed against other, more general moral rules. In this way it is possible to combine theories with principles, like honesty and truth, in order to reach a satisfactory outcome (Boyd *et al*, 1997). Nevertheless, tensions will always exist in practice between utilitarian theory and the duty-based emphasis present in deontological theory.

Deontology – duty-based ethics

Deontological, or duty-based ethics, operates on the basic premise that certain actions are in themselves inherently right or wrong and that consequences are largely irrelevant. In short, under this model some actions or choices simply cannot be justified by the consequences they achieve. The characteristics of the conduct concerned alone determine its moral acceptability and, as such, an action will be regarded as good because it is the right thing to do, and vice versa.

For example, we should always tell the truth simply because it is right to do so. Further, because telling the truth is the right thing to do we also have a duty to do so. In essence, then, deontology pertains to the morality of choices made rather than to the person or persons making the choices.

In respect of how we ought to treat others, deontology is regarded by some as based upon individual rights. Accordingly, the nature of deontological theory dictates that in making choices there are some basic or founding principles that should always be abided by. For those who adhere to a rights-based version of deontological theory, respect for persons and their rights is a central theme, and one that has been widely promulgated under the Kantian maxim that people should be treated as an end in themselves and never merely as a means to an end. More particularly, it involves a right of persons not to be used merely for the benefit of others. The components of this right are, however, rather complex when tested against a practical example, such as the now famous 'Trolleys and Transplants' hypothetical (Thomson, 1985). Thomson outlines a situation where a runaway trolley, or train, is destined to knock down and kill five workers. The train can be diverted into a siding to save these people, but in doing so it will inevitably kill one person who is working there. Intuitively it seems right to re-route the train. However, what of a situation where five patients waiting to receive transplanted body parts can be saved if a surgeon kills one patient in order to harvest her organs? Here it is intuitively wrong to kill the patient, even if five lives will be sacrificed otherwise. The difference lies in the complexities of deontological theory.

The victim in the transplant scenario is used as a means to an end whereby she is deliberately killed for the benefit of others. In the train or trolley scenario, however, the five workers will be saved by diverting the train regardless of whether the worker is present in the siding. Her presence in the siding is coincidental rather than deliberate or engineered, and her death is simply an unavoidable consequence of saving the other five. The consequences or outcomes of the actions involved are of course centrally important, but from a deontological point of view it is the intentional using of a human being without her consent and for the benefit of others that condemns the transplant surgeon.

Healthcare research frequently involves exposing its participants to potential harm in order to generate data that will hopefully benefit others in the future. It could be argued that the participants are being used as a means to an end, but so long as the participants' rights are upheld this is usually permissible. In other words, for deontologists it is generally justifiable to engage a participant in the research enterprise so long as to do so does not interfere with her rights. The fact of recognising and upholding individual rights is in itself a good that legitimates the conduct concerned. By implication, then, so long as the participant is enabled to exercise her right to self-determination by giving or withholding consent, her contribution to the research is morally permissible. However, this appears also to depend upon the level of harm to which the participant is exposed as it cannot be ethically right to permit a potential participant to agree to be subjected to unacceptable levels of harm. In some cases adherence to a pure deontological approach may result in an intractable *en passé* in the REC decision-making process. As a result it is often necessary to weigh up the potential good and bad effects of a research proposal by balancing deontological rights and wrongs against the possible and probable outcomes of the project.

Balancing deontology and consequentialism

It is abundantly clear from the preceding discussion that there are bound to be tensions and conflicts between the consequentialist and deontological approaches when applied to the ethical review of research. The almost polarised approaches of consequentialism, which focuses primarily on the interests of the collective, and deontology, which emphasises the rights and interests of the individual, may make consensus difficult to achieve. In practice, for example, there could be circumstances where a consequentialist approach might countenance recruiting research participants who have not consented, perhaps where the investigation requires the involvement of unconscious patients admitted to hospital for emergency treatment. For the deontologist, the end point, or consequences, do not justify the means by which they are achieved. Therefore, the violation of the rights or interests of the research participants in order to obtain the required data would be regarded as unacceptable. By contrast, the consequentialist would look to achieving the greatest good for the greatest number and measure the utility of the project as a whole, off-setting it against the possible harm to the participants.

A key aspect of the assessment of the ethics of a project lies in determining the level of harm that might occur through conducting the research in the absence of consent. This usually represents a value judgment based on one's own personal ethics, and can easily lead to disagreement amongst REC members. How, for example, can the possible hurt and distress caused to a participant who was enrolled in a study whilst unconscious be assessed? Clearly, an REC might insist that the researcher implement mechanisms to minimise this harm, by allowing the patient to require that her data is not used should she object to inclusion once she has regained consciousness, for example. But for some the damage, in terms of the violation of trust and abuse of a vulnerable person, has already occurred. At this point other factors, such as rights, dignity and welfare, must also be considered.

Rights

A rights-based approach to research ethics stresses the rights of individuals to exercise their autonomy and self-determination, not least through the giving or withholding of consent and the protection of their privacy. Founded primarily on liberal individualism, rights-based morality is regarded by some as an aspect of deontological ethics, which is certainly apparent from the foregoing discussion. It is also sometimes regarded as an aspect of the Kantian imperative not to treat persons as a means to an end. In fact, the classical interpretation does not focus on the rights of the individual; rather, it stresses the duty of others not to regard individuals in this way. A more contemporary interpretation of rights-based analysis tends to focus more on formal human rights and even legal rights, and has become the focus of some debate in the research ethics community.

Under GAfREC a central aspect of the responsibility of an NHS REC is to protect the safety, *rights*, dignity and welfare of actual or potential research participants. It has been suggested that this refers to moral rather than legal rights, which is an appropriate viewpoint (NRES, 2008: 4), but there is no explicit clarification to this effect in GAfREC. That said, the majority of the work of an REC is devoted to upholding and enhancing the research participants' moral rights, through maximising their autonomy and their ability to decide for themselves whether or not to take part in research. Aside from this, however, there are a number of legal rights that attach to various types and aspects of research. The right to privacy, for example, is a moral right protected by the law, and the law of consent acknowledges the right to self-determination. The relationship between ethics and law is complex, but in the context of research ethics it is perhaps important to recognise that the central rights with which an REC is concerned on behalf of potential participants are frequently recognised as legal rights based on morality. Some are enshrined in human rights legislation such as the Human Rights Act 1998, or other statutes, but many are supported by common law cases. The significance of these and other legal rights will be considered in subsequent chapters.

Virtue ethics

Virtue ethics is informed by the works of Aristotle and Socrates and looks to the motivation behind the action rather than its consequences (Gardener, 2003). As a result, virtue ethics, like virtues more generally, attach to the character of the person rather than to her conduct. Therefore, according to Campbell *et al*, a person who is 'a model of moral conduct' will exhibit virtuous traits such as compassion, kindness, fairness, honesty and respect for others and their feelings (Campbell *et al*, 2001: 8–9). With this as the starting point, a virtue ethicist attempting to determine the morality of any given situation would tend to enquire as to what a virtuous person would do in that particular scenario, and regard the impulse or rationale behind the conduct as the primary consideration in assessing its morality.

Close examination of the concept of virtue ethics in the context of healthcare research ethics gives rise to a number of relevant concerns. The first arises in trying to decide how to define what is meant by a virtue. By implication, in this theory virtues are always inherently good, or morally excellent, and therefore to be valued, but it is unclear whether the characteristics of a virtue are universal or if they are culturally or historically specific. Does every community value kindness, for example, and is the idea of fairness the same everywhere, or might different standards and ideals be ascribed to it? Secondly, there may be a danger that virtuous characteristics are used to justify actions that are in themselves immoral, at least to some. What of the freedom fighter or political activist who turns to violence to promote her cause? Commitment to a cause and courage in its pursuit may be regarded as moral ideals – virtues – but should they be revered if the result is harm to others? Arguably, therefore, well-motivated and otherwise virtuous conduct should be regarded as wrong if its consequences turn out to be bad. Similarly, it is difficult to condone an action born of 'bad' motives, even if its consequences are ultimately good. Furthermore, if, as some virtue ethicists claim, an act cannot be wrong if performed with good intentions, it is difficult to assess the usefulness of virtue ethics in relation to the ethical approval of healthcare research (Macintyre, 1984). In the context of healthcare research it can generally be assumed that the researcher is motivated by the inclination to do good, for instance by attempting to understand better the causes of ill-heath, or trying to contribute to knowledge about medicinal cures. This being the case, the value of virtue ethics to RECs would seem very limited.

However, not all virtue ethicists agree about the insignificance, or otherwise, of consequences. By stepping back from the concerns associated with conse-quences it is possible to focus on specific virtues, honesty or fairness for exam-ple, and uphold them as ideals in certain forms of conduct. In this way virtue ethics can provide a useful gauge against which RECs might measure a research proposal to assess its compliance with established ethical principles. More spe-cifically, what if, for example, a researcher sought to withhold information from her potential research participants fearing, legitimately, that providing complete information would bias the data? The REC would need to consider not only the impact this would have on the ability of the recruits to act autonomously and give an informed consent, but also how such an approach might affect the general attitude of future research participants. For instance, would it undermine the repu-tation of researchers generally by questioning their honesty and trustworthiness? Acting honestly and in a trustworthy manner is clearly a virtue that RECs should encourage researchers to practice, both for the general good and in order to pro-tect the interests of potential participants. However, there may well be legitimate circumstances where it is appropriate, even necessary, not to fully disclose the details of a research project.

The twin goals of maximising autonomy and trust in the participant and achieving the desired research results may be difficult to reconcile. The REC could, therefore, decline to give a favourable opinion in such circumstances, or it may insist that steps are taken to minimise any harmful effects, such as ensuring that the participants are fully de-briefed and informed of all the details, including the reasons for the 'deception', at the earliest possible opportunity. In this way it is again apparent that the practical work of an REC involves balancing competing ethical theories and approaches to research.

Feminist ethics – an ethics of care

Many commentators have argued that there is a close relationship between virtue ethics and what has become known as a feminist ethics of care (McHale and Fox, 2007: 111). These theories are born of a body of feminist academic thought that broadly revolves around the idea that gender bias is pervasive in society to the disadvantage of women. Adopting such a simplistic explanation is dangerous, however, since feminism in fact represents a diverse set of principles and ideals rather than a single thesis, the underlying premise of which is concerned with exposing and breaking down relations of dominance in all spheres. With this in mind, feminist ethics are often adopted, though perhaps not in name, in the process of ethical review. An obvious example concerns the insistence of many RECs that where a researcher is also the clinician responsible for the care of the potential patient participant, she should not be involved in the consenting process. In such a situation there is a clear power imbalance between the doctor researcher and the patient participant, which could disadvantage the patient. Further to this, it has been argued that women tend to adopt an ethic of care, known as a caring or relational approach, to problems, whilst men are more concerned with individual-istic justice-based solutions (Gilligan, 1982). On this basis, feminist ethicists tend to believe that the relational or caring emphasis encourages a holistic view that takes account of the human cultural and social aspects involved in any situation to achieve a more empathetic response. This is regarded as counter to the less-flexible, some would argue more male, approach inherent in the four principles espoused by bioethicists.

Whilst it is not possible, or appropriate, to generalise, research proposals submitted by members of the nursing professions often reflect these feminist ideals in the methodology adopted and the research questions to be addressed. For example, such research frequently involves qualitative methods designed to reveal detailed insights into specific issues relating to the experience of being a patient or a carer in particular contexts. Sadly, this emphasis has in the past cre-ated tensions and misunderstanding amongst REC members more used to assess-ing proposals that seek quantitative data capable of scientific statistical analysis. In many ways, such conflicts epitomise the discord between a more feminist ethic of care and the allegedly masculine, quantitative approach to research and research ethics. It is heartening to note, however, that RECs are developing greater expertise in the review of research, adopting qualitative methodologies; and consequently these enmities are being overcome.

Intuition

The gut reaction or intuitive morality is a common starting point in bioethics generally, and also in relation to research ethics. It relies on the fact that some practices and proposals instinctively simply seem wrong while others appear perfectly acceptable. The example of sham surgery is a case in point. The pros-pect of a surgeon deliberately cutting into a person's body for purely investiga-tive purposes that will have no therapeutic benefit offends one's sense of what is appropriate for a surgeon to do. But that in itself does not mean that a project involving sham surgery should automatically be rejected. Instead, a complex ethical analysis should be conducted to identify whether in fact it is justifiable to conduct the trial and expose the participant to the potential harm. The answer will depend on a number of factors, including the balance of risk to the participant against the potential benefit to be derived from the procedure. In short, even a proposal that instinctively appears to violate all ethical sensitivities should be subjected to scrutiny and evaluated according to established ethical principles. In this way it may be possible to overcome what Miller describes as an 'error in ethical judgment and reasoning derived from misguided moral intuition' (Miller, 2004: 111), whereby the ethics of medical research are measured according to standards normally adopted in the therapeutic context. Miller argues that it is a mistake to conflate research ethics and clinical ethics because medical research, unlike clinical practice, is not ruled by the therapeutic principles of non-maleficence and beneficence alone. Alongside this, moral intuition varies from person to person and according to cultural values and beliefs, leading to inconsistent and sometimes incoherent decisions. Accordingly, intuition will sometimes provide a basis at the outset of the decision-making process, but gut reactions should not be allowed to dominate.

The principles of medical ethics

Alongside the theories described above medical ethics has for some time been dominated by what is known as the four principles approach, and these are also relevant in the context of research ethics. Principlism, as some critics have termed it (Clouser and Gert, 1990), was introduced by Beauchamp and Childress in the late 1970s. Their book, *Principles of Biomedical Ethics*, is now in its sixth edition and has largely dominated bioethics ever since its initial publication (Beauchamp and Childress, 2006). The four principles described are beneficence, non-maleficence, justice and autonomy, and they provide an ethical framework applicable to medical practice that is also helpful in relation to research ethics.

Non-maleficence equates to the Hippocratic imperative *primum non nocere*, or first do no harm, whilst beneficence entreats the clinician or researcher to do good. In practice, there is an obvious tension between these two principles as it may be necessary to inflict some harm in order to achieve a 'good' outcome. Consider, for example, the situation where it is necessary to draw blood, or perhaps administer a drug by injection in clinical practice or as part of a research trial. The ultimate aim is to do good, either by obtaining research data that will inform the study being performed or by aiding diagnosis and treatment. Yet to do so it is necessary to cause harm by puncturing the skin and/or administering a noxious substance. Clearly, it is necessary to weigh the level of harm to be inflicted against the possible beneficial outcome in order to decide whether it is legitimate to stick the patient or research participant with a needle.

Similarly with autonomy, which is widely interpreted as allowing patients or research participants the right to decide for themselves whether to accept an intervention that is offered. In some contexts autonomy allows a kind of Millian libertarian approach that permits individuals to act however they choose, so long as their actions do not impinge on the liberty of others. In others, it may be tempered by a more deontological emphasis. It is unlikely, for example, that an REC would regard it as ethical simply to offer a potential participant the choice whether or not to sign up to a research project regardless of the level of harm she would encounter. More probably the REC would discern a duty to protect the interests of the participant, either by rejecting the proposal altogether if it was perceived as especially harmful, or, at a minimum, by ensuring that the participant was fully informed about the potential harm. In this way the participant could still exercise her autonomy, but she would be doing so on the basis of an informed choice.

The final principle of justice applies similarly in relation to research ethics, but has also been the basis of some controversy. Perhaps the most obvious application of justice or fairness in the context of healthcare research occurs with regard to the desire to spread the burdens and benefits of research as widely as possible across the community. This suggests that as far as is feasible within the confines of each research protocol, the inclusion criteria should be couched so as to make as broad a cross-section of society as possible eligible to take part. In other words, where the research population is not specifically limited by factors such as the condition being studied or the age range necessary to achieve the results, there ought to be few restrictions on who is eligible to participate. By implication this would mean that some groups who have traditionally been excluded from participation, such as adults with learning disabilities or others with limited mental capacity, would be permitted to become involved.

Both researchers and RECs are becoming increasingly familiar with research that is aimed at discovering more about people with learning disabilities and their health and care requirements. Specific guidance is also available on the application of the Mental Capacity Act 2005 in these circumstances, and expertise is being generated in relation to it. The issue here, however, concerns the inclusion of people with limited mental capacity as participants in research whose results are aimed at the general population. Researchers have traditionally shied away from including people with limited mental capacity because of the logistics of obtaining consent. It has been suggested, however, that to do so is to discriminate inappropriately against a significant proportion of the population. If research will genuinely have broad application across the community then all members and factions of the community ought to be represented in the research, including those who have learning disabilities or any other special characteristics. People from all walks of life suffer physical and mental ill-health so it is apposite to include everybody in healthcare research. Reflecting this view, several funding bodies now require the participation of people with learning disabilities as a precondition of financing projects (Walmsley, 2001). RECs are also able to insist, as far as practicable, on the inclusion of a broad cross-section of society in order to spread the burden of the research and ensure the generalisability of its results. However, the practicalities involved in obtaining consent and supporting people with learning disabilities throughout a study mean that many researchers remain resistant to the idea. In addition, legal issues are raised concerning the inclusion of people who lack mental capacity in research that will not benefit them or others with the same condition. These will be addressed in greater detail in Chapter 7.

Critics argue that the four principles approach does little to assist in decision-making since it often requires the practitioner, researcher or REC to prioritise particular principles, but fails to offer guidance as to when, and which, principles, should take precedence. It is clear that equality and justice is no less controversial than the other principles in this regard.

Conclusions

The preceding discussion demonstrates that no single theory or principle can be adopted as a guiding philosophy in relation to research ethics. Instead, REC decision-making will consist of balancing the various approaches to arrive at a consensus decision. In so doing three specific aspects of the proposed research will be scrutinised, including the efficacy of the research protocol, the qualification of the researcher to conduct the investigation, and the potential impact upon the participant. All are crucial to the aim of protecting the safety, rights, dignity and welfare of the potential research participant. In recent years the introduction of the NHS *Research Governance Framework for Health and Social Care* and the Clinical Trials Directive have diminished the necessity for RECs to assess the suitability of a researcher. Although it would clearly raise ethical concerns if a researcher was not qualified to perform the research, it is now the job of sponsoring institutions and governance departments to ensure that researchers are adequately qualified and properly supervised. Similarly, it falls to the researcher and her sponsor to assess the environment within which the research will be conducted with regard to physical safety and resource issues. Nevertheless, it remains the role of the REC to question these aspects of a proposal and ensure that they have been properly assessed. The standardised questions included in the NHS research ethics application form are designed to facilitate this and expedite the review process.

The recent proliferation of RECs into organisations such as universities and research-funding bodies means that some RECs may operate differently in practice and view their role differently depending on their defined remit. However, on the whole the general principles of ethical review are fairly consistent. As a result university, social science, social care and private sector Type I RECs all tend to apply the same basic principles as are adopted by the long-established NHS RECs. Within this, RECs conduct critical analysis balancing the needs of the researcher and society against the protection of the research participant to form an opinion as to the ethical acceptability of each proposal. However, in spite of the broad similarity of approach, RECs are still charged with producing inconsistent and sometimes eccentric outcomes. To some extent this is inevitable given the characteristics of ethical review and the principles and philosophies upon which it is founded. The formalities involved have been standardised with respect to procedure, but the nature of the process invites differences of opinion and interpretation amongst REC members and between different RECs. It is perhaps trite to state, therefore, that the nature of ethical review is such that differences of approach, opinion and sometimes outcome are to be expected. However, the mundanety of the claim does not alter its force. What is important is that RECs are prepared to question their own decision-making whilst understanding the reasons for differences between RECs and researchers and accepting criticism as inevitable. It is hoped that the remaining chapters will assist in this process.

Chapter 4

Legal liabilities of RECs

Introduction

This chapter will begin by outlining the statutory framework within which NHS research ethics committees (RECs) now operate to try to locate the responsibilities of RECs within their legal context. It will include some discussion of the background to the Medicines for Human Use (Clinical Trials) Regulations 2004, SI 2004/1031 ('Clinical Trials Regulations') and their relationship to the EU Clinical Trials Directive (2001/20/EC), the full title of which is the 'Directive of the European Parliament and of the Council on the approximation of laws, regulations and administrative provisions of the Member States relating to implementation of good clinical practice in the conduct of clinical trials on medicinal products for human use'. This will be followed by a detailed overview of the law of negligence in relation to the Clinical Trials Regulations. In order to provide some contextual analysis, the law will be examined by referring to a hypothetical case study whose aim is to demonstrate the ways in which the law might apply to any REC or REC member who neglected their basic duty to conduct a competent ethical review. The situation relating to breaches of statutory obligations under the Mental Capacity Act 2005 and the Human Tissue Act 2004 will be discussed in Chapters 7 and 8, and more general discussion of the common law that applies to consent and confidentiality will be discussed in Chapters 5 and 6 respectively.

The extent and legal implications of the regulation of NHS RECs has been the subject of much recent debate (Douglas, 2007; Roy-Toole, 2008: 114; Laurence, 2008; Taylor *et al*, 2008). The arguments stem in no small part from the fact that there is to date no case law to aid interpretation and add clarity to the statutory and regulatory obligations imposed upon NHS RECs. Some controversy, even confusion, about the circumstances within which RECs and their members might attract legal liability is therefore inevitable. This chapter will explore some of those controversies and confusions to attempt to explain the relationship between law and ethics in the context of the ethical review of healthcare research. Many of the principles underlying the common law position of NHS RECs, such as negligence and judicial review, also apply to committees that review research proposals outside of the NHS, including those responsible for the review of health and social care-related research and those in the university sector. However, much of the analysis here will focus on the regulation of clinical trials of investigational medicinal products (CTIMPs) and the responsibilities of NHS RECs in relation to them. There are two key reasons for this. First, the majority of the law surrounding healthcare research is statute law, which centres on medicinal products and product development, and there is at present no UK case law associated specifically with the work of RECs. Secondly, as explained in Chapter 3, it is a matter of policy that NHS RECs apply the standards and procedures required in the review of CTIMPs to all health and social care research they review. In addition, the ethical principles that underpin the work of NHS RECs are the same regardless of what kind of research is proposed, and the need to respect and protect the 'safety, rights and welfare' of research participants applies to all kinds of healthcare research. Hence, the guiding principles and standard operating procedures of healthcare RECs are the same irrespective of the specific details of the research intervention proposed.

The route taken by the Clinical Trials Directive to the UK statute books in the form of the Clinical Trials Regulations was long and complex. The central aim of the Clinical Trials Directive is to harmonise the conduct and regulation of clinical trials of medicinal products across the Member States of the European Community while simplifying the administrative provisions. More specifically, it is geared towards generating an economic and regulatory environment that promotes the conduct of clinical research and encourages the discovery and development of new medicinal products. The systematic changes introduced in the Directive are designed to promote harmonisation across the EU through the introduction of a uniform set of regulatory processes aimed at reducing administrative costs and uncertainties. Fostering greater co-operation between Member States involved in multi-centre, multi-national research was also a central aim of the Directive. As such, it is arguable that the Directive and the impetus behind it are 'industry led' in so far as it is designed to provide a legal framework through which clinical trials aimed at the development of new drugs can be conducted with minimal intrusion from regulatory bodies and government agencies (para 10 of the preamble). The Directive also aims simultaneously to protect human research participants (Art 3). Both aims are laudable, but their pursuit through statutory intervention inevitably introduces bureaucratic hurdles that require careful negotiation.

Conformity in the conduct of pharmaceutical research has long been the norm. Pharmaceutical companies tend to operate within a global market environment, wherein the guidelines for good clinical practice have been effective for many years (Baeyens, 2002). Large-scale trials across boundaries and borders (multi-centre, multi-national trials) are beneficial to the industry and their management is made easier by the relative homogeneity of licensing requirements. These, in turn, have been largely designed with the needs of the pharmaceutical industry in mind, making it possible to adopt practices in research and development that facilitate compliance with the regulatory and licensing requirements of large numbers of different countries and jurisdictions. Those involved in the industry recognise that the maintenance of high ethical standards helps their products obtain the required licences and also enables them to derive the public relations benefits associated with the promotion of best practice in research and development. It is perhaps no surprise, therefore, that the ethical and professional principles established in the Declaration of Helsinki and the International Conference on Harmonisation (ICH) Good Clinical Practice (GCP) Guidelines on the performance of clinical trials to ensure that trials comply with accepted ethical standards, represent a central plank of the Directive (Art 1 (2)–(4)).

In the United Kingdom the Clinical Trials Directive was transposed into UK law on 1 May 2004 in the form of the Clinical Trials Regulations. In most respects these Regulations mirror the provisions in the Directive, but some have argued that they diverge in important areas. Nicholson has claimed, for instance, that whilst the Directive defines ethics committees as 'an independent body in a member state . . . whose responsibility is to protect the rights safety and wellbeing of human subjects involved in a trial' (Art 2(k)) this independence is compromised in the UK Regulations (Nicholson, 2004). His main point is that the arrangements for the appointment of committee members, chairs and vice chairs contained in the Regulations will lead to a loss of 'independence' in contravention of the Directive. The thrust of this argument is that because the United Kingdom Ethics Committee Authority (UKECA), as the appointing authority, will have the power not only to set up and abolish RECs but also to appoint its members, the Regulations are out of step with the Directive's requirements that RECs be independent. Effectively, the concern is that appointments will be 'overtly political' (Nicholson, 2004: 1212). Whether or not this is a real concern is difficult to determine with any certainty. It is established practice that REC membership appointments are made at local level and this is set to continue. New members are generally recruited through public advertising with selection being made by interviews conducted by chairs, co-ordinators and Office of Research Ethics Committees (OREC) managers. Nolan principles regarding openness and competition in recruitment practices do appear to pertain. Perhaps the bigger question is whether any proposed appointees will subsequently not be ratified on the basis of 'political' interference. Without focused empirical research it would be difficult to gather evidence conclusively to demonstrate this, but given the complexity of the work and its voluntary nature it would seem unlikely that the process will be corrupted through interference by the UKECA.

One way in which it is arguable that the process of ethical review may have been corrupted, however, relates to the relationship between the Regulations and the ethical imperatives contained within the Declaration of Helsinki. This has also been called into question because the Regulations require 'that clinical trials be conducted according to the ethical principles of an out of date version of the Declaration of Helsinki, rather than the substantially rewritten version approved in 2000'. The preamble to the Directive itself specifies that:

> The accepted basis for the conduct of clinical trials in humans is founded in the protection of human rights and the dignity of the human being with

regard to the application of biology and medicine, as *for instance* reflected in the 1996 version of the Helsinki Declaration . . . '

(emphasis added)

The Directive was laid down in April 2001 but drafted prior to that, while the Edinburgh revision of Helsinki was approved in October of 2000, presumably during the process of drafting the Directive. The wording of the Directive, specifically, 'as for instance reflected in the 1996 version of the Helsinki Declaration', would appear to suggest an expectation that the Directive will be applied according to best practice at the time, rather than limiting its interpretation to that detailed in the 1996 revision of the Declaration of Helsinki. However, Sch 1, Part 1, para 2 to the Clinical Trials Regulations stipulate explicitly that:

'Declaration of Helsinki' means the Declaration of Helsinki adopted by the World Medical Assembly in June 1964, as amended by the General Assembly of the Association in October 1975, October 1983, September 1989 and October 1996.

At least in the context of clinical trials this seems, for the first time, to give the Declaration of Helsinki the force of law in the United Kingdom. If this is the case it is particularly notable because, in line with other ethical guidelines and codes, it had previously been regarded as merely 'soft law', that is to say, informative but not enforceable. That being the case, the amendments made in Edinburgh in 2000 and Seoul in 2008 would appear to have been deliberately excluded from the UK Regulations.

Given the controversy surrounding some aspects of the 2000 revision in particular (specifically the use of placebos where there is an established treatment, which remains controversial, especially in relation to licensing regulations in some jurisdictions, most notably the United States), it is easy to speculate that the emphasis on the 1996 version of Helsinki may be included for political reasons. Clearly, the single most important aspect of an REC's work relates to the independence of the review itself, which is fundamental to the quality of the review process and the safety of the system. Yet it is evident that in this regard RECs may feel that their independence is compromised if they favour principles adopted in Helsinki 2000 whilst the Regulations – the law – states that they should operate under the 1996 version. Cynics might argue that, combined with the fact that the Regulations stipulate that the UKECA, 'the authority', 'shall monitor the extent to which ethics committees adequately perform their functions', this potentially further undermines the independence of RECs.

Despite this controversy the Regulations do build upon established rules of good practice and ethics in clinical trials research and enshrine a great many concepts and practicalities associated with research ethics into UK law for the first time. Amongst these is the need for consent to be given voluntarily and for the interests of the subject to be held above those of society and science. Thus, the impact of the Regulations has been far reaching, not least in the major change they introduced to the status of NHS RECs, which became legally recognised bodies for the first time. The Regulations also include provisions defining the membership, constitution and operating arrangements of NHS RECs by law, and therefore give rise to potential new sources of legal liability. Some of the more significant implications of these changes will be explored below with a discussion of the public law of judicial review and potential liability in negligence as they affect RECs.

Aside from the Clinical Trials Regulations, recent years have also witnessed significant legal reforms in the area of healthcare more generally, and these have also had an impact on the operation of clinical and healthcare research and the role of RECs. Of particular note are the Mental Capacity Act 2005 and the Human Tissue Act 2004, which introduce new legal requirements and mechanisms governing these specialist areas of medical research. These will be considered in some detail in Chapters 7 and 8 respectively, but it should be remembered that the general common law principles, of negligence particularly, discussed in this chapter are also relevant. An NHS REC that fails to discharge its responsibilities under these statutes will be as likely to be liable in negligence as will one that breaches its duty under the common law of consent or confidentiality. An REC that was negligent in the performance of its duty prior to the implementation of the Regulations could theoretically always have been liable in law for that negligence. However, as will become clear later in this chapter, although there were numerous common law grounds upon which an REC might be held legally liable, negligence being the most likely, it would have been exceptionally difficult for a claimant to succeed in such a claim.

It is notable, however, that although this chapter takes as its focus the possible legal liability of RECs, no case has as yet ever been brought against an REC in the United Kingdom. This is undoubtedly in part due to the difficulty in so doing, but most overwhelmingly is the result of the good practice adopted by NHS RECs both before and after the introduction of the Clinical Trials Regulations. Since the Regulations have been in force, the system has been increasingly professionalised with greater emphasis on the responsibilities of RECs to observe guidance and meet legal deadlines in the process of ethical review. There is greater accountability through accreditation and monitoring and the review process has been standardised by the improved provision of training. Nevertheless, the more rigid legal structure within which RECs now operate gives rise to greater potential for legal action by both research participants and researchers, and it is these possible causes of action that will be explored in the remainder of this chapter.

Negligence

Civil or criminal liability may flow from negligent actions. However, criminal liability in relation to healthcare generally relates only to cases where there has been an extremely serious failure to adhere to accepted standards of professional conduct. Criminal liability is therefore very rare and usually applies only in cases where grossly negligent conduct has caused death, and is exceptionally unlikely to apply to RECs. By comparison, however, although there are to date no recorded cases in the United Kingdom, it is relatively easy to envisage a situation where civil (tortious) liability for negligence might be imposed where an REC has failed in some way adequately to perform its duty.

What follows is a brief exposition of the ways in which the law of negligence might apply to RECs that fall short of their professional duty. This must be premised by the caveat that the increased regulation and professionalism of RECs since the implementation of the Clinical Trials Directive means such that action is not only very unlikely to be brought, but also incredibly unlikely to be successful. Perhaps the best way to illustrate the reasons for this is by referring to specific hypothetical scenarios. Imagine then the following situation:

> Sam has entered into a research project to investigate a new treatment for tennis elbow. Sam suffers from the condition and, as she has tried all other treatment options, she falls squarely within the inclusion criteria for the study. She is given an information sheet, which she reads. The research nurse then goes through the details with her verbally and Sam agrees that she understands the implications of participation and signs the form. The new intervention is to be administered weekly by injection. One arm will receive the active agent whilst the other will be injected with a placebo and act as a control. The procedure will be blinded so that neither Sam nor the investigator knows which arm is receiving placebo and which the active agent. Sam will be required to complete a diary recording her symptoms. Her elbows will be examined and her diary monitored at every 'treatment' appointment.
>
> Initially all goes well, but after several weeks Sam's left elbow becomes very painful and stiff. She records the symptoms as requested and reports the deterioration at her next appointment. The investigator notes her condition and advises her to continue with the study routine as 'there is nothing serious to worry about'. A few days later Sam's elbow becomes excruciatingly painful. She calls the telephone number on the information sheet and is advised to take some pain medication and to attend the clinic for her regular appointment two days later. By the time Sam arrives at her next appointment her arm is hot and very swollen. An infection in the bone is diagnosed and she is admitted to hospital. After a week in hospital Sam is discharged but never regains the function in her elbow. Other participants also experience similar symptoms but are treated more quickly and recover completely. The trial is halted.
>
> Sam claims that the treatment under investigation was dangerous and that the study should never have been allowed to go ahead. She alleges, *inter alia*, that the REC which gave the study a favourable opinion was negligent.

For Sam to succeed in her claim against the REC she will first need to establish the basic components of negligence. She must ascertain that the REC owed her a duty of care, that there was a breach of that duty and that the injury she suffered was caused by the breach. Each of these elements will be considered in turn.

Duty

It is not automatic in English law that persons or citizens owe a duty of care to one another. In the absence of such a duty it is by now trite to explain that a bystander may stand idly by while an unrelated child drowns in three inches of water, or an unseeing person walks blindly towards the edge of a cliff and impending doom. This remains the case even if the observer would put themselves at no risk by intervening to prevent the harm, or by going to the rescue. Essentially, therefore, where no duty of care exists, no care need be undertaken and no help offered, so it is important to recognise the circumstances within which a duty will arise.

It is perhaps most obvious that a duty of care will arise where there is a special relationship between the parties involved. For example, if the bystander was the parent or guardian of the drowning child, then she most certainly would be under a duty to attempt to rescue her unfortunate offspring. Similarly, a duty of care will arise where there is no familial relationship but the observer has voluntarily assumed a duty to care for the child concerned, such as in a baby-sitting situation, or, to change the scenario, where a person undertakes to care for a sick or infirm person. A duty can also arise through a contractual relationship where the duty is imposed by virtue of mutual agreement, or perhaps a contract of employment. In the case of professional relationships, including RECs and their members, however, a duty will arise from the fact that those concerned have held themselves out as being peculiarly suited to perform the task by virtue of qualifications, skill or expertise (*R v Bateman* (1925)). In addition, a person in this kind of relationship would owe a duty to anyone who she could reasonably foresee might be injured or harmed through her actions. This is the so-called neighbour principle, whereby the possibility of the kind of harm that resulted must have been reasonably in the contemplation of the party in breach, that is, the REC. The principle was clearly enunciated by Lord Atkin in *Donoghue v Stevenson* (1932):

> The rule that you must love your neighbour becomes in law that you must not injure your neighbour . . . you must take reasonable care to avoid acts and omissions which you can reasonably foresee would be likely to injure your neighbour. Who then in law is my neighbour? The answer seems to be – persons who are so closely and directly affected by my act that I ought to have them in my contemplation as being so affected, when I am directing my mind to the acts or omissions which are called into question.

Having established that it must be foreseeable that somebody in Sam's position could be harmed and that the neighbour principle is satisfied, under *Caparo Industries plc v Dickman* (1990) it must also be regarded as reasonable, just and fair to impose such a duty on the defendant or REC. That said, it seems self-evident that an REC, whose primary role is to protect the dignity, rights, safety and welfare of actual and potential research participants, would owe a duty of care to somebody like Sam. On the face of it, then, Sam appears to have passed the first hurdle in establishing that the REC owes her a duty of care. That is, however, merely the first step towards establishing liability.

Having confirmed that a duty of care does exist, Sam will next need to show that the REC was in breach of that duty. To determine whether this is the case it is first necessary to identify the parameters of the duty of care owed by an REC, which will be achieved by measuring the conduct of the REC concerned against that of any reasonable REC. In large part this entails applying the criteria established in *Bolam v Friern Hospital Management Committee* (1957), where the court held that a doctor 'is not guilty of negligence if he has acted in accordance with a practice accepted as proper by a responsible body of medical men skilled in that particular art' (the *Bolam* test). This principle now applies to all professional groups and would therefore require that for an REC to avoid being found negligent it must have operated in accordance with standards adhered to by other RECs.

To achieve this, an REC will first have to be compliant with the Clinical Trials Regulations with respect to its membership and constitution. It will then also have to perform the process of ethical review in a manner commensurate with its responsibilities according to the National Research Ethics Service (NRES), *Standard Operating Procedures for Research Ethics Committees* (NRES, April 2009). Before considering this in detail it is necessary to explain that guidelines such as those published by the NRES do not ordinarily have the force of law. The REC must apply established ethical principles and guidelines, and take account of applicable regulations and laws in order to protect the rights, safety and welfare of Sam and other participants. That said, it must be acknowledged that where a specific guideline is regarded as strongly informative, or even directive, and is adhered to by most, if not all practitioners to whom it applies, then to deviate from it may be regarded as deviating from a practice accepted as proper, and therefore negligent under the *Bolam* test. So, what precisely would a claimant like Sam need to show to establish that an REC had been negligent in the performance of its duty?

She could argue that the REC was not competent to conduct the review, possibly because it was not properly constituted or because it had not received proper training, or that it had failed to apply recognised principles and so did not perform the review according to accepted standards. She may even allege that the REC had neglected to conduct a review at all. As the claimant, the burden of proof would be on Sam to show that the REC had acted negligently. This, in itself, would be a barrier to her chances of succeeding in her claim but, if successfully proven, any of these claims could result in the REC being found negligent.

Probably Sam's best hope of demonstrating negligence would be to show that the REC had given a favourable opinion but failed to conduct a review at all. However, this seems too fanciful to contemplate. Equally, a claim based on the incompetence of the REC appears whimsical on the face of it, but if shown would certainly give rise to a plausible claim. To be competent the NHS REC members need not only to possess their own individual skills and expertise but must also have undertaken training specific to their role as REC members. Such training involves obtaining knowledge and understanding of the basic ethical principles that relate to the ethical review of research involving human participants. It should also ensure that REC members recognise and understand the role and remit of an NHS REC and the regulatory requirements associated with its function. Training is required to assure the quality of the service provided by RECs and to promote consistency of decision-making. Sam may therefore be able to prove negligence if she can show that the REC that gave a favourable opinion for the study through which she was injured had not received adequate training. A vast array of training is currently available to NHS REC members and they receive enormous encouragement to attend, so it would seem unlikely that Sam could succeed with such a claim. In addition, the consensus decision-making process adopted by RECs means that it is not necessary for every member to be trained in each specialty or aspect of the review process. Sufficient understanding and safeguards should be in place so long as some members of each committee have received adequate instruction.

Liability relating to an REC not being properly constituted to perform the review would probably attach to the appointing authority rather than to the REC itself, for example where the authority had appointed a committee with too few members or lacking in the requisite mix of expertise. Alternatively, an REC that complied with the Regulations but undertook a review when it was not quorate could be regarded as not properly constituted. The Regulations explicitly stipulate, in Sch 2, para 6, that at least seven members must be present, including one lay+ member and one expert member, for a valid decision to be taken. The members of the REC themselves may be liable in negligence because they ought to have been aware that they were in breach of the Regulations and so should have declined to give an opinion. More specifically, the REC co-ordinator should have advised that the members present were not authorised to conduct the review and suspended the meeting. It does, however, seem extremely unlikely that such a situation could arise, given the level of competence of REC co-ordinators and the now routine adherence of RECs to their standard operating procedures.

The second head of Sam's possible claim would be that the REC failed to perform the review according to accepted ethical standards. This may appear to be a more easily imaginable occurrence, but nevertheless it is still difficult to envisage that an REC would act this way, and even more unlikely that the action would succeed.

To be successful Sam would almost certainly need to demonstrate that the REC disregarded established ethical principles in the process of its review. It may, for example, have prioritised the research over the interests of the participants, thereby subjecting Sam and others to unacceptable risks of harm. Schedule 1, Part 2 para 3 to the Clinical Trials Regulations stresses that the research subject's rights, safety and well-being 'are the most important considerations and shall prevail over the interests of science and society'. Therefore, any neglect of the duty to protect these rights and interests would constitute a clear breach of the REC's statutory duty, as well as a breach of its common law duty.

Alternatively, the REC may have neglected to pay sufficient attention to the seriousness of the potential harms to which the participants may have been exposed, either by misunderstanding the intricacies of the proposal, not appreciating the possible dangers, or by failing to request revisions to the protocol. There has been some speculation that this could easily happen, for example where an REC fails to ascertain that clinical equipoise exists or fails to establish that the risk to participants is minimal (Laurence, 2008: 70). To succeed here, Sam would have to show that other RECs would have recognised the risk to the participant and acted differently, either requiring amendments to the protocol or by rejecting the application. Put simply, the *Bolam* test would be applied to ascertain whether this particular REC was out of step with others in the performance of its review. Under the ruling in *Whitehouse v Jordan* (1981), however, it should be noted that it would not of itself amount to negligence if an REC mistakenly gave a favourable opinion because its members had misunderstood guidance or misapplied principles. As long as the REC had conducted itself according to the standard operating prodcures and attempted to follow appropriate guidance, albeit mistakenly, it would not be culpable. However, an REC probably would be negligent if it failed to address a matter that it is required to consider by law.

With respect to this, it has recently been alleged that an REC may expose itself to claims of negligence by not ensuring that adequate arrangements are in place to provide compensation for anybody harmed as a result of their participation in a study via proper indemnity arrangements:

> An ethics committee that fails to direct its mind to these matters and issues a favourable opinion regardless is . . . failing in its legal duty.
>
> (Roy-Toole, 2008: 114)

Indemnity may be described as a method used to protect people, such as employees, from the effects of compensation claims made against them for negligent actions in the course of their employment. It is an established principle in the NHS more broadly, that the NHS is vicariously liable for the negligent actions of its employees. As a result, a clear policy of indemnity has been developed (DoH, 1996). This helps to ensure that a successful claimant will receive the compensation to which she is entitled if clinical negligence is proven, regardless of whether the individual employee has the funds available to pay. Research is regarded as 'a core NHS activity' and 'is therefore treated in the same way as any other NHS activity in relation to potential liabilities for clinical negligence' (DoH, 2005: 1). Indemnity is relevant here in two ways: first, because of its role in ensuring that research participants who are harmed as a result of their involvement in research are able to obtain compensation for injuries suffered; and, secondly, because it is the mechanism through which members of NHS RECs are protected from being personally liability for paying compensation if they are found negligent in the performance of their duty as members. In short, the NHS indemnity arrangements cover negligent harms caused by members of NHS RECs as well as those that might be caused by NHS researchers.

Under the Clinical Trials Regulations it is a requirement that all clinical trials include provision for 'insurance or indemnity to cover the liability of the investigator and sponsor which may arise in relation to the clinical trial' (Taylor *et al*, 2008). This is incorporated into reg 15(5) of the Clinical Trials Regulations, which stipulates that:

> In preparing its opinion, the committee shall consider, in particular, the following matters:
>
> . . .
>
> (i)   provision for indemnity or compensation in the event of injury or death attributable to the clinical trial;
>
> (j)   any insurance or indemnity to cover the liability of the investigator or sponsor; ...

Further to this, Sch 1, Part 2, para 16 requires that 'provision has been made for insurance or indemnity to cover the liability of the investigator and sponsor which may arise in relation to the clinical trial' as is required under the ICH GCP; it does not specify that this must be checked or monitored by the REC. However, Sch 3 to the Regulations deals with particulars and documents that must accompany an application for an ethics committee opinion, and within this, Sch 3, Part 1, para 1(g)(iii) stipulates that this includes details of 'any provision for compensation in the event of injury or death attributable to the trial'. Similarly, Sch 3, Part 1, para 1(g)(iv) requires details of 'any insurance or indemnity to cover the liability of the sponsor and investigator' to be provided to the REC, and Sch 3, Part 1, para 3(c) requires documentary evidence of insurance covering liability of sponsor and investigator. All of which suggests that the REC should obtain and assess these documents unless the application contains instead 'an explanation of why that information is not provided' (Sch 3, para 1).

The claim that an REC that neglects explicitly to consider the arrangements for indemnity before issuing a favourable opinion about a research proposal may be failing in its legal duty has, however, been soundly refuted in a letter jointly authored by the Department of Health, the Royal College of Physicians, London and the NRES. Here it is contended that:

> As long as the REC is satisfied that a suitable sponsor is in place and that the sponsor will make appropriate arrangements for the management and monitoring of the research in conjunction with the research governance offices at each host organisation, then it fulfils its legal responsibility to protect the legal rights of research participants.
>
> (Taylor *et al*, 2008: 66)

In practice it is evident that for most NHS research, responsibility for assessing that the researcher has adequate indemnity is generally fulfilled by the research support office or the research and development department. In circumstances where this occurs the REC has effectively delegated authority for this function to the relevant research governance officers. Of course, the practicalities of decision-making of this type often dictate that delegation is necessary as a matter of expediency, but the legal position with regard to authority to delegate is complex. Indeed, it is questionable how far an obligation imposed by statute may legitimately be delegated to another body.

In general, 'only a body or person in whom a power is vested is entitled to exercise that power' (Leyland and Woods, 2002: 308), and the exercise of that power by another could be viewed as acting *ultra vires*, or beyond their authority. In this context the key principle may be that the body making the decision should act in such a way that it does not undermine the purpose of the statute. With that in mind, it is then clearly arguable that, so long as the arrangements for insurance, indemnity and compensation arrangements are subjected to appropriate scrutiny, the purpose of the statute is upheld, even if responsibility for so doing is delegated to a part of the NHS other than an ethics committee. In cases involving entirely different factual circumstances, it has been held, however, that judicial functions that affect the rights of individuals cannot properly be delegated (*Barnard v National Dock Labour Board* (1953); *Vine v New Zealand Dairy Production and Marketing Board* (1967)). That said, if the assessment of factors such as insurance cover and the qualifications of investigators is regarded as administrative, where, for example, it is considered simply a matter of gathering information, then it may be permissible to delegate that responsibility (*R v Race Relations Board ex p Selvarajan* (1975)). To add to the controversy, it appears that some RECs do scrutinise the indemnity arrangements, while others do not. Should a court be called upon to adjudicate on the issue, this may lead to doubts about what is proper practice in this regard. In the meantime, the absence of case law relating directly to this point adds to the uncertainty regarding the requirement for RECs to explicitly satisfy themselves that appropriate arrangements have been made for indemnity. Similarly, the possibility remains that an REC that fails adequately to scrutinise a researcher's indemnity arrangement could be held in neglect of its legal duty.

Concerns of a similar nature may also be voiced about the REC's responsibility for assessing that the chief investigator is appropriately qualified and experienced to carry out the study. Schedule 3, Part 1, para 1(s) to the Regulations details the need for this assessment, and documentary evidence of such in the form of *curriculum vitae* is required by Sch 3, Part 1, para 3(k). Such claims can be countered in the same manner, namely that as long as proper governance arrangements are in place the REC is entitled to expect that the checks will be conducted by the governance office. In addition, whilst in practice it probably makes little difference who complies with these statutory requirements as long as somebody does, volunteer members of NHS RECs might wish to be reassured that their committee is complying with its statutory responsibilities.

Despite the controversy over indemnity, the prospects of Sam being able to demonstrate that the REC that reviewed the study which resulted in her being harmed was in breach of its duty to her, are relatively slight. However, even if it can be demonstrated that the REC failed to operate according to appropriate standards and so was clearly in breach of its duty, Sam will still need to prove that the harm she suffered was directly caused by the negligence of the REC.

Causation

In all medical negligence cases a claimant must show that her injuries were caused by the breach. The test employed to demonstrate causation is generally known as the 'but for' test. Put simply, the claimant must show that 'but for' the negligence, the harm or injury would not have occurred. In Sam's case, therefore, she must first demonstrate that the injury she suffered to her elbow was a direct result of the intervention she was subjected to by participating in the clinical trial. In other words, 'but for' taking part in the research she would not have suffered this harm. Although this might appear to be self-evident, it is not as straightforward as it appears.

The main complicating factor in medical negligence cases is the difficulty of establishing that no other factors were responsible for the harm suffered. For example, it would seem beyond question that a doctor would be guilty of negligence if a patient she failed to examine and diagnose died of poisoning soon after. However, on these facts in *Barnett v Chelsea and Kensington Hospital Management Committee* (1968) the claimant did not succeed in negligence even though the doctor concerned was clearly in breach of his duty. The difficulty was that the patient, who was subsequently shown to be suffering from arsenic poisoning, was beyond help at the time of his admission to the hospital. He would therefore have died even if the doctor had attended him appropriately. The cause of death was poisoning rather than the lack of treatment.

In Sam's case it seems probable that a causal link would be established between her injury and the fact that she participated in the research. But that in itself would not mean that the REC would be held liable for the harm she suffered. To establish that the REC was liable Sam would be required to prove in court that there was a causal link between harm she has suffered and the REC's breach of duty. The court will use one of two possible approaches to assess her evidence: the 'all or nothing' approach, or the 'material increase in risk' approach.

The 'all or nothing' approach to causation demands that the claimant shows, on the balance of probabilities, that it was the defendant's breach, rather than some other factor, that caused the harm. *Hotson v East Berkshire AHA* (1987) involved a 13 year-old boy who fell from a tree and injured his hip. At hospital he was misdiagnosed and therefore did not receive proper treatment until five days after the injury. Consequently avascular necrosis occurred and by the age of 20 he was permanently disabled. On the facts it was found that the claimant had a 25 per cent chance of making a full recovery and avoiding disability if he had been diagnosed promptly. In the House of Lords it was held that the claimant failed to demonstrate that the injury was caused by the negligent delay in treatment. Because there was a 75 per cent chance that the avascular necrosis would have materialised even without the delay, it could not be shown, on the balance of probabilities, that the delay caused the harm suffered. The injury, and the subsequent disability, was therefore deemed to have been the result of the fall from the tree.

By contrast, the 'material increase in risk' approach takes a different stance. In *McGhee v National Coal Board* (1973) the claimant was exposed to brick dust in the course of his work and eventually suffered dermatitis. The exposure was an inevitable aspect of the job, therefore the employers were not negligent in that respect, but it was argued that the lack of washing facilities at work meant that the claimant's skin was coated with brick dust during his journey home at the end of his day's work, and that this exacerbated his condition. The National Coal Board agreed that the failure to provide washing facilities was negligent, but countered that this was not the cause of the claimant's disease because the dermatitis might have occurred regardless of the lack of washing facilities. The House of Lords held that it could not be established that the inability to wash the dust off at the end of the working day due to lack of facilities was the actual cause of the injury. The defendants had, however, created the risk that dermatitis would occur by failing to offer the opportunity to wash the dust off. As it was this specific injury that had materialised in the claimant they could be found to have materially increased the risk of it happening. Lord Wilberforce stated at p 6 of the judgment that:

> . . . where a person has, by breach of a duty of care, created a risk, and injury occurs within the area of that risk, the loss should be borne by him unless he shows that it has some other cause . . .

The same material increase in risk approach was initially adopted in the case of *Wilsher v Essex AHA* (1988). Here it was claimed that a child born prematurely suffered retrolental fibroplasia and near blindness as a result of receiving too much oxygen due to medical negligence. It was alleged that one of the doctors caring for the child had been negligent in not realising that the catheter supplying the oxygen was inserted into a vein rather than an artery. Because of this the readings from the monitoring equipment were misleading and too much oxygen was given. The claimants sued, arguing that the retrolental fibroplasia was caused by the excess of oxygen. However, although this was a possible cause, it was not possible to demonstrate that it was *the* cause. Many premature babies suffer retrolental fibroplasia even if no oxygen is administered, and there are causal connections associated with several other conditions affecting pre-term babies. It was argued that the raised oxygen levels had materially increased the risk of the condition occurring, and this was accepted in the lower courts, but the House of Lords rejected the argument and instead substituted the 'all or nothing' approach to causation. Accepting that this was a cruel outcome in the circumstances, Lord Bridge delivered the following statement at p 1092 of the judgment:

> . . . the law, which only Parliament can change, requires proof of fault causing damage as the basis of liability in tort. We should do society nothing

but disservice if we made the forensic process still more unpredictable and hazardous by distorting the law to accommodate the exigencies of what may seem hard cases.

The above are, of course, only the most obvious examples of these kinds of cases, but they do reveal the complexity of the assessment of causation and the complications that face a claimant seeking to prove the cause of an injury. On close scrutiny of *McGhee* it is arguable that the biggest decider of which test to adopt is public policy and the need to ensure that employers are required to treat their employees fairly in relation to injuries sustained in the course of their work. How, for example, could the court demonstrate conclusively that Mr McGhee's dermatitis was the result only of the increased exposure to brick dust during his cycle ride home from work, rather than resulting from the unavoidable exposure during working hours? The prolonged exposure was clearly one of the factors, but in *Wilsher* the excess oxygen level was also one of the factors known to cause retrolental fibroplasia. This controversy was revisited in *Fairchild v Glenhaven Funeral Services Ltd* (2003) where the claimants suffered mesothelioma following exposure to asbestos during their working lives. The difficulty was that they had been exposed to asbestos whilst working for several different employers and it was impossible to establish which individual employer was responsible for the exposure that had resulted in the cancer. As all the employers admitted breach of their duty of care to protect their workers from exposure the court held that each of them had increased the risk of mesothelioma for the claimants and found them all liable. In this way the *McGhee* principle was upheld and the burden of proof placed on the claimants extended only to proving that there had been a material increase in the risk of developing the disease.

In relation to Sam's case, because the burden of proof in a case such as this always falls upon the claimant, it will be necessary for her to show that the alleged negligence on the part of the REC caused the harmful effects she suffered. This will be a difficult task. In the first place Sam's claim will be hindered by the fact that there are a number of possible causes for the condition of her elbow. Amongst these are the fact that her arm was already affected by tennis elbow before the research intervention; that she had received invasive treatment for that condition prior to entering into the research project; that the research involved invasive procedures; and that the procedures used in the research were experimental and administered directly by researchers, all of which factors render the REC's involvement somewhat remote. Further, the fact that Sam complained of symptoms in her arm at an early stage and the research team failed to take immediate action to examine the arm or investigate the reasons why, suggests a cavalier, possibly negligent, approach to a possible adverse event in the study.

The later suspension of the trial after other participants suffered similar events also suggests that the research intervention is the most likely cause of the harm suffered. With this in mind it seems highly probable that the actual damage sustained was more immediately the result of the research intervention than the actions of the REC. It is true that the research could not legitimately have been conducted 'but for' the favourable opinion given by the REC, but notwithstanding that, it was not the REC which administered the agent that seems most likely to have caused the harm.

In addition to the problem of multiple possible causes, the issue of which approach the court might take to causation must be considered. If the 'all or nothing' approach is adopted there would seem to be very little chance for Sam to succeed against the REC. It is clear that the REC sanctioned the trial, but even if its favourable opinion was based on negligence, the court would have difficulty concluding that its action was more likely than not to have resulted in her injury. Some other participants suffered similar, but less-severe symptoms, but it is by no means certain that the mere fact of entering the study led to the injury suffered since some participants seemed not to have experienced these effects. Therefore, the REC is unlikely to be held liable. The scenario may be different if the court takes the increase of material risk approach. Here it is feasible that all possible contributors to the adverse outcome will be held liable, in which case the REC may be implicated as a contributor to the harm suffered. It is, however, possible that despite negligence in the performance of its review, the REC will escape liability even in these circumstances.

Sam's claim against the REC will almost certainly be only one of a number she will have made as a result of suffering injury. This will include a claim against the investigator conducting the research, who has greater proximity to the harm suffered and is therefore more likely to be liable. The law relating to causation has long accepted that where there has been a series of actions, a later act may intervene to break the chain of causation. This complex area of law is known as the doctrine of *novus actus interveniens* and can operate in such a way that earlier causes are overshadowed by those that occur later in the chain. Where, as here, the intervening act is that of a third party, several types of intervention are recognised: instinctive or natural intervention, deliberate acts of wrongdoing and (the one that is most relevant here) negligent interventions.

The impact of intervening acts in cases of medical negligence is complex. Generally, the existence of medical negligence will not disrupt the chain of causation to absolve the perpetrator of a crime from responsibility (*R v Smith* (1959); *R v Blaue* (1975); *R v Cheshire* (1991)), but there is more uncertainty in relation to cases in the tort of negligence such as Sam's. In *Hogan v Bentinck West Hartley Collieries Ltd* (1949) the claimant was a minor who was unable to return to his job after his thumb was negligently amputated following an injury sustained at work. The House of Lords decided by majority decision that the cause of his incapacity was the negligent amputation rather than the original injury, but authority subsequent to this suggests that in principle the circumstances within which negligent treatment ought to be permitted to break the chain of causation are extremely limited. In Sam's case it will be important to ascertain whether this REC, or others, would have issued a favourable opinion when acting non-negligently, especially since any breach by the REC is most likely to be procedural. If so, it would seem possible that the actions of the researcher would be regarded as a *novus actus interveniens* breaking the causal link between the REC and Sam's injury. The fact that Sam was injured after voluntarily participating in a research study may also be persuasive in a finding against the researcher. Justice would appear to dictate that a remedy ought to be available to her.

Damages

A successful case under the tort of negligence would provide Sam with the opportunity to obtain damages. Damages are financial compensation, the purpose of which is to put the claimant, so far as money can do so, back into the position she would have occupied had the negligence not occurred – in other words, to compensate the injured party for harm suffered or losses incurred rather than to punish the tortfeasor. Damages can be awarded for expenses relating to the injury, such as any medical costs incurred, pain and suffering, loss of amenity, loss of earnings where applicable and any potential future losses. Quantifying such losses in cases involving physical injury like this is always problematic since no monetary sum will restore the use of Sam's elbow. As a practical solution a tariff system has been developed which provides an arbitrary, but consistent level of compensation depending on the kind of injury sustained and its impact. Clearly, special considerations need to be applied in exceptional cases, for instance Sam might expect her award to be adjusted if she were an athlete or a musician who relied on her arm, but this would also be influenced by the fact that she was already debilitated in her ability to perform because of her pre-existing condition.

In negligence cases involving healthcare it is rare for a claimant to sue an individual practitioner personally. Instead, an action is more likely to be brought against an employer, who would be vicariously liable for the actions of the practitioner. In brief, this means that the employer is held liable for the actions of the employee, which gives the claimant access to greater means of redress since the individual employee is usually much less able to pay damages. In the case of an REC, the appointing authority would be vicariously liable for the actions of the REC and its members and should provide indemnity for all volunteer REC members to provide cover should such a claim be made. Researchers will usually be covered for negligence in the performance of their profession by their employer. Researchers are also responsible for ensuring that arrangements are in place to provide indemnity to compensate participants like Sam for any harm suffered in the course of the research. As previously discussed, RECs are required to check that such arrangements are in place and that they provide adequate cover in the event of a participant being harmed.

It is notable that, ordinarily, the indemnity provided only offers compensation cover for negligent harm and does not extend to non-negligent harm. Clearly, it would not be feasible or appropriate to provide indemnity for non-negligent harm resulting from deliberate or malicious misconduct in relation to research. Such situations are alluded to in *NHS Indemnity: Arrangements for Handling Clinical*

Negligence Claims Against NHS Staff (DoH, November 1996) which, in Annex A, para 18, distinguishes legitimate actions taken in the course of NHS employment from those where civil or even criminal action may be taken against the individual. Excepting those circumstances, it is of some concern that the standard NHS indemnity does not allow for compensation in other cases of non-negligent harm resulting from research. It is easily foreseeable that in some circumstances a research participant may be harmed as a result of her involvement in a study even if no negligence has occurred. In clinical trials, for instance, harm could arise from the use of a novel preparation or an established pharmaceutical compound in a new application, even in the absence of negligence. In such circumstances it would be entirely appropriate to provide the injured participant with compensation, and arguably scandalous not to. Indeed, according to *Research in the NHS: Indemnity Arrangements:*

> A research ethics committee may decide that a study cannot go ahead unless participants are assured of compensation for non-negligent harm. In that case the research can proceed, only if a non-NHS body is willing to make the required arrangements for compensation.
>
> (DoH, 2005: 2)

Despite this, in cases where indemnity per se is not provided for, *NHS Indemnity Arrangements for Handling Clinical Negligence Claims Against NHS Staff* suggests that '[I]n exceptional circumstances (and within the delegated limit of £50,000) NHS bodies may consider whether an ex gratia payment could be offered', but 'NHS bodies may not offer advance indemnities or take out commercial insurance for non-negligent harm' (DoH, November 1996: Annex A, para 16). Instead, it is expected that the pharmaceutical industry will make arrangements in relation to such harms resulting from clinical trials, usually following a standard format drawn up with the agreement of the Association of the British Pharmaceutical Industry. This is generally adequate to protect participants, be they patients or volunteers in clinical trials of medicinal products, but the arrangements for sponsors of research conducted in the NHS by the independent sector, such as universities and medical research charities, is less formalised. The majority of such bodies do not offer indemnities or take out commercial insurances in respect of this type of harm. Some, like the Medical Research Council, for example, do offer assurances of a sympathetic hearing of cases involving non-negligent harm in studies it has funded, but there are no guarantees. The uncertainty here is compounded by the fact that the guidance insists that 'NHS bodies should not make ex-gratia payments for non-negligent harm where research is sponsored by a non-NHS body' (DoH, November 1996: Annex A, para 17). Where harm results from defective products or equipment, NHS indemnity does not apply, but special arrangements operate under consumer protection legislation.

The lack of available remedies following deficient ethical review has long been recognised (Brazier, 1990), and Sam will clearly have very mixed fortunes in her claim against this NHS REC. On the positive side, her claim against the research team involved in her case is much more likely to succeed. In practice, however, it is not only a participant like Sam who may wish to bring an action in negligence against an REC. Pharmaceutical research is big business, which means that researchers have a lot at stake and may be prepared to bring legal action against an REC that is thought to be responsible for causing losses. Perhaps the most obvious situation where this may occur is if an REC negligently caused a delay in issuing a favourable opinion, for example where the REC acted in contravention of its obligation to give an opinion within the 'specified period' under reg 15 of the Clinical Trials Regulations. Generally, the specified period is 60 days, but exceptionally, under reg 15(10)(a)(i) and (ii), the time can be extended to 90 days where the trial involves a medicinal product for gene therapy, somatic cell therapy or a product containing a genetically modified organism. Additionally, if it is necessary to consult a specialist committee or group, that time period can be further extended to 180 days. An REC that caused an inappropriate delay in the ethical review process would therefore be acting in a manner contrary to the Regulations and in breach of its responsibilities. It is easy to envisage that a pharmaceutical company could suffer financial loss as a direct consequence and therefore damages would be readily quantifiable. No legal action of this type has yet been reported, and the likelihood of a case being brought is remote given the adherence of NHS RECs to the Regulations through their standards of procedure, but the theoretical possibility remains.

Public law and judicial review

Aside from liability in tort it is also possible that a decision taken by a public body such as an NHS REC may be subjected to a legal challenge through the process of judicial review. This challenge is available to persons who have an interest in the decisions or actions of a public body and permits them to request that the lawfulness of a decision is reviewed by a judge. An action like this against an REC is likely to be brought by a researcher whose proposal has not received a favourable opinion from the REC concerned. However, simple rejection of a proposal would not raise an entitlement to judicial review. Instead, the claimant would usually have to demonstrate either that the decision was illegal, for example outside of the remit of the REC, that there had been some impropriety during the REC's decision-making process, which could have interfered with the outcome, or that the decision was unreasonable or irrational. In determining whether a decision is unreasonable the test of *Wednesbury* unreasonableness, arising from the case *Associated Provincial Picture Houses Ltd v Wednesbury Corporation* (1947), will apply. This means that the decision must be shown to be 'so unreasonable that no reasonable person acting reasonably could have made it'. In essence this is a stricter test than merely reasonableness, since it recognises that no decision-making body acting reasonably could have reached a similar decision. Usually a judicial review would only be expected after all other avenues have been exhausted and there is no further right of appeal. In practice the case would need to have been pursued through the entire NRES appeals process before it could be referred for judicial review.

If such a challenge were to be successful against an REC, the outcome would usually be that the REC would be required to revisit its decision by conducting a further review according to proper processes so that a lawful decision is reached. In essence, even if the aggrieved party was successful, with the judicial review finding in her favour, the court could not overturn the REC's decision. As a result the eventual outcome may remain the same, and the research proposal may still be rejected. *R v Ethical Committee of St Mary's Hospital (Manchester) ex p Harriott* (1988) is a clear example of this process in practice. In this case a woman who was refused access to fertility treatment because of her criminal record requested a judicial review of the decision made by the clinical ethics committee, alleging that she had been unreasonably discriminated against. The court ruled that the unit concerned was not entitled to formulate policy on grounds that were discriminatory, and required the case to be re-decided. Ultimately, however, the original decision was upheld.

Conclusions

NHS RECs have existed for many years, but, unlike other countries, their formalisation is a relatively recent phenomenon. In the United States, for example, the National Research Act was passed in 1974 following revelations about poor research conduct in a large number of studies involving human participants in the United States. Amongst its key initiatives was the requirement that Institutional Review Boards (IRBs) be constituted to assess the ethical implications of research in every institution where wholly or partially federally funded research is conducted. By law the IRBs function in a similar way to NHS RECs. Researchers are obliged to apply for initial approval of their proposals as well as for any subsequent amendment to the research protocol. They are also required to report adverse events and to suspend the research if serious threat to the human participants is detected. In addition, unlike UK NHS RECs, IRBs also fulfil a monitoring role conducting annual reviews of research projects. IRBs have subsequently been described as 'the cornerstone of the Federal regulatory process' (Chalmers, 2006: 86). It is useful to note here, however, that in the United States, IRBs are conceptually distinct from ethics committees, which are generally more akin to the clinical ethics committees now becoming established in the United Kingdom. By comparison with the United States, the introduction of a centralised system of ethical review in the United Kingdom in 1991 was relatively late, and the formal legal regulation of RECs long overdue.

NHS RECs have always been required to work within established law and according to recognised guidelines, whilst having 'due regard for the requirements of relevant regulatory agencies and of applicable laws' (GAfREC, 2001). But recent years have witnessed a great deal of turmoil and consternation in the research ethics community associated with changes imposed by the Clinical Trials Directive. Subsequent to its implementation in the United Kingdom in the form of the Clinical Trials Regulations, the shape and contours of NHS RECs have altered and adapted to the new legal environment within which they need to operate.

While the core work – the process of ethical review of research – remains unchanged, the administration and governance of the process has become the subject of greater regulation and management than ever before. Following the inception of the Central Office for Research Ethics Committees (COREC), which then morphed into the NRES, the first incarnation of GAfREC, which is expected to be updated in 2009, new standards of procedure, the accreditation of committees and increased opportunities for training, a new professionalism has been welcomed into the system. In addition, the revised legal status of committees and their members has focused the minds of volunteer members on their own vulnerabilities and potential liability. This is perhaps unsurprising given the increasingly litigious nature of society and professional life generally. It may also have been fuelled by the recognition that criminal penalties can be imposed for some breaches of obligations under the Clinical Trials Regulations. This chapter has sought to allay some of those concerns whilst setting the responsibilities of RECs within their legal context. The following chapters will build on this by examining the application of the basic law discussed here in the context of specific issues such as consent, confidentiality and the responsibilities imposed under the Human Tissue Act 2004, and in the context of research involving vulnerable populations.

Chapter 5

Consent

Introduction

Consent has been described as 'a precondition for autonomous decision-making' (Pattinson, 2006: 97). As such, both ethics and law demand that persons have a right to self-determination and choice about matters relating to their personal and physical integrity, including their participation in research. There is, however, no specific statute-based law of consent in the United Kingdom, and the concept has developed through common law judgments. Similarly, there is no UK case law pertaining explicitly to consent in research. However, many influential judicial statements have concerned the relationship between autonomy and consent in the context of medical treatment, and have been informed by ethical principles to the effect that informed consent 'ensures that due respect is given to the autonomy and dignity of each patient' (*Chester v Afshar* (2004), para 18).

In addition, a number of the more recently enacted statutes in the field of healthcare locate consent at their core. For example, the Human Tissue Act 2004, which will be discussed in Chapter 8, the Human Fertilisation and Embryology Act 2008, the EU Clinical Trials Directive (2001/20/EC) and the Medicines for Human Use (Clinical Trials) Regulations 2004, SI 2004/1031 ('Clinical Trials Regulations'), all revolve around the issue of consent. Despite this there is little statutory guidance in relation to what consent means and how to obtain a valid consent. Practical guidance on this is largely the domain of professional guidance such as that issued by the General Medical Council (GMC, 2008) and the Medical Research Council (MRC, 1967, 2000, 2004), together with guidance published by the National Research Ethics Service (NRES) pertaining specifically to clinical research (NRES, May 2007 and May 2008). This chapter will begin with an outline of the law and ethics surrounding informed consent, followed by an analysis of its practical operation in relation to research, touching on notions such as voluntarism and information provision. These will be addressed in the context of the detailed requirements set out in the Clinical Trials Directive and the Clinical Trials Regulations, and their relationship to the common law more generally. Some additional issues will be considered in the discussion of 'appropriate consent' as contained in the Human Tissue Act in Chapter 8.

Legal and ethical imperatives

Broadly speaking, obtaining consent from a research participant authorises a clinician or researcher to have physical contact with the participant. It also protects the rights of participants to exercise their own autonomy and retain control over what happens to them. In the words of the Nuremberg Code, research participants should not be subjected to 'force, fraud, deceit, duress, overreaching, or other ulterior form of constraint or coercion' (BMJ editorial, 1996), and obtaining consent helps to protect against these abuses. More generally, legal authorisation is required for any intervention involving interference with the physical integrity of the body, its tissues and fluids, or access to personal data and records. Aside from the kinds of physical contact that are inevitable in ordinary life, such as jostling on public transport or in crowded places, this principle applies regardless of whether the intrusion is performed for treatment, research or any other purpose. Unauthorised interference with the bodily integrity or liberty of a person is regarded as trespass. It is based on the premise that people have the right to individual autonomy, which should be respected by others.

Autonomy was recognised as a key aspect of medical law early in the history of medical law in the US case of *Schloendorff v Society of New York Hospital* (1914), where Justice Cardozo proclaimed that 'Every human being of adult years and sound mind has the right to determine what shall be done with his own body'. Ian Kennedy has stated that in English law, '[P]erhaps the most fundamental precept of the common law is respect for the liberty of the individual. In a medical context this means that a person's right to self-determination, to deal with his body as he sees fit, is protected by the law' (Kennedy, 1991: 320). However, the relationship between autonomy and consent is complex, and although the recognition of the right to give consent permits the exercise of choice, it may not, as will be considered later, automatically enhance individual autonomy. Nevertheless, consent is now revered as the cornerstone of English medical law and the right to decide whether or not to accept treatment or participate in research is regarded as fundamental. Hence, the ethical imperative to obtain consent as enshrined in the Nuremberg Code, the Declaration of Helsinki, and all other influential codes of ethics relating to health research is clearly reflected in the law.

In recent years a number of influential cases concerning medical treatment have led to this position. For instance, in *Re T (Adult: Refusal of Treatment)* (1992) it was held that in principle 'an adult patient who suffers from no mental incapacity has an absolute right to choose whether to consent to medical treatment, to refuse it or to choose one rather than another of the treatments being offered' (p 652). In practice, other factors, such as the capacity to make the decision, will influence whether or not a consent or, as in this case, a refusal, is upheld as legally valid. Despite the court acknowledging this particular patient's absolute right to consent or refuse, the complexities of the facts surrounding the case meant that her refusal was overruled by the court. Perhaps more significant to an understanding of the role of consent in research is the legal response to situations where consent has not been obtained, or a refusal has been ignored.

Failing to obtain consent prior to interfering with a person's physical integrity can potentially lead to liability in crime or tort. Liability will depend upon the particular circumstances of the case and the context within which it applies. For example, in the medical context generally, unauthorised touching can be regarded as criminal battery, for which 'it is sufficient that the touching is against the will of the person being touched' (*Bartley v Studd* (1995)). There is no need to demonstrate that the person doing the touching does so with deliberately malevolent motivation. The law has tended to regard criminal battery as an inappropriate cause of action in cases involving medical treatment, largely due to problems associated with the need to demonstrate criminal intention. Because treatment is ordinarily performed for the benefit of the patient and in accordance with her interests, it is difficult to attribute maleficent motives to a clinician, even one who administers treatment without consent. However, the position is different with regard to research. The regulatory requirements for consent and the provision of information prior to involving any participant in health and social care research are now so well-established that failure to obtain consent must surely be regarded as wilful. Given this, and the trend in recent healthcare-related statutes towards imposing criminal penalties for non-compliance, it would not seem out of step with current policy to impose criminal liability upon researchers who fail to obtain valid consent.

Alternatively, a clinician or researcher who neglects to obtain consent from a patient or participant may be found liable under the tort of battery (trespass to the person) or the tort of negligence. In *Freeman v Home Office* (1984) it was held that tortious battery is 'the unconsented to intrusion of another's bodily integrity' (p 539), demonstrating that mere touching will suffice to succeed in a claim of battery provided the claimant can show that it was non-consensual. To paraphrase the words of José Miola, trespass will apply where the courts regard any consent given as so invalid that it is as if no consent had been given at all – for example, in a case where a participant agreed to participate in a research study on X, but was instead subjected to a different trial. The extreme example of a case where, due to an administrative error, a child was circumcised instead of having his tonsils removed, was cited in *Chatterton v Gerson* (1981) to illustrate the point. Because of the serious nature of the wrong in such cases the claimant will not need to demonstrate that any loss has been suffered in order to succeed. However, the claimant may, as in the case of *Ms B v An NHS Trust* (2002), only receive nominal damages as a result. In a battery case, punitive damages may be awarded alongside compensation. Such cases are, however, relatively uncommon and usually limited to situations where there has been deliberate misrepresentation or fraud (*Potts v NWRHA* (1983); *Appleton v Garrett* (1995)). It is not inconceivable that such a case could result from deliberate research fraud whereby a researcher deliberately misled or misinformed a participant. This would certainly seem the most appropriate response, but to date no cases have been brought.

It is more usual for cases to be brought under negligence, and arguably more appropriate (Brazier, 1987). As explained in Chapter 4, negligence demands that the defendant owed a duty of care to the claimant, which was breached causing some harm or loss for which the claimant may be compensated. With regard to consent, aside from deliberate cases of fraud, or very poor practice, such as those described above, the issue is not usually about whether consent was given, but whether it was properly informed and therefore legally valid. Put simply, the claim will usually be that the professional who obtained consent failed to provide the patient, or in this case the research participant, with sufficient information of a quality that was adequate to enable the participant to make a fully autonomous decision. In other words, the consent obtained was not a fully informed consent and therefore not legally valid.

In order to succeed in a claim of negligence the participant would need to prove that her agreement to take part was based on inaccurate or incomplete information and was therefore not a legally valid consent. Such circumstances could lead to a criminal case if the participant was misled by a researcher who deliberately withheld information or misinformed the participant. This would be a clear example of research misconduct, or even fraud, and will be dealt with in Chapter 9. A successful negligence claim requires the participant to show that the researcher had a duty to provide her with full information, and that, as a consequence of the researcher's failure to do so, she was harmed. Furthermore, she would need to demonstrate that had proper information been furnished she would not have agreed to participate and so would have avoided the harm that subsequently occurred. Depending on the circumstances, she may also allege that the research ethics committee (REC) was negligent by, for example, failing to ensure that the participant information sheet contained sufficient detail to enable her to make a fully informed decision. Such an allegation would be founded on a perceived inability to act autonomously, but the legal response to such claims in the United Kingdom has typically been less than supportive.

Informed consent in law

The legal recognition of informed consent can trace its roots to the US case of *Salgo v Leland Stanford Junior University Trustees* (1957) where it was held that there is a duty to 'inform the patient of any facts that are necessary to form the basis of an intelligent consent'. *Salgo* concerned the quality of information required before a person could be said to have validly consented to participating in medical research. The case does not, of course, have authority in English law. Such cases, and the principles contained within them are, however, often regarded as informative in the juridification of similar issues in England, and over the last 35 years there have been a string of cases concerning the place of informed consent in relation to treatment, attempting to enshrine the doctrine of informed consent in English law. To date none has concerned research, and none has succeeded in securing the primacy of the doctrine in English law. As a result, many medical law scholars (Jones, 1999; Jackson, 2006) insist that 'the law in England and Wales does not recognise the so-called "doctrine of informed consent"' (Herring, 2008).

Chatterton v Gerson (1981) was the first case to explicitly consider this issue. Disappointingly for advocates of informed consent, it held that 'once a patient is informed in broad terms of the nature of the procedure which is intended and gives her consent, that consent is real, and the cause of action for failure to go into risks and implications is negligence, not trespass'. Following this case, the now infamous case of *Sidaway v Bethlem Royal Hospital Governors* (1985) examined in detail the standard of information required to support a valid consent. Mrs Sidaway underwent an operation on her spine, which carried an inherent risk of between 1 and 2 per cent that damage to the spinal cord and nerves would occur. When this risk materialised and Mrs Sidaway was left partially paralysed, she alleged that the surgeon had been negligent in not adequately warning her of the risk. There was no suggestion that the surgery itself had been negligently performed, her case was simply that had she been fully appraised of the risk she would not have had the surgery and would not have suffered the resulting paralysis. The case went to the House of Lords, and was no doubt complicated by the fact that the surgeon had died before it got to court. Nevertheless, despite a number of apparently supportive judgments, including Lord Bridge's statement (p 663) that a judge:

> ... might in certain circumstances come to the conclusion that disclosure of a particular risk was so obviously necessary to an informed choice on the part of a patient that no reasonably prudent medical man would fail to make it

every judge rejected Mrs Sidaway's claim.

Following *Sidaway* a number of subsequent cases in the 1980s reached similar conclusions. In *Blyth v Bloomsbury Health Authority*, decided in 1987, shortly after *Sidaway*, but not reported until 1993, the patient asked detailed questions concerning possible side-effects of the proposed treatment, but received incomplete answers. When the side-effects materialised she claimed that the judgment in *Sidaway* demanded that attention should be paid where information was specifically sought. This was rejected. Similarly, in *Gold v Haringey Health Authority* (1988) the claimant tried to distinguish therapeutic and non-therapeutic procedures, arguing that the level of information provided should necessarily be higher where the procedure was not medically required. Had Mrs Gold succeeded this would clearly have been significant for the law of consent in relation to research; unfortunately, she also failed.

The law has paid scant regard to the need for full information to be provided in order to ensure that the ethical imperative of self-determination and autonomous decision-making is upheld. More bluntly, it could be argued that the rights of patients to exercise their individual autonomy based upon full and frank disclosure have been flouted, or at least avoided, in these cases. However, since the 1980s, when these influential cases were decided, professional and ethical guidance relating to both treatment and research have acknowledged the need for a move away from medical paternalism towards patient autonomy and self-determination. Consequently, in medical practice today there is generally a greater recognition of individual patient's rights, as is evidenced to some extent by recent guidance issued by the General Medical Council (GMC, 2008). It is arguable that as practitioners pay greater respect to individual autonomy the application of the *Bolam* test will cause the law to pay greater heed to the concept of informed consent. Indeed, the case of *Chester v Afshar* (2004) may illustrate this point.

The facts were not dissimilar to those in *Sidaway* but Ms Chester argued that although she believed she was not furnished with adequate information, she would still have undergone the surgery, albeit at a different time. On this basis one would expect her claim to fail for want of a clear causal relationship between the failure to warn and the harm she suffered, but instead the court adopted a novel approach to the situation, stating that:

> There would be a danger . . . of an honest claimant finding herself without a remedy in circumstances where the surgeon has failed in his professional duty, and the claimant has suffered injury directly within the scope and focus of that duty. . . . such a claimant ought not to be without a remedy, even if it involves some extension of existing principle . . . Otherwise the surgeon's important duty would in many cases be drained of its content.

Ms Chester thereby succeeded in her claim and the courts appeared to be moving towards a clear recognition of a right to full disclosure. However, subsequent cases have thrown this development into some confusion (*Al Hamwi v Johnson and another* (2005)).

The dearth of case law on research means that all the cases and associated guidance on consent discussed so far have concerned medical treatment, rather than focusing primarily on research, and careful distinctions must be drawn between the two at this stage. By implication, treatments offered to a patient are expected to generate benefits for the patient and therefore are generally broadly construed as being in the patient's best interests. By comparison, although some research may have advantageous consequences, it is not presumed to hold out the prospect of benefit to the participant. There is at least a possibility, therefore, that the need for full disclosure of risks and implications is more imperative in relation to research than it is with regard to treatment. Ethically, however, if autonomy counts for anything it cannot be the case that it may be afforded more limited respect in some situations as opposed to others; it should be applied consistently.

From this, and the ongoing academic debate about the efficacy of informed consent, it is apparent that the relationship between autonomy and informed decision-making is complex. In the context of treatment, for example, José Miola has claimed that 'the informed nature of the decision . . . based on all relevant facts and opinions, can . . . be seen as a gateway towards autonomy'

(Miola, 2009: 76). But others have raised doubts as to whether informed consent can actually safeguard and enhance individual autonomy (Manson and O'Neill, 2007). Two main obstacles operate to impede the relationship between informed consent and autonomy. The first concerns the nature of autonomy itself; the second focuses on the informational element of informed consent – what information is necessary and how much detail should be disclosed? Both are muddled and, as the earlier brief review of UK case law concerning treatment reveals, often contested (Pattinson, 2009).

The pertinent issues are whether, in practice, informed consent is used appropriately to achieve the aim of enhancing personal autonomy, and whether the provision of information is a vehicle capable of delivering the ideal of autonomous decision-making. As Onora O'Neill states, the claim that informed consent 'is the key to respecting patient autonomy . . . is endlessly repeated but deeply obscure' (O'Neill, 2003). Her argument is complicated, but largely founded upon the fact that informed consent is often thought impossible, or not necessary, for example where persons lack the capacity to consent, and that the procedures relating to informed consent protect non-autonomous choices as well as autonomous ones. She explains that by this she means that choices that are 'timid, conventional and lacking in individual autonomy' will be thought of as equally as sound as those that are 'self-assertive, self knowing, critically reflective, and bursting with individual autonomy' so long as the form and procedures associated with informed consent are adopted (O'Neill, 2003: 5). In this she is particularly concerned that what she terms 'the ritual of informed consent' may not demonstrate the absence of coercion and deception.

It is axiomatic, however, that respect for individual autonomy requires that voluntary informed consent should be obtained from research participants prior to their involvement in the study. This is embedded in all national and international guidance since the Nuremburg Code, and is fundamental to the International Conference on Harmonisation (ICH) Good Clinical Practice (GCP) Guidelines on the performance of clinical trials, the Clinical Trials Directive and the Clinical Trials Regulations. The Regulations define informed consent in Sch 1, Part 1, para 3(1). It maintains that a 'person gives informed consent to take part in a clinical trial only if his decision . . . is given freely after that person is informed of the nature, significance, implications and risks of the trial'. This must also be evidenced in writing either by the person herself or by a witness to that person's oral consent where she is unable to sign or make a mark to indicate consent. This provision implements Art 2(j) of the Directive. Aside from the requirement in Sch 1, Part 3, para 3 that 'the subject has given his informed consent to taking part in the trial', a number of further conditions are also imposed upon the process of obtaining this consent, namely that:

2. The subject has been informed of his right to withdraw from the trial at any time.

. . .

4. The subject may, without being subject to any resulting detriment, withdraw from the clinical trial at any time by revoking his informed consent.

5. The subject has been provided with a contact point where he may obtain further information about the trial.

These requirements reflect the routine expectations of RECs reviewing research proposals, and give them force of law in relation to clinical trials. In addition, Sch 1, Part 3, para 1 makes it mandatory that 'the subject has an interview with the investigator, or another member of the investigating team, in which he has been given the opportunity to understand the objectives, risks and inconveniences of the trial and the conditions under which it is to be conducted'. Whether this will ensure that the participant gives an informed consent is questionable.

The language of informed consent in relation to healthcare interventions implies not only that a person is furnished with the information, but also that she has engaged with it and developed an understanding of what is proposed. Indeed, the common law test for whether or not a person has decision-making capacity demands the presence of the ability to comprehend and retain the relevant information and weigh it in the balance to arrive at a decision (*Re MB* (*Adult: Medical Treatment*) (1997)), which suggests more than that the person has been passively informed. By merely requiring that the potential participant is given 'the *opportunity* to understand the objectives, risks and inconveniences of the trial and the conditions under which it is to be conducted' (emphasis added), the wording of Sch 1, Part 3, para 1 implies that simple notification of these factors is sufficient. There is apparently no requirement to ensure that the details are understood or retained, which is at odds with the common law understanding of what it means to have decision-making capacity.

In *Re C* (*Adult: Refusal of Medical Treatment*) (1994), a 68 year-old man who suffered from paranoid schizophrenia had been an in-patient at Broadmoor secure mental hospital for 30 years. His doctors recommended that he needed an operation to amputate his leg, which had become gangrenous. However, Mr C argued that he 'would rather die with two feet than live with one' and refused to consent to treatment. It fell to the court to decide whether he was competent to make this decision. The judgment established that for a person like Mr C to be competent he would need to understand the nature, purpose and effects of the proposed treatment, understand the information provided in relation to that, and believe it, albeit in his own way, so that he could make a choice as to whether or not to accept it. Merely being provided with the relevant information was inadequate for this assessment; the person also needed to engage with it and use it to inform his reasoning. Subsequent cases, including *Secretary of State for the Home Department v Robb* (1995), involving a prisoner on hunger strike, *Re MB* (*Adult: Medical Treatment*) (1997), where a woman with a needle phobia refused a caesarean section, and *Re JT* (*Adult: Refusal of Medical Treatment*) (1998), involving a woman with learning difficulties who was permitted to decline kidney dialysis, have upheld this position. Moreover, Chapter 4 of the Code of Practice to the Mental Capacity Act 2005 adopts a similar approach, insisting, amongst other things, that the ability to make a decision depends on whether the person 'is able to understand, retain, use and weigh up the information relevant to the decision'. Seemingly, therefore, decision-making capacity is dependent upon a person comprehending and appreciating the detail of what is involved.

Furthermore, with specific regard to research, the Declaration of Helsinki insists (at para 22) not only that subjects should be 'adequately informed' but also that '[A]*fter ensuring that the subject has understood the information*, the physician should then obtain the subject's freely-given informed consent, preferably in writing' (emphasis added). Yet, according to the Clinical Trials Regulations, participation in clinical trials research requires only that the potential participant has been given 'the *opportunity* to understand' and includes no requirement to ascertain that she has actually understood. This clearly resonates with the earlier discussion demonstrating that, with regard to treatment, the common law in the United Kingdom gives only limited credence to protecting individual autonomy through the doctrine of informed consent. Arguably, however, despite the centrality of the concept in all ethical guides relating to research, the Clinical Trials Regulations pay even less heed to it, and thereby afford the research participant and her autonomy far less-stringent protection than might be expected and ought properly to be demanded.

The second problem with informed consent is located within the informational aspect of the doctrine and is articulated within the questions, what information is necessary, and how much detail should be disclosed to a person contemplating participating in research? Despite O'Neill's reservations about consent procedures becoming ritualistic, it does seem obvious that sufficient information needs to be imparted to enable the person to exercise her autonomy by at least making a considered choice; but how much information is enough to facilitate this?

It is informative to refer back to the Nuremberg Code at this point. The first standard articulated in the Code states that before it is possible to give a voluntary consent a person 'should have sufficient knowledge and comprehension of the elements of the subject matter involved as to enable him to make an understanding and enlightened decision' and that:

> there should be made known to him the nature, duration, and purpose of the experiment; the method by which it is to be conducted; all inconveniences and hazards reasonably to be expected; and the effects upon his health or person which may possibly come from his participation in the experiment.
>
> (BMJ editorial, 1996)

Paragraph 22 of the Declaration of Helsinki (2008 version) reflects similar principles:

> In any research on human beings, each potential subject must be adequately informed of the aims, methods, sources of funding, any possible conflicts of interest, institutional affiliations of the researcher, the anticipated benefits and potential risks of the study and any discomfort it may entail. The subject

should be informed of the right to abstain from participation in the study or to withdraw consent to participate at any time without reprisal.

From this it is apparent that very detailed information should be provided to any potential research participant if her involvement is to be regarded as ethical. But this is not necessarily reflected in UK law.

There is, as has been stated, no case law in the United Kingdom upon which to judge the level of information necessary to constitute a fully informed consent to research. It is known that in the United States, where informed consent is an established legal concept in relation to both treatment and research, the courts have required a much higher level of disclosure for research than for treatment (*Whitlock v Duke University* (1987)). Similarly, in Canada, in *Halushka v University of Saskatchewan* (1965) it was held that even where the research is effectively a therapeutic experiment the ordinary standards of disclosure should be observed, and 'the subject of medical experimentation is entitled to full and frank disclosure of all the facts, probabilities and opinions which a reasonable man might be expected to consider before giving his consent' (pp 443–444). Where clinical trials of investigational medicinal products (CTIMPs) are concerned the Clinical Trials Regulations provide greater legal certainty than does the common law in relation to treatment. Schedule 1, Part 3, para 1 requires the disclosure of 'the objectives, risks and inconveniences of the trial and the conditions under which it is to be conducted'. This is combined with the ICH GCP 'Elements of Informed Consent' which, along with the ethical principles inherent in the Declaration of Helsinki, are incorporated into the Clinical Trials Directive and the Clinical Trials Regulations in Sch 1, Part 2. However, no explicit detail is provided as to the specific factors that should be disclosed.

More generally, the NRES has issued extensive guidance on the compilation of information sheets and consent forms, which provides detailed explanations of the type and quality of information that should be provided to research participants (NRES, May 2007). With regard to information sheets it advises that 'one size will not fit all' and states:

> brief and clear information on the essential elements of the specific study: what the research is about, the condition or treatment under study, the voluntary nature of involvement, what will happen during and after the trial, what treatment may be withheld, the participant's responsibilities, the potential risks, inconvenience or restrictions balanced against any possible benefits and the alternative(s) …
>
> (NRES, May 2007: 8–9)

It also recommends that a model information sheet be adopted containing headings to a standardised pro-forma, although it is noted that studies involving minimal intervention or risk will require less-detailed information sheets.

Additionally, the way in which information is presented is known to influence accessibility and understanding. For example, Gunn *et al* observe that simple language and pictorial representations can help to enhance comprehension (Gunn *et al*, 1999: 283), and the NRES guidance suggests that for adult studies 'the language level used should be no more difficult than that used in the information leaflets of medicines for the general public or in tabloid newspapers' (NRES, May 2007: 9). Different standards will clearly be required for children and adults with impaired capacity. Where the participants have limited English language skills the documents should be translated into relevant dialects. Simply providing comprehensive information presented in an accessible manner, and obtaining a consent, will not necessarily be sufficiently robust to ensure the protection of the participants' rights. In order to be certain that the consent is ethically effective and legally valid, the NRES also advises that the language 'must not be coercive' (NRES, May 2007: 9), which introduces a further aspect to the consent process.

Clearly, the terminology used within information sheets and consent forms should leave potential participants in no doubt that they have a free choice to decide whether or not they wish to be involved with the research. It is possible, however, that persons who are unwell or otherwise disadvantaged might feel pressure to accept experimental treatment simply because existing regimes are ineffective or have unpleasant side-effects. Put simply, the surrounding circumstances may have a coercive effect on the person's ability to act autonomously. Ferguson discovered that this was indeed a factor in 74 per cent of the patients she interviewed, with some believing that their involvement was 'their only chance of a cure' (Ferguson, 2006: 169). The issue of consent being vitiated by coercion has rarely been considered by the courts in the United Kingdom, and with uncertain results. In *Freeman v Home Office* (1984) a prisoner claimed that he had agreed to undergo treatment proposed by a prison doctor because he felt he had no option. However, the court held that this did not invalidate his consent. Conversely, in *Re T (Adult: Refusal of Treatment)* (1992) it was decided that the patient's refusal of consent had occurred as a result of pressure, or undue influence, from her mother, and her refusal was overridden. Both ethically and legally, therefore, researchers should avoid overstating any suggestion that participation might be beneficial, especially since the outcomes of research are necessarily unpredictable.

Other considerations must be taken into account where participants are also patients. For example, it has been known for some considerable time that:

> . . . patients who like their doctors and have confidence in them are inclined to agree to proposals to take part in research . . . patients may feel gratitude for attention received, or hope to secure extra attention in future; they may simply wish to please their doctor.
>
> (Royal College of Physicians (RCP), 1990: para 7.75)

Ferguson found this to be relevant in 44 per cent of her sample (Ferguson, 2006: 172). Consequently, it is particularly important that patients are advised that their right to care or treatment, both in the present and the future, will be unaffected, regardless of their decision. Outside the medical arena, and depending on the circumstances, possible recruits should know that their employment, education, eligibility for finance or access to services will be unaltered. That said, simply providing the information in a non-directive fashion and making statements of this kind will not necessarily overcome any impressions held by potential recruits that their agreement or refusal to participate may have an impact upon their entitlements. It is also necessary, therefore, to consider who delivers the information about the study, and whether any power imbalance exists between the researcher and the potential participant that might have an impact upon the decision to be made.

It has long been recognised that the power imbalance between doctor and patient can be a bar to patient autonomy (Shultz, 1985; Montgomery, 1988). Consequently, if the researcher is also the clinician treating the participant there is a strong possibility that the patient will feel some obligation to consent to joining the study. It is recommended that information about the study should be delivered by a third party who is outside of this dependent relationship. Conversely, it can be argued that the fact that there is a pre-existing relationship between the parties might be an advantage, since ordinarily clinicians are obligated to act according to the best interests of their patients. As an aside to this point, there has in recent years been a move away from the language of subjects towards 'participant' in an attempt to overturn traditional power imbalances in the relationship between the researcher and the 'researched on'. It is notable, however, that the Clinical Trials Regulations adopt the terminology of doctor and subject and thereby intrinsically perpetuate stereotypes and power imbalances associated with such relationships.

Other factors may also influence the quality of consent given by a participant. It seems self-evident, academically, that participating in clinical research is likely to mean more frequent clinic visits and by implication that greater attention will be paid to the participant's health needs. Interestingly, however, Ferguson's research indicates that this is not necessarily recognised by participants as 25 per cent of her respondents did not regard this as a motivation for entering the study. More worrying is the impression given by one respondent that this fact might have been used as an *incentive* to encourage participation:

> This didn't occur to me [as a reason for taking part], but the doctor pointed it out . . . my doctor more or less said that I'd be getting better taken care of.
>
> (Ferguson, 2006: 174)

It is easy to speculate that such factors may be less influential in a publically funded health system like the NHS, but their significance should not be overlooked in the process of ethical review.

Ethics committees are also sensitive to the possible impact of external factors on a potential participant's ability to give an effective informed consent. In this regard the physical and emotional state of the potential participant at the point of recruitment is especially important. Ferguson highlighted this in relation to pain, where several of her respondents commented that they would 'do anything you want' or say '"yes" to anything' because they were in such pain at the time they were approached (Ferguson, 2006: 179). It is because of this kind of pressure that NHS RECs recommend that patients should ideally be allowed time to decide whether or not to participate. Unless there are reasons relating to the particular project which prohibit it, RECs will therefore insist that potential participants are given at least 24 hours to decide. Whilst this seems manifestly obvious, and the NRES guidance *Information Sheets and Consent Forms version 3.2* (May 2007) includes a model form of words that entreat those invited to participate to take time to read the information and discuss it with others, there is very limited acknowledgement of this safeguard elsewhere.

Notwithstanding the previous discussion, there are some situations where explicit informed consent is *not* required. These areas will be discussed in detail in other chapters, but it is worthwhile noting them briefly here. The first is where data has been completely and irrevocably anonymised so that it is no longer personal data as defined within the meaning of the Data Protection Act 1998 (DPA 1998). The key aspect of this is that the data has been entirely divorced from those to whom it relates and therefore can be manipulated and transferred without infringing anybody's rights. Similar issues apply where approval for the processing of personal data without consent is given by the National Information Governance Board for Health and Social Care (NIGB), formerly known as the Patient Information Advisory Group (PIAG), under s 251 of the NHS Act 2006. Issues relating to anonymisation and public interest defences to potential breaches of data protection law will be covered more fully in Chapter 6. Two other exceptions to the need for informed consent pertain to the Human Tissue Act 2004 (HTA 2004). The first concerns 'existing holdings' of tissue, known as 'relevant material' under the HTA 2004, that was already held prior to 1 September 2006, the second relates to the use of tissue from the living that is not identifiable by the researcher, which does not require consent as long as the research is ethically approved by a NHS REC under s 1(9) of the HTA 2004. These examples will be considered in Chapter 8, but before concluding this chapter it is necessary to consider some difficult ethical situations within which consent may be compromised.

Consent conundrums

The nature of the research project proposed may dictate that fully informed consent from potential participants is in many respects an impossible ideal. In any study where genuine equipoise exists, it is at least arguable that participants cannot give a genuine informed consent because the outcomes are not known, so the information provided can never adequately describe what will actually occur. Pattinson (2009) has considered this issue in relation to the debate about face transplants following concerns expressed by the Royal College of Surgeons in 2003 that 'patients will not be able to choose . . . in an appropriately informed way' (Royal College of Surgeons, 2003: 19). The issue was that the risks associated with this largely experimental procedure were not sufficiently well-understood for any surgeon to be capable of 'coherently aggregating' them and presenting them to a potential transplant recipient 'for the purposes of informed decision making' (Royal College of Surgeons, 2003: 19). This is not an isolated example.

Research into xenotransplantation, broadly defined as 'the transplantation of body tissue between "foreign" or different species' (McLean and Williamson, 2005: 41), exemplifies similar and additional concerns. This technique is championed by its advocates as a potential solution to the shortage of human organs for transplant, but as a novel experimental treatment option it raises complex issues in relation to consent. As well as raising concerns about the difficulties of providing sufficient information upon which a potential xeno recipient could base her consent, this intervention would also clearly be a last hope attempt at treatment for any potential recipient. As such, their ability to give a voluntary consent, uncoerced by the gravity of their medical condition, is also questionable (Fovargue, 2005). Furthermore, xenotransplantaion poses the spectre of diseases crossing the species barrier and subsequently infecting the population at large. This kind of public health concern accordingly gives rise to questions as to whether the wider population ought properly to be included in some kind of democratic agreement prior to its use in individuals (Fovargue and Ost, 2009).

The two examples above may appear to be extreme scenarios involving situations where gaining or giving informed consent is problematic. However, similar concerns can arise in relation to many circumstances that are relatively mundane in the world of clinical research. Arguably, all phase 1 trials of medicinal products fall into this category since the effects of a novel chemical on the human body can never be predicted with absolute certainty, even though *in vitro* and animal studies will have been conducted. The most obvious recent example to illustrate this point is the trial of TGN1412 at Northwick Park Hospital in March 2006, which resulted in six participants becoming seriously ill and requiring intensive care. The case will be discussed again in Chapter 9, but it is of interest here because it illustrates the fact that grave side-effects may be entirely unforeseen. In addition, subsequent claims made by the subjects raised concerns about the quality of their consent. For example, the fact that one young man's motivation for entering the trial was to pay for driving lessons (BBC, December 2006) suggests that 'volunteers' pay insufficient attention to the information provided when financial incentives are provided (Morin *et al*, 2002; Grady, 2005).

Related issues arise where researchers deliberately illicit so-called 'broad consent' rather than explicit informed consent. This approach is particularly adopted in relation to biobank-type research involving tissues and data that are incorporated into large-scale research studies, and involves the participant's agreement for unspecified future research uses of the tissue or data. The participants are merely informed that their samples, whether tissue or data, will be used for future unspecified research, and asked for their broad agreement. The technique is defended on the basis that long periods of time are involved and it is not always possible to foresee the direction the research will take, in which case broad consent protects the interests of the participant, especially if the approval of an ethics committee is obtained (Hansson *et al*, 2006). Conversely, opponents argue that the premise behind the concept is flawed because it ignores a fundamental aspect of informed consent, that of understanding, and frequently downplays the risks associated with the research (Hofmann, 2009). In addition, by not asking for consent to additional procedures, experiments or investigations it is impossible to know whether the participant has objections to that research. Hofmann likens this to obtaining consent to withdraw £900 from a person's bank account and then claiming that it is legitimate to take £9,000. Clearly, simply giving a broad consent does not authorise any and all subsequent actions. When combined with the concerns expressed earlier about paying inadequate attention to whether participants fully understand the implications of their involvement in research, broad consent seems a dangerous practice that is detrimental to autonomy. It is one thing to avoid ascertaining whether a potential participant understands the risks and implications of engaging in a project, but quite another to deliberately disregard their rights whilst claiming that they have broadly consented.

Similar problems have been articulated about the practice of obtaining so-called provisional consent in relation to research in the emergency context, for example where the research needs to be conducted in the emergency department and the participants are unconscious patients. Until recently in the United Kingdom there was no mechanism for 'proxy consent' whereby another adult could authorise treatment or research involving an incapacitated adult. However, the situation has been altered significantly in England and Wales by the Mental Capacity Act 2005 (MCA 2005), in Scotland by the Adults with Incapacity (Scotland) Act 2000, and by the Clinical Trials Regulations. Their implications are discussed in detail in Chapter 7; however, the recommendations offered by para 26 of the Declaration of Helsinki, the ICH GCP, and other influential guidelines remain influential. In response to these guidelines RECs have traditionally taken the view that the research may commence, so long as it has ethical approval, relates to the particular condition involved and cannot be conducted in any other population. The additional safeguard that as soon as the person is able to give her consent to continue in the study, her authorisation should be sought for continuation and for use of data previously generated, is also insisted upon. This is a pragmatic response to difficult circumstances and has been widely established as acceptable. However, the implementation of the MCA and the Regulations may simply cause confusion for RECs.

Aside from these examples some commentators also argue that seeking consent may render the research impossible (Foster, 2001: 124). More specifically, Tobias and Souhami claim that informed consent is 'a major barrier to the successful conduct of randomised clinical trials in cancer' (Tobias and Souhami, 1993: 119). At the core of their assertion is evidence that demanding that full information is provided can result in limited recruitment, especially where very sick patients are involved. These kinds of situations are rare in healthcare research but may be more prominent in social science and psychology research. They are rarely seen by NHS RECs, and are more likely to involve the avoidance of providing complete information rather than not seeking consent at all. Foster discusses this as a balancing act, where respect for the rights of the participant are weighed against the needs of science as competing moral claims. It may, she says, be ethical to conduct the trial in circumstances where there is no risk, but the answer to the research question is important. However, 'if your overriding concern is that the wishes of people being used as a means to someone else's ends should first be consulted then you would not consider this research to be ethical' (Foster, 1996: 817). RECs faced with the ethical review of this kind of project may be confronted by a tension between law and ethics. It may genuinely not be possible to answer the research question if fully informed consent is sought, either because the results will be biased through the provision of information or because recruitment will prove impossible. However, even if the REC is minded to approve the project, believing that the importance of the question outweighs the rights of the participant, this will not be permissible if the study falls under the Clinical Trials Regulations because it involves a CTIMP, or is subject to the MCA 2005.

Conclusions

Although consent is regarded as the cornerstone of medical law and ethics, the above discussion has highlighted some of the issues raised by its application in practice. Doyal has commented that:

> [O]ur ability to deliberate, to choose, and to plan for the future are the focus of the dignity and respect which we associate with being an autonomous person capable of participation in civic life. Such respect is now widely regarded as essential for good medical practice and should dominate the practice of medical research.
>
> (Doyal, 1997: 1108)

However, the foregoing discussion demonstrates that in many respects the law as presently constructed is imperfect in protecting the rights of research participants and promoting their autonomy. Consent is widely regarded as the legal expression of autonomy, but the ability of consent to protect the interests and safety of research participants is highly contingent. It depends primarily on the quality of the information provided, the way it is communicated and the capacity of the subject to understand it and act upon it autonomously. These aspects form an established part of the process of ethical review, but it is evident that the law does not always uphold that ideal.

Furthermore, in relation to the requirement to provide fully informed consent, some scholars believe that 'consent has become an ethical device for making research ethically acceptable' (Hofman, 2009: 128). Others hold the view that everybody has a moral responsibility to participate in research that is of itself beneficial to society and offers minimal risks to the individual, which implies that consent might be waived in some circumstances (Harris, 2005), particularly where the patient is benefiting from previous research (Evans, 2004). Such arguments have also been decisively countered (Perna, 2006), but ideas such as these will be problematic for RECs that encounter them.

It is many years since Doyal wrote that denying volunteers appropriate information 'is a clear breach of their moral rights' (Doyal, 1997), and even longer since Nuremberg, but the lessons learned must not be forgotten. Despite concerns about the nature of autonomy and the practicalities of information provision, it is essential that the dignity, safety and welfare of anybody who considers participating in research are properly protected. Informed consent may not be perfect, but it is the best means we have for enabling research participants to exercise their self-determination or autonomy by deciding whether or not to be involved in the research.

Chapter 6

Confidentiality issues in research ethics

Introduction

Research involving human beings raises issues about confidentiality in relation to the recruitment of participants, protection of their data during the research process, and protection of their identities when the research findings are being disseminated. Therefore, like consent, confidentiality plays a major role in the work of research ethics committees (RECs). In general, the duty of confidence requires that certain information is kept secret, and as such it is also a crucial aspect of many types of professional relationship. For example, Lord Keith claimed in *Attorney General v Guardian Newspapers (No 2)* (1988) that:

> [T]he law has long recognized that an obligation of confidence can arise out of particular relationships. Examples are the relationships of doctor and patient, priest and penitent, solicitor and client, banker and customer.

In the context of healthcare more broadly, it is settled law 'that there is an abiding obligation of confidentiality as between doctor and patient' (*Ashworth Security Hospital v MGN Ltd* (2000), p 527).

Individuals clearly value the ability to protect their privacy, which is widely regarded as a fundamental right. In relation to medical practice generally, this means that patients are reluctant to disclose sensitive information relevant to their medical diagnosis and treatment, unless assured that the details will be kept confidential and private (*W v Egdell* (1990); *Z v Finland* (1997)). Such reticence may as a consequence disadvantage the individual patient by precluding accurate diagnosis and appropriate treatment. It could also have an impact on public health more generally if, for example, it resulted in preventable infectious diseases spreading unchecked, or that epidemiological research is hampered. Confidentiality is therefore clearly based on both consequentialist and deontological reasoning. It also plays a key role in healthcare, and, along with consent, is a cornerstone of healthcare law.

There are, however, some situations where the individual's right to privacy may be legitimately overridden, and information legitimately disclosed, despite ethical and legal restrictions on the use of confidential information. These include circumstances where the person who is the subject of the information gives her consent to its disclosure, when the law requires disclosure, and when disclosure would be in the public interest. More specifically, a large number of statutes and regulations do not merely permit disclosure, but actually require it. There are, for example, regulations and requirements that require that statistics on the incidence of infectious diseases are recorded and collated, that births and deaths are notified and that information is documented about numerous other aspects of social life and medical care. Anonymous data is gathered in relation to many of these applications, but, regardless of anonymisation, the details recorded may make it possible to trace individuals, their doctors or locations, raising the possibility of breaches of confidentiality.

The anonymisation of data is a useful tool in the process of research if used effectively. More specifically, where the identity of the individuals who are the source of the data is protected and cannot be discovered, the data is not regarded as confidential, and can therefore be disseminated freely (*R v Department of Health ex p Source Informatics Ltd* (1999)). Furthermore, properly anonymised data is outside of the scope of the European Data Protection Directive (95/46/EC), and the UK Data Protection Act 1998 (DPA 1998) which implemented it into domestic law. Hence, the restrictions imposed by these legislative instruments will not apply. However, it is important to recognise that not all forms of apparent anonymisation are effective for these purposes (Kalra *et al*, 2006).

A number of different techniques can be applied to render data non-identifiable, but not all will achieve true anonymisation. For example, anonymisation can be achieved by simply removing explicit identifiers, such as name and address, from the data without making further changes or adding additional protection. This leaves open the possibility that contextual information, for example pertaining to the individual's medical condition or medical practitioner, may make identification possible. Moreover, if a researcher is conducting a study about a very rare condition with few sufferers, it is not beyond the bounds of possibility that the identity of research participants could be discovered by examining the locations within which the work was carried out, or making some other connection (Kent, 2003).

Another common way of anonymising research data is to codify the data, so that each participant is represented by a coded identity rather than personal information. This is a perfectly adequate approach, especially where there is a need to retain a record of the identity of participants, but adequate safeguards must be put in place to ensure that the coded data and the identifiable information are kept separate. It is also necessary to ensure that the code can be easily broken to enable identification of the participants should the need arise, in case, for example, serious adverse events occur in clinical trials of medicinal products. This type of anonymisation is therefore reversible, and as such the information retains the status of personal data under the DPA 1998 and must be protected accordingly.

Particular difficulties arise in relation to the anonymisation of data relating to genetic information about individual people. Every person's genetic make-up is unique but is closely related to that of other members of the same family. Consequently, the discovery of genetic information about one person can reveal characteristics about their family members, such as predispositions to certain medical conditions or surprising indicators of their paternity. If, in the course of research, genetic testing exposes the fact that the person concerned has an inherited condition, concerns arise as to how to deal with that information. Should it be conveyed to the person concerned, to her family members, or should it be kept secret? Imagine, for example, that a person discovers through her involvement in research, that she is carrying a gene that means that her life-expectancy is limited. Her outlook on life and the choices she makes – whether to marry or stay married, whether to procreate, how to relate to her children if she has any – will all be influenced by this knowledge. The same is true for the family if they have the same awareness. It may be better if they did not know. However, it is arguable that if crucial information is known by others it ought morally to be shared with those who will be most affected by it (O'Donovan and Gilbar, 2003).

The alternatives for the researcher are to inform the potential participant that no genetic information generated through the research will be disclosed to her. In these circumstances the participant exercises her autonomy by agreeing to this stipulation, or not. This is a widespread and accepted technique adopted by the developers of many tissue banks and databases used for research. For example, UK Biobank, which is a large-scale study involving the compilation of a database including genetic information, informs its participants that they 'will not be able to tell individual participants the results of any tests which may be done on their samples'. This is the case even though '[O]nce you have given us your consent, we will continue to use your information up to and after your death, unless you withdraw from UK Biobank' (UK Biobank, 2009). Conversely, if a researcher wishes to be able to make disclosures to the participants, they would need to include mechanisms in the study to ensure that the knowledge received would not disadvantage those involved. For example, detailed information would need to be provided to explain the possible implications of receiving such information. In addition, genetic counseling may be required, or referral to specialist medical services for advice or treatment.

Besides these concerns, it is self-evident that some groups or organisations will have a special interest in acquiring genetic data if it is available. Insurance companies, for example, may argue that the calculation of actuarial risk is more accurately assessed if they have knowledge of predispositions to specific inherited conditions, which would be an advantage to their business. Employers may also wish to benefit from the acquisition of knowledge about the future health prospects of potential employees, to maximise the benefits in taking on workers who are less likely to become sick and minimise costs associated with staff illness. Research participants who undergo genetic tests that reveal their DNA profile therefore need to be informed about the potential implications, both to themselves in terms of knowledge they may acquire about their future health status, and with regard to their insurance and employment prospects.

Genetic testing for research also raises concerns with regard to possible breaches of confidentiality through poor data security, which may permit unauthorised access to genetic information. RECs therefore need to keep in mind that even where DNA is extracted from samples or tissues and codified, all that is required to identify the person concerned is a matching sample. It is, of course, arguable that identification made in this way is still largely the stuff of science fiction, yet this kind of technology is used routinely in criminal investigations that have access to specific databases. Concerns have already been raised following the reported use of a diagnostic biobank to identify the murderer of Swedish politician Anna Lindh (Hofmann, 2009: 126). Awareness of the controversies surrounding different methods of anonymisation, and the use of databases, especially in relation to genetic information, is therefore a vital aspect of the work of RECs. Knowledge and understanding of the intricacies associated with this type of research will enable them to consider the specific confidentiality issues that arise and to ensure that potential participants are adequately informed about the implications.

Data protection and anonymisation issues have also been contentious in relation to some types of epidemiological research. This field of research aims to discover factors affecting health and illness in the general population. It studies the occurrence, distribution and prevalence of diseases, and other health-related conditions across populations to identify the incidence, spread and causes of specific diseases, infections and contamination. Anonymised data can be used in this type of research, but patients generally need to be identified, so that it is possible to gain initial access to the information. However, the potential public health benefits of the research are often thought to outweigh concerns about breaching individual privacy and a utilitarian approach may be used to justify breaching confidentiality. Given the abundance of legislation to protect the right to privacy, it can be difficult to construct an argument that gives the needs of society priority over the rights of the individual. Consequently, some commentators have argued that epidemiological research has been hindered, or even stifled, because of restrictive legislation and the overly protective attitudes of RECs (Kmietowicz, 2001). These concerns will be discussed below in some depth to demonstrate that a sound understanding of the law and its application should facilitate most types of research without compromising the rights of participants.

Researchers also have a right to confidentiality, which includes a right to expect that the details of their research proposals will be securely guarded by RECs charged with reviewing them. RECs must therefore be aware of the extent of their ethical and legal obligations in this regard. Included amongst these obligations, aside from the general duty to observe confidentiality and privacy to be discussed in detail below, is the need to understand the impact of the Freedom of Information Act 2000 (FOI Act), which came into force in 2005. This Act permits any member of the public to make enquiries about the business of public bodies such as government departments, health authorities and associated organizations, including NHS RECs. Therefore, as information about these RECs and their membership is readily available in the public domain, any NHS REC member could be approached and questioned about the work of her REC.

The FOI Act does not require that all and any information should be publically available. Consequently, organisations that may be subject to FOI Act requests have designated officers whose job it is to respond to such requests as appropriate. Since it is a legal requirement to respond within 14 days of receipt of a request, REC members need to be aware of who, within the organisation, has responsibility for handling such approaches and to refer FOI Act requests accordingly. In the NHS REC system this person will generally be the REC co-ordinator. In addition, concerns about privacy issues, whether related to the role of the REC or associated with specific research proposals, can be referred to the office of the Information Commissioner. This is an independent authority that reports directly to Parliament, whose role is to oversee and enforce the DPA 1998 and FOI Act and works in an advisory capacity to assist individuals or organisations in assessing the extent of their duty of confidentiality.

Confidentiality issues arise frequently in relation to research and are particularly relevant to the process of recruitment, access to records and the storage and dissemination of research findings. This chapter will therefore examine the law and ethics associated with confidentiality and the protection of data pertaining to individuals in the context of research. In so doing it will begin with an overview of the main statutes and cases that make up the legal framework in the United Kingdom, and the ethical codes and guidelines that inform and govern research practice. From there, some of the practical controversies that arise in relation to specific types of research will be examined. The chapter will conclude with some comments on the effectiveness of confidentiality in protecting the rights of research participants and how these can be balanced against the wider public interest.

Ethics and law in confidence

At the outset it is important to define what is meant by confidentiality, and how it relates to privacy. The distinction between the two is self-evident if one considers that an idea, thought or piece of information is private as long as it is kept to oneself or is known only to a very limited group of people. However, once that same thought, or information, is shared more widely amongst others who are required or expected to limit its further disclosure, it becomes confidential. For example, when a woman discovers that she is pregnant this is an entirely private matter as long as it is known only to herself and perhaps a partner. Nevertheless, as soon as her medical practitioner is informed and undertakes to care for her during the pregnancy it becomes a confidential matter, the details of which may only be shared in limited and highly restricted circumstances, such as where other clinicians need to be informed in order to assist in her treatment. In this situation the professional relationship between the patient and her doctors gives rise to a professional duty of confidence whereby her private information may only be legitimately disclosed in certain prescribed circumstances, and to specific individuals or groups. Put more simply, individuals can rightly claim control over information about those areas of their lives that they regard as personal or private. Generally, this control extends to excluding others from having access to the information, and this is protected by law.

Confidentiality is enshrined in the codes of conduct published by the professional bodies that govern the practice of healthcare professionals. Indicative of this is the code issued by the governing body of doctors in the United Kingdom, the General Medical Council, *Confidentiality: Protecting and Providing Information*, which dictates that its members 'must treat information about patients as confidential'. The code goes on to demonstrate the contingent nature of confidentiality in practice by explaining that:

> [I]f in exceptional circumstances there are good reasons why you should pass on information without a patient's consent, or against a patient's wishes, you must follow our guidance . . . . and be prepared to justify your decision to the patient, if appropriate, and to the GMC and the courts, if called on to do so.
>
> (GMC, 2004)

The GMC guidance is under review in 2009, but it seems unlikely that these basic principles will change significantly in any future revision. From this it is apparent that the right to privacy through confidentiality is not absolute, and that there are some circumstances in which it is permissible, both ethically and legally, to breach confidences. These circumstances, including certain types of research, are well-defined, and will be discussed in detail below. In the meantime, the situations where breach of confidentially may be permissible, as well as those where it is not, and the mechanisms that can be employed to avoid inappropriate breaches, will be considered more generally.

The ethical imperative to respect privacy and confidentiality is widely recognised and included within all national, international and professional codes of ethics. The Declaration of Geneva, for example, requires doctors to declare that '[A]t the time of being admitted as a member of the medical profession . . . I will respect the secrets which are confided in me, even after the patient has died' (World Medical Association, 2006). The Hippocratic Oath takes a similar approach, with the words, 'whatever, in connection with my professional practice . . . I see or hear in the life of men, which ought not to be spoken of abroad, I will not divulge'. With specific reference to research, the Medical Research Council (MRC) has issued guidance that relates specifically to confidentiality and emphasises its significance with the words:

> Respect for private life is a human right, and the ability to discuss information in confidence with others is rightly valued. Keeping control over facts

about one's self can have an important role in a person's sense of security, freedom of action, and self-respect.

(MRC, 2000)

Individual autonomy provides the ethical foundation of confidentiality and requires that persons should be in control of information about themselves, and determine who should have access to it, and in what circumstances. This is recognised as a right protected by law and largely exercised through the law of consent whereby access to data is permissible if the individual who is the subject of that data agrees to its dissemination. The sources of the legal protection of confidentiality are many and various, involving several areas of common law as well as a number of statutes aimed specifically at regulating the transfer of data between individuals and organisations. The ethical codes and guidelines previously mentioned are also influential in informing professional regulation and non-statutory professional guidance, such as that published by the National Health Service and similar bodies. All of these sources of the right to confidentiality are founded upon basic principles of justice, fairness and equity. Hence, although contract law, tort law and a number of important statutes operate to help maintain and protect the right to privacy that underpins the duty of confidentiality, it is equitable obligations of confidence that might be regarded as its main legal source. The law of equity provides the opportunity to obtain injunctions to prevent one's legal and equitable rights being infringed, which is not particularly helpful in cases where confidentiality has already been breached. However, it is through the common law of equity that the basis of the legally enforceable duty of confidentiality is defined. Therefore, this analysis will commence with a discussion of these equitable obligations and their legal basis before moving on to consider the role of the various statutes that impose obligations of confidentiality with regard to research, and the contractual and tortious duties that apply to researchers and RECs.

Four criteria lie at the heart of the equitable obligation of confidence in the common law, all of which must be satisfied before a legal breach of confidence can be established. First, the information must be of a private, personal or intimate nature, in order to possess the necessary quality of confidence (*Stephens v Avery* (1988); *Campbell v MGN* (2004)). In addition, according to Lord Goff in *Attorney General v Guardian Newspapers* (*No 2*) (1990), the information must not already be in the public domain or trivial in nature. There is some debate as to precisely what kind of information might attract these characteristics in the medical context. In *Campbell*, for example, Lady Hale considered situations when there may be a legitimate public interest in knowing certain information, claiming, in the context of disclosures about celebrities like Naomi Campbell, that 'not every statement about a person's health will carry the badge of confidentiality or risk doing harm to that person's physical or moral integrity' (*Campbell* (2004), para 157). This is at odds with British Medical Association (BMA) guidance, which regards the simple information that a person is registered with or has attended a particular doctor as attracting the duty of confidence (BMA, 2004: 167). The BMA is focusing solely on the nature of the information and clearly takes no account of the celebrity status of the person concerned, whilst Lady Hale seems to imply that the extent of the right to privacy may depend upon the person's personality:

> The privacy interest in the fact that a public figure has a cold or a broken leg is unlikely to be strong enough to justify restricting the press's freedom to report it. What harm could it possibly do?
>
> (*Campbell* (2004), para 157)

We will return to the possible harms caused by breaches of confidence later in the chapter.

The second criterion is that the information has been imparted in circumstances that import an obligation to maintain confidence, which today is very broadly construed. In the past it was necessary to demonstrate that a confidential relationship, such as doctor and patient, existed between the parties concerned. However, following *Wainwright v Home Office* (2003) this no longer applies. Instead, following *Campbell*, it must simply be established that the person knows when she receives the information that it should be regarded as confidential. This applies however the information is received. As such, the duty of confidence will arise even if the information is discovered by chance, provided it is obvious from the nature of the information that the person to whom it pertains would wish it to be private (*AG v Guardian Newspapers Ltd (No 2)* (1990), p 281). This has very clear implications for researchers and members of research teams, and for RECs that are charged with protecting the interests of potential and actual research participants. In practice, all concerned must be aware of their obligations and mechanisms must be in place to avoid breaches of confidentiality, whether foreseeable or inadvertent.

In order for a claim of breach of confidence to succeed, it is necessary to show that there has been a disclosure to a person who was not authorised to have access to the information concerned. This may present evidential problems, particularly as there is no requirement to prove that the information has fallen into the public domain.

The final criterion associated with the equitable duty of confidence is that the subject of the information, the person who originally communicated it, would suffer some harm from its revelation. Some controversy surrounds this requirement. In *R v Department of Health ex p Source Informatics Ltd* (1999), for example, it was held that no breach of confidentiality resulted from the disclosure of anonymous data. However, judgments in other cases have taken the view that harm may be construed more broadly. For example, *Stone v South East Strategic Health Authority* (2006) suggests that potentially causing harm to public trust, for instance in the inviolability of the doctor–patient relationship, could be regarded as a public harm and thereby necessitate the protection of the information in question. It is not difficult to anticipate that public trust might be damaged if confidences were breached through engagement with the research process, which explains the centrality of confidentiality in the process of ethical review.

The common law of equity and equitable obligations in the context of confidentiality is just the starting point when it comes to understanding the legal framework within which research involving confidential data operates. Ethics dictates that the use of identifiable patient information by any part of the NHS or research community is governed by the overriding principle of respect for autonomy, which operates largely through the mechanism of informed consent. In practice this means that no data should be disclosed for research purposes without the explicit consent of the individual concerned. In this regard, the common law principles relating to consent discussed in the Chapter 5 also apply. In addition, a number of highly influential government reports and statutes inform the regulatory environment that governs confidentiality in research. These will be examined in turn, before some of the more controversial aspects associated with their practical application are outlined.

Research in the NHS must comply with the basic principles of confidentiality and data protection contained in a series of NHS policy documents. The most pertinent are *Confidentiality: NHS Code of Practice* (DoH, 2003) and *The Protection and Use of Patient Information* (DoH, 2004). Both are founded upon principles developed in an earlier document known as the *Caldicott Report*, named after its author (Caldicott, 1997). The report was commissioned by the Chief Medical Officer at the time following concerns about the extensive use made of patient identifiable information in the NHS, and the potential for breaches of confidentiality. In line with its remit the Caldicott Committee reviewed issues relating to identifiable information about patients that passes from NHS organisations to other NHS or non-NHS bodies. It developed a number of principles relating to the transfer of information designed to ensure that patient-identifiable information is only transferred for justified purposes and that only the minimum necessary information is transferred in each case. The basic principles are that such data should only be transferred when absolutely necessary, in other words, when there is no alternative. Only the minimum amount of information should be transferred, meaning that only strictly relevant data must be passed on. Access to such data must be strictly on a 'need-to-know' basis, so that inadvertent communication is avoided, and every body concerned must know their responsibilities.

The major initiative under the Caldicott Report was the requirement for health service providers to establish a 'framework of individual responsibility' under the leadership of guardians of patient information, who have come to be known as Caldicott guardians. These are generally senior health professionals whose role is to safeguard and govern the uses made of patient information. Each NHS body therefore has a Caldicott guardian who takes responsibility for information transfer and data protection in their institution. National frameworks have been developed to facilitate this and NHS organisations are accountable for the preservation of confidentiality through clinical governance. It is of note that the Caldicott Committee was charged with developing guidelines in relation to data transfer for purposes other than direct care, medical research or where there is a statutory requirement for information. Theoretically, therefore, the principles do not apply to research. However, since the Caldicott principles adhere to fundamental ethical beliefs and standards, and are enshrined in the majority of ethical codes, they reflect the stance adopted by RECs and are relevant for that reason. Furthermore, Caldicott guardians are generally an invaluable source of advice for both researchers and RECs, particularly where difficult issues arise in relation to recruitment of research participants or access to data.

The core principles of the Caldicott Report also play a key role in the DPA 1998, which is regarded by many as the most crucial piece of legislation in this area. Indeed, in relation to clinical trials of investigational medicinal products (CTIMPs), the requirements of the DPA 1998 are specifically incorporated into Sch 1, Part 2, para 11 to the Clinical Trials Regulations. Its primary aim is to ensure the security of personal information and, unlike its predecessor, the Data Protection Act 1984, which applied primarily to electronic data, this is an all-embracing statute. It imposes duties on everybody who handles, processes and stores personal information about anybody, whether manual or electronic data. The DPA 1998 imposes criminal penalties on those who infringe its requirements. In brief, the Act incorporates eight principles, which require that all information must be:

- processed fairly and lawfully;
- obtained for specified and lawful purposes and not processed in a manner incompatible with those purposes;
- adequate, relevant and not excessive;
- accurate and up to date;
- kept no longer than necessary;
- processed in accordance with subjects rights;
- protected by appropriate security;
- not transferred without adequate protection.

The first principle is the overarching provision that data is processed fairly and lawfully according to the subject's rights. By implication, then, and under Sch 33 to the DPA 1998, the common law rights of the individual to whom the data pertains must be upheld if the data is to be processed fairly and lawfully, as must the rights which attach under the Human Rights Act 1998. The easiest way for a researcher to ensure compliance with this requirement is to obtain explicit consent from the subject of the data for its use in the research. This will authorise its use for the specific research purposes. In these circumstances it is incumbent upon the REC to ensure that the participant who is being asked to allow the researcher to access her data is properly informed of the kind of information sought, the uses to which it will be put, and the methods that will be taken to ensure its security.

Particularly relevant in the context of research is the requirement that data handlers, that is anybody who collects, collates, stores or transfers data relevant to the Act, must ensure that data is only obtained and processed for specified purposes.

Some researchers mistakenly believe that personal data that has been consensually recorded, for example in a patient's medical records or on a university database, is readily available for use in research. But unless explicit consent was obtained for its use in research applications at the time the data was acquired, this is not the case, as the second data protection principle explicitly forbids the use of data for any purpose other than that which was specified when it was obtained. With regard to medical research this clearly means that information entered in medical records for the purpose of diagnosis and treatment is not available for research without further authorisation.

The remaining data protection principles become relevant to all aspects of the collection, storage and use of data generated in the research process. These principles require that only data that is relevant to the research is gathered; for example, if details such as the participant's age or date of birth are superfluous to the project, they should not be obtained. Further, all data received should be securely stored with security that is appropriate for the kind of data, and retained for no longer than is necessary. In practice this means that RECs should enquire of investigators as to the measures in place to protect confidential data during the research process. For example, will computer files be encrypted or password protected? Where and how will audio or video recordings be stored and for how long? There are also practical issues surrounding the destruction of data of all kinds, and RECs will wish to be reassured that specialist techniques will be employed where necessary. It is in relation to questions of this type, and with regard to the requirement to ensure that data is not transferred without adequate protection, that experienced RECs can often advise and support researchers. This mirrors one of the key Caldicott principles and has become especially pertinent in relation to electronic data transfer. How, for instance, can research data be transferred by email or fax in such a way that breaches of confidence can be avoided? The most obvious method is by ensuring that the individuals who are the subject of the data cannot be identified, either by anonymising the material or by encoding it and sending the code by separate communication. In addition, practical security techniques, such as ensuring that fax machines are not in public access locations and that the intended recipients of any transmission are aware of their impending arrival, are useful methods of protecting communiqués by fax. It is questionable whether disclaimers at the foot of email messages requesting that information received in error be destroyed or returned to the sender provide adequate safeguards, but this has yet to be tested in court.

The courts have now firmly established that the principles enshrined within Article 8 of the European Convention on Human Rights and the Human Rights Act 1998, buttress the equitable foundations of the duty of confidentiality (*R (B) v Stafford Combined Court* (2006)). The right to privacy contained in Article 8 can only be enforced against a public authority, which excludes private individuals but includes bodies such as hospital trusts, GP surgeries, universities and RECs. Article 8(1) proclaims that 'Everyone has a right to respect for his private and family life, his home and his correspondence', which upholds confidentiality by ensuring that unauthorised disclosures are actionable. Alongside this, however, Article 8(2) adds a utilitarian provision that severely limits the apparently all-embracing character of Article 8(1), by providing that 'there shall be no interference by a public authority with the exercise of this right except such as in accordance with the law and is necessary in a democratic society'. With obvious utilitarian intent, this allows the public interest to outweigh the rights of the individual in circumstances that would otherwise amount to a breach of privacy and thereby renders the protection offered by Article 8 as highly contingent.

The contingent and complex nature of the legal protection of privacy and confidentiality was also reflected in the common law, even before the enactment of the Human Rights Act 1998 and the DPA 1998. For example, in *AG v Guardian Newspapers* (*No 2*) (1988) Lord Goff explained that:

> although the basis of the law's protection of confidence is that there is a public interest that confidences should be preserved and protected by the law, nevertheless that public interest may be outweighed by some other countervailing public interest which favours disclosure.

The practical ramifications of this are vividly portrayed in the advice to participants in the UK Biobank project in response to a question about whether the police will have access to the information held in the database:

> We will not grant access to the police, the security services or to lawyers unless forced to do so by the courts (and, in some circumstances, we would oppose such access vigorously).
>
> (UK Biobank, 2009)

There are a range of circumstances under which the Biobank may be required by law to disclose confidential information, including health information such as DNA. And, despite the assurances that allowing such access would be vigorously resisted, the legal obligation to do so under legislation such as the Police and Criminal Evidence Act 1984 and the Terrorism Act 2000 is at least equally as stringent. On considering ambiguities present here, and the conditional nature of the right to privacy more generally, the simple ethical principles upon which data protection is founded tend to lose their persuasiveness.

Nevertheless, the duty to maintain confidences is often more pervasive than is at first evident. For example, aside from the obvious ethical obligations and those imposed by statute discussed above, many professional people also have the duty of confidentiality embedded in their contracts of employment. When combined with the Caldicott requirements, this means that those employed in the NHS should receive training to ensure that they understand their responsibilities and will potentially be in breach of their contract of employment and subject to disciplinary action or even dismissal if they breach confidentiality. In addition, professionals engaged in activities where the duty of confidence arises will also be bound by the obligations imposed upon them by their governing professional bodies: the General Medical Council in the case of doctors, and the Nursing and Midwifery Council for members of the nursing professions. Breaches of these obligations may invoke professional disciplinary responsibility or liability in negligence.

Any professional person whose work requires that she maintain confidentiality is potentially liable under the tort of negligence if she fails to observe her duty of confidence. This will apply where she has either revealed confidential information herself or has failed to ensure its protection (*Swinney v Chief Constable of Northumbria Police* (1996)). Such liability could even apply to REC members who inappropriately disclose information about research applications submitted to them for approval. Consider, for example, the situation where a researcher submitted her PhD research to an REC, and its substance was subsequently revealed to another person who managed to conduct the project first. Depending on the details of the project it is possible that the original researcher would be unable to publish her research because it was not regarded as original to her. That being the case, she might also be unable to obtain her PhD. To succeed in a claim of negligence in such a case, the claimant would need to overcome the same difficulties as for any other negligence action, with regard to demonstrating that a duty owed was breached and caused harm to ensue.

Demonstrating that a harm capable of being compensated has been suffered as a consequence of breach of confidence usually poses an additional problem. In tort, damages are usually only available to compensate for physical or quantifiable financial losses, which would not easily apply in a case of breach of confidence. Consequently, unless it was possible to show such losses, only minimal compensation would be available. The PhD candidate might be able to demonstrate that she has lost the chance of a sparkling academic career, but under tort law the courts are generally reluctant to compensate for a lost chance.

The chances of success might be higher had a pharmaceutical company found itself in a similar position, and was able to demonstrate that information about a novel, and potentially highly lucrative chemical compound, had been revealed to a rival company. If the person who committed the breach benefited financially she might be required to make recompense to the victim under the ruling in *Blake v Attorney General* (2003), but this would be ineffective if the profit was made by the rival company rather than the REC member who breached the confidence. It is more likely that action would be taken under the DPA 1998, which would impose a criminal penalty, although in these circumstances it may also be necessary to consider whether the breach was deliberate or merely negligent.

However, a New Zealand court did find that the revelation of a person's health status could cause them to suffer losses (*Furniss v Finchett* (1958)). Moreover, with regard to the negligent failure to ensure that proper precautions are taken to keep confidential information secure, damages were paid in a case where adequate measures were not taken to prevent a computer printout containing confidential information about a prisoner falling into the hands of a fellow inmate

(*H v Home Office* (1992)). It is also possible that in the wake of the Human Rights Act the courts will come to recognise a new tort of breach of privacy at some point in the future, although the House of Lords declined to do so in *Wainwright v Home Office* (2003). In the meantime, damages are now available for breach of confidence in equity, but the awards tend to be paltry (*Cornelius v Taranto* (2001); *Campbell v MGN* (2004)). Despite this, the potential for breaches of confidentiality to cause harm have been particularly controversial in the context of healthcare research, and it is to these controversies that the discussion will now turn.

Confidentiality controversies

It has been claimed that '[A]nxiety about public attitudes towards the use of health information in research has created disproportionate constraints on research compromising its quality and validity' (Royal College of Physicians, 2007: 24). The implication behind this is that concerns about the possible harms caused by breaches of confidentiality in the academic community, and presumably in the REC community, are not in accordance with the views of the public, and may therefore be overblown (Barrett *et al*, 2006). Accordingly, the Royal College of Physicians argues that there is evidence to show that few people decline to participate in epidemiological studies when asked, suggesting that in practice the regulatory framework may be too heavy handed (Royal College of Physicians, 2007: 24; Iverson *et al*, 2006).

The main thrust of the controversy about what has come to be regarded as the unnecessarily burdensome nature of privacy laws and policies stems from the introduction of the DPA 1998. At the time of its enactment it was widely felt that its provisions would prevent much, if not all, valuable epidemiological research from taking place, and impose undue restrictions upon other areas of research (Health Service Journal Editorial Report, 2000). More specifically, many prominent researchers feared that the requirement to obtain explicit consent for the use of personal data would prohibit access to certain information about individuals, and the conditions from which they suffered, which as a result would be lost to certain databases and cancer registries. Consequently, there was a high profile campaign to have medical research excluded from the DPA 1998 altogether. Although this would have been contrary to Article 8 of the Human Rights Act (Beyleveld, 2006), the Government of the day were sympathetic to the idea and took legislative action.

At that time the Health and Social Care Act 2001 was part way through the parliamentary process and it was decided to introduce a new section dealing with the control of patient information. This ultimately became s 60 of the Health and Social Care Act 2001, which was a temporary measure designed to introduce a mechanism through which the Secretary of State could regulate the disclosure of confidential patient data for research without consent. Effectively, s 60 would permit the use of patient identifiable information. The relaxation of general principles of confidentiality was only permissible, however, where it was in the interests of improving patient care, or where there was a genuine public interest in so doing. The provisions of s 60 could only be invoked where anonymised information would not suffice, or if it was clearly impracticable to obtain consent.

To provide an additional protection, s 61 of the Act instituted the Patient Interest Advisory Group (PIAG), whose primary role was to advise the Secretary of State on whether and when it would be appropriate to allow consent to be evaded. In practice, researchers seeking to use s 60 had first to obtain REC approval for the project, and then make a case to the PIAG in support of their application to use identifiable information. The request would go initially to the Department of Health and be referred to the PIAG if it was felt appropriate. It would not be regarded as appropriate to forward an application that had not first gained REC approval in principle. Acceptance by the PIAG would then need to be referred to the Secretary of State who would seek parliamentary approval. In effect the PIAG became a gate keeper in an extensive bureaucratic process (Turnberg, 2003).

Section 60 of the Health and Social Care Act 2001 has now been superseded by s 251 of the NHS Act 2006 respectively. More recently, in January 2009, the PIAG was replaced by the National Information Governance Board for Health and Social Care (NIGB) under s 158 of the Health and Social Care Act 2008. This body now has responsibility for the administration of powers under s 251. Immediately upon its establishment the NIGB launched an ethics committee to review s 251 applications, inviting existing members of the PIAG to become its members in order to promote continuity. The committee meets bi-monthly to consider applications for s 251 support, and applicants are recommended to submit applications at least one month prior to the meeting at which they wish their application to be considered (DoH, January 2009). It seems that the process still takes time. Furthermore, the NIGB apparently expects that very few situations will warrant s 251 support. Barely a month before the NIGB's inception, the PIAG responded to the General Medical Council's public consultation on its revised confidentiality guidance, stating that:

> In general, many secondary uses of data and medical research in particular, are unlikely to meet the public interest test threshold, to warrant disclosure on public interest grounds.
>
> (PIAG, 2008: 3)

It is also at pains to explain that s 251 may 'only be used as a permissive gateway' and cannot be invoked where patients have explicitly refused to give consent. In addition, it stresses that it is always preferable to avoid the need to use s 251. The document also invites enquiries:

> from those seeking to use identifiable patient data to advise on how an activity may be undertaken without recourse to S251 powers or minimising

the extent of their use to where using pseudonymised information or seeking consent are genuinely not practicable.

(PIAG, 2008: 5)

It is too early to draw any conclusions about the operation of the NIGB specifically. However, given its genesis and composition it seems likely that little will change.

Whilst some still clearly regard the NIGB, formerly the PIAG, and the associated regulation and process of ethical review, as overly burdensome and restrictive of the research process (Randerson, 2006), to others the existence of the NIGB might be regarded as comforting. Those who are concerned about the disclosure of information for research purposes in the absence of participant consent will no doubt be particularly supportive, and prepared to find ways to facilitate research and the review process (Pegg, 2006). With this in mind it is significant that, in spite of suggestions that patients are often unconcerned about the use of their data for research, it is generally accepted that people do wish to control whether and when their samples and data are used in research (Royal College of Physicians, 2007: 24). Some commentators have expressed concerns that the relationship of trust between doctors and patients may be damaged as they come to be 'regarded by some as part of the conspiracy to deprive patients of informational autonomy' (Case, 2003: 235). Yet, as has been shown, several legal provisions exist, including s 8(2) of the Human Rights Act, which permit breaches of confidentiality subject to a public interest defence. This has also been firmly acknowledged by domestic law in *W v Egdell* (1990), and applies most obviously in situations where disclosure is justifiable in order to protect others from harm – a position that has been supported and defended by both the GMC and the BMA (GMC, 2004; BMA, 1999). It is evident, therefore, that the maintenance of confidentiality requires careful balancing of the interests of individuals against those of the wider community, and the best way to achieve this is by obtaining properly informed consent, which will usually ensure that individual autonomy is upheld. However, situations have been reported where this process has been seen to be woefully inadequate, to the potential detriment of both the research participant and the researcher.

A specific and controversial example of a case of this type occurred at Simon Fraser University in Canada in 1994 (Lowman and Palys, 2000). The researcher, Russel Ogden, had conducted interviews with people involved in the suicides and euthanasia of AIDs sufferers as part of his criminology Masters project. After completing his studies he was subpoenaed by the Vancouver coroner to provide evidence to an inquest, which would have required him to disclose the identities of his research participants. Ogden had assured his participants that he would keep their identities 'absolutely confidential' and so, although he was prepared to discuss the research generally, he declined to reveal their names or any confidential information that could be connected to them. He then found himself embroiled in a protracted court case to determine whether he could be forced to make the disclosures.

It was ultimately accepted that under Canadian law communications relating to his research were privileged and the court could not compel him to reveal the participant's identities.

Further controversy followed because the Simon Fraser University provided only very limited support to the researcher, and subsequently introduced a policy requiring researchers to offer only limited confidentiality to their research participants, acknowledging that researchers may be required by law to divulge information gathered in the course of research. Commentators on the case have rightly described the situation as one in which ethics and the law conflict. The question is, should ethics prevail so that participants who give their time and share their knowledge and experiences are properly protected? The similarity between the facts in the Ogden case and the emphasis behind the myriad of UK legislation on disclosure in the public interest is stark. Similarly, the quote from Biobank, cited above, reflects the legal position in the United Kingdom, but may be at odds with some researchers' sense of ethical duty. The question then becomes, is it unethical to refuse to comply with the law in circumstances such as this?

Interestingly, the suggested form of words in the National Research Ethics Service (NRES) document *Information Sheets & Consent Forms: Guidance for Researchers and Reviewers* (2007) seems to accord more with the ethical view than that of the law:

> All information which is collected about you during the course of the research will be kept strictly confidential, and any information about you which leaves the hospital/surgery will have your name and address removed so that you cannot be recognized.
>
> (NRES, 2007: 27)

The recommended wording for drug trials is slightly less categorical, recognising that the data may need to be reviewed by 'regulatory authorities' although 'all will have a duty of confidentiality to you as a research participant and we will do our best to meet this duty' (NRES, 2007: 26).

Much of this discussion turns on ideas of harm and whether the damage done by breaching confidentiality might be greater than the harm, or potential harm, to the public interest that is protected by law. If we reconsider Ogden's case the issues are even more complex than they first appear. On the surface the issues seems to revolve around Ogden's duty to those who participated in his research, whose interests he had promised to protect by maintaining confidentiality. This is balanced by the public interest in ascertaining whether any, and perhaps which, of those participants had been involved in crimes that may have resulted in deaths. But there is also a third interest to be considered, which is the intrinsic value of research of this type and its findings.

A similar controversy would arise if, for instance, a researcher sought to discover how many doctors had engaged in assisting patients to die. Assisted suicide is currently unlawful and therefore those involved will be understandably reluctant to admit to it. However, reliable statistics about its incidence to determine how prevalent the practice is would be incredibly helpful in informing the debate about whether it should be legalised. It seems likely that the only way to obtain such data would be to guarantee that the results were anonymised and the participants' identities protected. At the same time, there would be an obvious and profound public interest in revealing which doctors had assisted patients to die, and the surrounding circumstances. This would be balanced by the researchers' explicit duty to maintain confidentiality and also by the fact that this invaluable data would not have been produced without the pledge to keep the identities secret. As we have seen, the duty of confidence is never absolute and can never be certain, but in this case the same is true of the public interest. On the one hand the public interest in detecting and punishing wrongdoers is strong, but on the other the need to discover the extent of this kind of criminal misconduct may outweigh the first imperative (Cecil and Wetherington, 1996).

Ethically, it is clear that the level of protection afforded to confidential disclosures made in the process of research should be proportionate to the degree of risk of harm associated with the type of data collected. However, this can be problematic when it needs to balanced against the legal requirement to protect the public interest, especially when the potential to destroy the trust between the researcher and the research community, and research participants is factored in. In this environment it is perhaps not surprising that the concept of limited confidentiality, whereby caveats such as UK Biobank's promise that '[W]e will not grant access to the police, the security services or to lawyers unless forced to do so by the courts (and, in some circumstances, we would oppose such access vigorously)' (UK Biobank, 2009), becomes an attractive, if somewhat unsatisfactory, proposition.

Conclusions

The relationship between the law relating to confidentiality and data protection is poorly understood and often misconstrued. The sad consequences of this were evidenced by several recent examples of public authorities failing to share information that may have saved lives due to their flawed understanding of their legal obligations in relation to data protection (Taylor, 2003; Walker, February 2004; Walker, March 2004). The situation is no better in relation to healthcare, as a recent example involving Gwynedd hospital in Wales demonstrates. Here hospital staff believed that it would be contrary to data protection legislation to continue with the hospital policy of displaying patient's names on boards above their beds. They therefore removed all the identification boards with the result that patient safety was seriously compromised, prompting one official to comment that 'since these changes have been made, we have misplaced patients as no-one was aware they were still in hospital' (Gudena *et al*, 2004: 1491). A subsequent survey of the views of patients and relatives about the policy revealed that the vast majority were entirely unconcerned about having their names displayed.

And, of course, by law all that was required to avoid any breach of confidence was the patient's consent to display the information. This level of confusion over privacy and misunderstanding of data protection principles and the role of confidentiality is perhaps hardly surprising when one considers the ambiguity in some legal judgments (Biggs, 2008). Nevertheless, although, and perhaps because, it is apparent that the right to confidentiality is often highly contingent, it is crucial that researchers and RECs understand the fundamental principles involved and how they operate in practice so that the individual's right to privacy can be appropriately protected.

At present, despite calls to the contrary (Harris, 2005), there is no obligation for anyone to participate in research, and all participants should be regarded as volunteers, acting altruistically. Therefore, no matter how potentially beneficial the project may be, it is ethically problematic to countenance deliberate, or even inadvertent, breaches of confidence in the name of research. Whilst there may be an understandable public interest in the disclosure of personal information with regard to epidemics, for disease prevention, or in order to protect the health or life of known individuals, such as for child protection issues, breaches of confidence in order to facilitate research are of a different order of magnitude.

RECs therefore need to continue to be vigilant about ensuring, for example, that data necessary for recruitment purposes is accessed ethically. It is particularly important that data protection principles are observed with regard to privacy of clinical information. This means that explicit consent should be obtained from participants before data can be collated for research purposes. Once the research is underway, RECs must be reassured that researchers intend to adopt methods to ensure that the data is protected by adequate security measures and that investigators and their teams are aware of their responsibilities. Beyleveld rightly calls for 'a broad concept of privacy to be deployed' in this regard (Beyleveld, 2006: 163). By this he means that it should be recognised and accepted that anonymisation is often insufficient to protect privacy interests and that, consequently, explicit consent should always be obtained in order to foster not only 'an atmosphere of trust which is necessary for medical research to flourish' but also a culture where people will be willing to participate in research (Beyleveld, 2006: 163). This, he argues, is the position adopted by human rights law at domestic and European levels because the right to privacy is a right that is always engaged in relation to health-related data. The discussion above suggests that the NIGB broadly agrees.

Breaches of confidence cause harm and offence to those involved. The unfairness, hurt and mistrust associated with assaults on personal privacy are deeply damaging, both to the individuals concerned and to the reputation of research and researchers more generally, even though this is often not recognised as harm capable of legal compensation. As such, the ethical foundations of the duty of confidentiality and the right of privacy ought properly to be prioritised to protect both the autonomy and liberty of research participants, and the interests of the research enterprise more broadly.

Part II

Specialist concerns

Chapter 7

Researching vulnerable groups

Introduction

The nature of vulnerability has been much debated (Liamputtong, 2007) and is not the primary focus of this chapter, although more will be included in Chapter 9. Instead, this chapter will concentrate on specific groups for whom particular legal rules apply, namely children, and adults who lack decision-making capacity. Vulnerability in these groups stems chiefly from their limited ability to exercise individual autonomy, either through immaturity or because of impaired mental capacity. As a consequence, people in these groups have traditionally been thought of as requiring special protection, especially in the context of research. Despite this, research involving members of groups who are viewed as vulnerable because of their inability to give a legally valid consent has been regarded as important, and ethical guidelines have been developed to support its facilitation. In 1964, for example, the World Medical Association's Declaration of Helsinki endorsed research in these populations if 'the research is necessary to promote the health of the population represented and this research cannot instead be performed on legally competent persons'. The EU Clinical Trials Directive (2001/20/EC), preamble, para 3 states that:

> Persons who are incapable of giving legal consent to clinical trials should be given special protection. It is incumbent on the Member states to lay down rules to this effect. Such persons may not be included in clinical trials if the same results can be obtained using persons capable of giving consent.

As previous chapters made clear, research involving human participants in the United Kingdom today is governed largely by the law pertaining to the clinical trials of medicinal products alongside the common law, and is heavily informed by ethical guidelines. In the NHS, the National Research Ethics Service (NRES) policy stipulating that the requirements of the Medicines for Human Use (Clinical Trials) Regulations 2004, SI 2004/1031 ('Clinical Trials Regulations') should be adopted even if the study does not involve investigational medicinal products provides a unitary starting point. However, the situation is complicated by the legal and ethical complexities surrounding research on children and adults who lack capacity. With regard to children and consent, the common law revolves largely around best interests, and has recognised circumstances whereby minors may be deemed competent to make their own decisions., This is at odds with the provisions contained in the Clinical Trials Regulations. By the same token, and almost perversely, the Mental Capacity Act 2005 was enacted shortly after the Clinical Trials Regulations, and introduces rules for the involvement of non-competent adults in non-clinical trials research that operate distinctly from those contained in the Regulations.

This chapter will be divided into two parts. The first will offer an assessment of the situation regarding the involvement of children in research, including some controversies around the status of a child's assent. The second will discuss the legal framework surrounding research involving adults who lack capacity. Following that, some general conclusions will be drawn.

Children

Children are rightly regarded as a particularly vulnerable population. They are often unable to make their views known, especially those of early years, and, as has been shown in Chapter 2, they have in the past been the victims of research abuses. As a result, concerns about exposing children to risks associated with research have been cited as a reason for not involving them in clinical trials. However, failing to involve children in clinical research and trials of medicinal products means that reliable evidence about the efficacy and safety of interventions used in their treatment is either limited or unavailable. Similarly, failing to conduct systematic assessment of other healthcare interventions designed to be applied in the treatment of children can lead to the introduction of ineffective, or perhaps even harmful, treatment regimes (Mulhall *et al*, 1983).

There is now a wealth of evidence to show that because of a dearth of research involving children a large proportion of treatment decisions are not supported by validated clinical evidence (Rudolf *et al*, 1999; Conroy, 2000; Smyth, 2001). Consequently, children may be exposed to risks every time a drug is prescribed off-label or effectively administered 'blind' when unlicenced medications are given in everyday practice. In these circumstances sick children are subjected to potentially ineffective treatments, possibly with unknown side-effects, at a time when they are already in a weakened and vulnerable condition due to their illness.

Concerns about the failure to involve children in research have been voiced increasingly over recent years (Caldwell *et al*, 2004), and para 3 of the preamble to the EU Clinical Trials Directive acknowledges the real need to conduct research involving children:

> ... there is a need for clinical trials involving children to improve the treatment available to them. Children represent a vulnerable population with developmental, physiological and psychological differences from adults, which make age- and development-related research important for their benefit.

With this in mind Council Regulation (EC) 1901/2006 on medicinal products for paediatric use came into force in January 2007. Article 1 states that the Regulation:

> . . . lays down rules concerning the development of medicinal products for human use in order to meet the specific therapeutic needs of the paediatric population, without subjecting the paediatric population to unnecessary clinical or other trials and in compliance with Directive 2001/20/EC.

The central aim of the Regulation is to facilitate paediatric trials so that children have greater access to medicines that are specifically designed or adapted and licensed for their use, and 'to improve the information available on the use of medicinal products in the various paediatric populations' (preamble, para 4). The regulation of clinical research on children involving medicinal products is therefore governed by several overlapping pieces of legislation. In the United Kingdom, the Clinical Trials Regulations, which implement the EU Clinical Trials Directive, is probably the most significant. In addition, Regulation 1901/2006 operates in tandem with the Clinical Trials Regulations specifically to promote research on the paediatric population. Alongside these the common law also applies to consent arrangements and pertains to all other types of research. The regulatory environment is therefore highly complex in relation to medical research involving children.

One area that might be expected to be uncomplicated concerns the definition of what it is to be a child for the purposes of medical research. There is a presumption in law that once a person attains adulthood they are entitled to make decisions on their own behalf, but socially the demarcation between adult and child is far from clear in the United Kingdom. The age of majority is 18, but a person needs only to be 17 to drive a car, 16 to consent to sexual relations, and must pay full adult ticket prices for public transport and entry to venues such as cinemas from the age of 14. With regard to healthcare in Scotland, the Age of Legal Capacity (Scotland) Act 1991 sets the age at which one attains full decision-making capacity at 16 years. In England and Wales, however, the Family Law Reform Act 1969, s 1(1) defines the age of majority as 18, but under s 8 permits those aged 16 and 17 to consent to medical treatment that is of direct benefit to the person. With regard to medical research, the legal position is further complicated by reg 2(1) of the Clinical Trials Regulations, which stipulates that '"adult" means a person who has attained the age of 16 years', and also by Art 2(1) of Regulation 1901/2006, which states that '"paediatric population" means that part of the population aged between birth and eighteen years'. Further, under the common law a minor under the age of 16 will be able to make medical treatment decisions if she is competent to do so under the rules established in *Gillick v West Norfolk and Wisbech Area Health Authority* (1985). The court recognised (p 421) that attaining maturity is a gradual and flexible process whose progress depends on the attributes and experience of the individual concerned:

> If the law should impose upon the process of growing up fixed limits where nature knew only continuous process, the price would be artificiality and a

lack of realism in an area where the law must be sensitive to human development and social change.

It will become clear from the discussion of the *Gillick* case below, that, in some circumstances, minors may attain the capacity to make decisions for themselves before they reach the age of 16. There is, however, a presumption in law that below this age consent for medical and other physical interventions must be given by an adult who has responsibility for the child. As with adults, legal authorisation must be obtained for the participation of minors in research before any research can be lawfully conducted. It is therefore very important to know who has the power to give consent for a minor to participate in medical research, and whether and when a minor can consent on her own behalf. In order to explain the intricacies of consent in relation to children, this discussion will begin with an analysis of the situation where the minor is not competent to decide, and then move on to discuss the position as it relates to those who have attained decision-making capacity. An assessment of the role of assent will also be included as this forms a major controversy in relation to the Clinical Trials Regulations.

The non-competent minor

Immaturity prevents very young children from exercising individual autonomy and demands that the child's welfare is protected by the adults responsible for them. Where a minor is below the age of 16, the law bestows this responsibility upon the parents, or another person with legal guardianship, or occasionally the courts. The applicable law in this regard is the Children Act 1989 in England and Wales, the Children (Scotland) Act 1995 in Scotland and the Children (Northern Ireland) Order 1995 in Northern Ireland.

The law is further reinforced by Article 8 of the European Convention on Human Rights and, although the United Kingdom is not currently a signatory, it is notable that Art 6 of the European Convention on Biomedicine applies the same approach. However, each of these legal measures relates to the provision of medical treatment and is based on the presumption that the treatment concerned will be in the best interests of the child. Similarly, the right to authorise treatment under the common law exists only so far as what is proposed advances the welfare of the child. Accordingly, in *Secretary of State for Health and Community Services v JWB and SMB* (1992), it was asserted that in relation to surgery the right did not extend to authorising that which was perceived to be 'in the interests of those responsible for the care of the child or in the interests of society in general' (p 295). Consequently, concerns have been raised about the legitimacy of parental proxy consent as a means of authorising a child's participation in a research project from which the child may not benefit.

In the context of research it cannot be presumed that the child's best interests will be served by participating in the study. Medical research is conducted in order to investigate certain aspects of conditions or treatments where the results are either unknown or uncertain.

In some cases it may be possible to argue that participation was in the best interests of the child. For example, in the study of a medicinal product that is designed to treat the condition from which the particular child suffers, where the drug proves to be effective and the child was in the active treatment arm, a claim that the trial was in the child's best interests may be acceptable. However, the drug may prove ineffective or even harmful. Alongside this, some of the participants will undoubtedly be in a control, or even placebo arm, and in many cases the data generated will benefit only future child patients rather than those participating in the research. Given the level of uncertainty about whether the child will derive any benefit, it is difficult to argue that involvement in research is demonstrably in the individual child's best interests, and the legitimacy of parental proxy consent is therefore highly questionable in relation to clinical research.

In the United States, the validity of parental consent in non-therapeutic research was challenged in *Grimes v Kennedy-Krieger Institute; Higgins v Kennedy-Krieger Institute* (2001) following what became known as the Kennedy Krieger lead paint study. The research took place in an area of Baltimore where there were high levels of lead poisoning in children. It sought to assess and compare different methods of lead reduction in social housing dwellings, and landlords recruited to the study were given incentives to encourage them to let their properties to families with young children. Some of the children involved would potentially have been exposed to lead poisoning regardless of the study, but parents later complained of being inadequately informed about the risks of participating in the study and the levels of lead to which their children were exposed. The court was emphatic that:

> It is not in the best interests of a specific child, in a non-therapeutic research project, to be placed in an environment, which might . . . be, hazardous to the health of the child . . . the 'best interests of the child' is the overriding concern of this court in matters relating to children.

The absence of any specific case law on this point in the United Kingdom makes it difficult to speculate as to the legality of parental consent in this type of circumstance, but Mason and Laurie suggest that 'the same sentiment underlies legal framework in the United Kingdom' (Mason and Laurie, 2006: 686).

Despite this, all of the major national and international guidelines on research involving children who are unable to give consent adopt a model that permits research on condition that it has the potential to benefit children as a group, cannot be conducted in any legally competent group, and consent is given by a parent or legal guardian. For example, the Medical Research Council specifies that 'consent is legally valid and professionally acceptable only where the participants (or their parental guardian) are competent to give consent, have been properly informed, and have agreed without coercion' (MRC, 2004: 21). Similar provisions are included in guidelines issued by the Royal College of Paediatrics (2000) and the British Medical Association (BMA, 2001), amongst others. Similarly, the Department of Health counsels that:

> Where children lack the capacity to consent for themselves, parents may give consent for their child to be entered into a trial where the evidence is that the trial therapy may be at least as beneficial to the patient as standard therapy.
>
> (DoH, 2001: para 9.1)

Guidelines, however, are not in themselves legally binding or regarded as representing the law. Therefore, whilst it may be ethical to adopt a practice that reflects professional guidance, this may be at odds with the law. That said, in respect of clinical trials of medicinal products, the EU Clinical Trials Directive and the Clinical Trials Regulations in the United Kingdom operate explicitly on the premise that parents will give proxy consent. Article 4(a) of the Directive requires that 'the informed consent of the parents or legal representative has been obtained' and that this consent 'must represent the presumed will of the minor'. This is mirrored exactly in Sch 1, Part 4, para 13 to the Clinical Trials Regulations, and therefore stands as legal authority for parental proxy consent in relation to clinical trials of medicinal products.

The provisions in the Directive and the Clinical Trials Regulations also stipulate that valid consent from the parent or legal guardian is contingent upon a number of further requirements. Specifically, notification must be given that they have the right to withdraw the minor from the trial at any time by revoking their consent and no incentives may be given to the minor or the person with parental responsibility (Sch 1, Part 4, paras 3, 5 and 8). In addition, the clinical trial is regarded as necessary to validate data obtained in other clinical trials or by other research methods (Sch 1, Part 4, para 11) and the parental representative has been provided with 'a contact point where he may obtain further information about the trial' (Sch 1, Part 4, para 2).

These provisions are relatively uncontroversial, and accord with the ethical principles that any research ethics committee (REC) may apply to research involving children. More contentious, however, is the statement that the informed consent given by a person with parental responsibility will represent the 'presumed will' of the minor. Further detail follows in the discussion of the competent minor and assent from the minor, but it is sufficient to state here that this provision is at odds with the widely promulgated ethical approach which advises that, where possible, researchers should always request and obtain the agreement of children being recruited into research studies (Royal College of Paediatrics and Child Health, 2000). The inclusion of the words 'presumed will' seems to suggest that the parents will be assumed to be acting in the interests of the child, and that the child is accepting and compliant. However, this may not necessarily correspond to a legal understanding of what amounts to the *best* interests of the child and be at odds with the child's perception and opinion of what is involved. Furthermore, the legal position regarding consent is unclear in the event that there is disagreement between parents as to whether the child should participate in the research.

Where the parents disagree in relation to the provision of treatment, the position is settled. In *Re R* (*A Minor*) (*Wardship: Medical Treatment*) (1994) (p 184) the Court of Appeal stated that:

> . . . the doctor will be presented with a professional and ethical but not a legal problem because, if he has the consent of one authorised person, the treatment will not without more constitute a trespass or criminal assault.

Along with other common law pronouncements, however, this applies in the context of medical treatment that is regarded by a clinician as demonstrably in the child's best interests. The same cannot be said of research, and a researcher would face a difficult problem if one parent declined or actively sought to withhold consent. Ethically, it would seem inappropriate to conduct research on a child whose parent was opposed to the child's participation, even if the other parent consented. Legally, the primary concern would be for the welfare of the child, rather than in resolving any dispute between the parents, since, as Lord Fraser explained, 'parental rights to control a child exist not for the benefit of the parent but for the child' (*Gillick* (1985) (p 413)). The Clinical Trials Regulations are silent on this point, although they make provision for alternative arrangements for consent where the parents cannot be contacted, or are otherwise unable to consent. In these circumstances, under Sch 1, Part 4, para 1 to the Regulations, a legal representative will act for the child. This individual will be a person who has knowledge and understanding of the trial and its aims and objectives, including any 'risks and inconveniences', and 'the conditions under which it is to be conducted'. It is envisaged, however, that this will occur in only very limited circumstances, such as where the research is of an emergency nature and there is insufficient time to obtain parental consent.

Therefore, the general position regarding the involvement of children in research under the Clinical Trials Regulations is that parental consent must be obtained and that this will represent the 'presumed will' of the child. It must be stressed, however, that, although the NRES requires NHS RECs to apply the standards adherent in the Clinical Trials Regulations to all research they review, NHS RECs, and others, will tend, rightly, to follow ethical and professional guidance in relation to non-clinical trials research. Furthermore, some commentators argue that the ethical approach that maximises child and adolescent autonomy is to be preferred (Elliston, 2007). This will inevitably include the involvement of legally competent mature minors in the consent process and require assent from those who are unable to consent, even though ostensibly the Clinical Trials

Directive and the Clinical Trials Regulations do not require it. The law and ethics that apply in these circumstances will be discussed below.

The competent minor, consent and assent

In relation to medical treatment, the legal presumption that minors below the age of 16 are not competent to make decisions on their own behalf is rebuttable if it can be shown that a minor has attained sufficient maturity to be capable of making autonomous decisions. Indeed, in Scotland, under s 1(2) of the Age of Legal Capacity (Scotland) Act 1991, parents' rights to make decisions for their children cease at 16, although under s 2(7) they retain responsibility to provide parental guidance until the child reaches 18. Therefore, where a minor has developed sufficiently to be able to exercise her own autonomy, it is at least arguable that she should be permitted to decide for herself whether or not to participate in a research study. Notably, Sarah Elliston argues that a child who wishes to decide and is competent to do so 'should be at liberty to do so' (Elliston, 2007: 193). Furthermore, the MRC alleges specifically that 'where children have sufficient understanding and intelligence to understand what is proposed, it is their consent and not that of their parent/guardian that is required by law' (MRC, 2004: 23). Conversely, the General Medical Council advises that in relation to children below the age of 18, even if they are 'able to consent for themselves', the doctor 'should still consider involving their parents, depending on the nature of the research' (GMC, 2007: para 38).

As has been noted above, *Gillick* (1985) provides authority for the proposition that some young people are capable of making informed decisions for themselves. To avoid any confusion it should be noted that the leading judgment in *Gillick* was delivered by Lord Fraser, hence the term 'Fraser competence' is sometimes substituted for the more usual '*Gillick* competence'. Here, Lord Fraser held that minors would be competent to make valid treatment decisions providing they demonstrate 'sufficient understanding and intelligence to know what they involve' and that the intervention proposed is in their best interests (p 423). Lord Fraser's judgment reflects the general proposition that parental consent will be valid provided what is proposed is in the child's best interests. By contrast, Lord Scarman, who supported the majority judgment in the case, spoke of the minor understanding not just the nature of the treatment proposed, but also its implications. He was silent, however, with regard to the issue of best interests.

Subsequent authority suggests that when assessing whether or not a child has capacity, the *Gillick* criteria, as laid down by Lord Fraser, are definitive, but that these ought to be applied in conjunction with Lord Scarman's statements (*R v Secretary of State for Health and Family Planning Association ex p Axon* (2006)). Essentially, this implies not only that the minor must be competent to understand what is proposed, but also that the procedure must be in her best interests. Taking this into account, Mason and Laurie claim that it is now 'established beyond doubt that the best interests test is the legal determinant of acceptable treatment with regard to children' (Mason and Laurie, 2006: 689). Accordingly, the inclusion of the test of best interests in *Gillick*, in line with the Family Law Reform Act 1969 and the equivalent Scottish legislation, precludes competent minors from legally consenting to research and other non-therapeutic interventions, because these are not demonstrably for the individual minor's benefit and therefore cannot be regarded as in their best interests. In line with this, some commentators have questioned the view that competent minors can give valid consent to participate in research, on the basis that they cannot have adequate experience to fully comprehend what may or may not be in their best interests (Wedler and Shah, 2003). Yet ethically, denying children the opportunity, if not the right, to participate in the decision about whether or not to be involved in research may be overly paternalistic. Consequently, the majority of guidelines from professional bodies and research councils advise that even if a child cannot give a legally valid and binding consent, the child's assent should be obtained before she is enrolled into a study.

European legislation is, at best, inconsistent on the issue of assent from the minor. Although the EC recommendations define assent as 'the expression of the minor's will to participate in a clinical trial', the Clinical Trials Directive itself is silent. Instead, in common with Sch 1, Part 4, para 7 to the UK Clinical Trials Regulations, it states that the trial may proceed if:

> The explicit wish of a minor who is capable of forming an opinion and assessing the information . . . to refuse participation in, or to be withdrawn from, the clinical trial at any time is considered by the investigator.

It is to be hoped that within that consideration an investigator would observe guidance from the Council for International Organisations of Medical Sciences (CIOMS), amongst other authorities, to refrain from including a child who objected to participating, and withdraw one who wished it, so that 'a child's refusal to participate in the research will be respected' (CIOMS, 2002: guideline 14). However, there is no requirement within the Clinical Trials Regulations for researchers to do so. It is also important to recognise that assent is not the same as simply not dissenting. Indeed, the GMC has advised that children 'should not usually be involved in research if they object or appear to object in either words or actions, even if their parents consent' (GMC, 2007: para 38). In other words, if a child actively dissents then, arguably, she should not be included, or should be withdrawn.

Clearly, this stance raises practical implications about what is meant by dissent, for example where a child is afraid of needles and objects to having injections or the taking of blood samples. Here the relationship between the researcher and the child participant is crucial because of the requirement in the Regulations to 'minimise pain, discomfort, fear and any other foreseeable risk in relation to the disease and the minor's stage of development' in the design of the study. It is difficult to understand how this can be achieved unless the child is actively involved in the consenting process. Consequently, despite the silence of the Directive and Regulations with regard to obtaining consent or assent from the minor, it is impossible to envisage a practical process which will satisfy ethical criteria without engaging the child in an effective dialogue about her participation in the study. Moreover, to this end Sch 1, Part 4, para 6 to the Regulations requires that the minor will be given information about the trial and its risks and benefits, 'according to his capacity of understanding, from staff with experience with minors'. Whilst it would seem entirely appropriate for those conducting research involving children to have experience of dealing with them this may not extend to the skills required to assess the mental capacity of minors.

Additionally, it has been suggested that the researcher is not ideally placed to judge the competency of the child participant because of the potential conflict of interests created by the researcher's vested interest in conducting the research (Hunter and Pierscionek, 2007). Further, the extent of the potential risks and benefits associated with the study may be speculative and therefore not only difficult to ascertain, but also problematic to convey to a minor. The need for RECs to satisfy themselves that appropriate members of the research team have the required experience and understanding to comply with this measure will, together with other regulatory and ethical imperatives, represent a heavy burden.

Implications for the process of ethical review

It is apparent from the foregoing discussion that there are a number of tensions between the law, ethics and practicalities associated with research involving minors. The key issues of concern for RECs relate to the obvious points of divergence between the law as outlined in the Clinical Trials Directive and the Clinical Trials Regulations, and the myriad of ethical guidance in the area which are compounded by the dearth of specific case law on children's involvement in research.

It could be argued that RECs can simply distinguish between research that involves clinical trials of investigational medicinal products (CTIMPs) and research that does not, applying the regulatory framework to the former and other guidance to the latter. However, the insistence by the NRES that the same standards will be applied to the process of ethical review regardless of whether or not the research involves CTIMPs makes this problematic. Following the Regulations implies that detailed arrangements to obtain consent or assent from minors are not required, but this would offend all ethical guidelines pertaining to children and research, and is therefore likely to be resisted by RECs, and properly so. Furthermore, the emphasis on best interests in the legal assessment of when an intervention is appropriate for a child raises questions as to how research can be legitimated and who can give valid consent for the participation of a child.

An issue that complicates the matter further stems from the fact discussed briefly in Chapter 4 that the Clinical Trials Regulations purport to incorporate the provisions contained in the Declaration of Helsinki as amended in 1996 (Clinical Trials Regulations, Sch 1, Part 2, paras 1 and 2). Paragraph I.11 of the 1996 version of the Declaration of Helsinki stipulates that when a 'minor child is in fact able to give consent, the minor's consent must be obtained in addition to the consent of the minor's legal guardian', which suggests that consent from the minor is a requirement of her participation in any research if she is competent. Without definitive guidance from the courts in this regard, the legal role of parental consent and its relationship to consent from a competent minor, and assent from a minor who lacks capacity, is a matter of mere speculation. This leaves RECs with a difficult task. Ethical guidance suggests, even requires, that children ought properly to be included in any decision as to whether or not they should participate in research, yet the legal regulation of research involving investigational medicinal products fails to make adequate provision for their involvement.

Since Nuremberg, if not before, it has been trite to insist that no person should be expected to participate in research without first giving their voluntary, informed consent. It is therefore understandable, 'because we care' (Bridgeman, 1998), that we seek to protect children from exploitation in relation to research. This is reflected in the requirement, prevalent in all ethical guidelines, that the interests of the research participant should not be subordinated to those of society or science. Yet, in this context, being overly protective may in fact amount to paternalism, which may be disadvantageous to children as a whole. In this regard the legal requirement that consent to the involvement of children in research is legitimate only if it promotes the child's *best* interests may be too high a threshold. If, as was outlined at the beginning of this section, it is essential for the good of children generally that they are included in research, then it is imperative that a way is found to facilitate this without disadvantaging children individually.

It is arguable that, provided the research is scientifically sound and ethically approved, where a child is capable of understanding the implications of her participation her own informed consent should be sought, and should be authoritative. Accordingly, if a minor is competent to give consent she should be trusted to do so, and permitted not only to make self-interested decisions, but also to act altruistically for the benefit of others (Baylis and Downie, 2003). Where the minor is not capable of providing a legal consent, then parental consent should be obtained, and deemed legally valid, provided the child's assent is forthcoming.

From the above, it is evident that any REC responsible for the review of such research must also be aware of the intricacies and inconsistencies in the law and regulation relating to the process. This would be encouraged by ensuring that each REC that deals with research involving children includes a member with paediatric expertise. It is recommended that this expertise should be based upon education and qualifications, and, where possible, should also include experience of the research context. This is clearly a significant factor in recruiting members of RECs, and could potentially limit the number of RECs regarded as properly constituted to conduct the review of research involving children. By comparison, it has been alleged that in the United States, institutional review boards (IRBs), which are equivalent to RECs in the United Kingdom, operate differently (Kaufman, 2002), and are often under-resourced, ill-prepared and over-burdened.

As a result their reviews tend to focus more on procedural formalities at the expense of issues concerned specifically with patient protection. Lack of training and understanding of the complexity of assessing risk and benefit in paediatric research has also been identified as contributing to these shortcomings. To avoid similar problems in the United Kingdom, NHS RECs must be properly constituted and obtain good quality training if they are to provide adequate protection to children who participate in research.

Once this has been taken into account the additional protections required by the governing conditions in the Clinical Trials Regulations, such as the fact that the trial relates directly to the condition from which the child suffers or can only be carried out on minors, and that some direct benefit will be obtained for children, should provide satisfactory safeguards. Further, the ethical imperative to obtain consent from competent minors, and assent from those who lack legal decision-making capacity, should be bolstered by acquiring legal legitimacy. In this respect the position in the United States, where it is expected that researchers will seek assent from children above the age of seven (Singh, 2007), is preferable. RECs should continue to demand that children consent or assent to their participation in research as appropriate and become more insistent about the third governing principle contained in the Clinical Trials Regulations, which stipulates that the 'risk threshold and degree of distress have to be specially defined and constantly monitored'. When these measures become commonplace the way will be open to overcome the dangers inherent in current prescribing for children whilst enhancing the autonomy of child research participants.

Researching with adults unable to consent for themselves

Many different types of research participant fall into the category of adults who are unable to consent for themselves. Amongst these are people with severe learning disabilities, those whose capacity is affected by degenerative brain diseases such as Alzheimer's dementia, and others who are unable to communicate by reason of trauma or unconsciousness. It is essential to conduct research in these groups in order to increase and enhance our understanding of the illness and disabilities from which they suffer, as well as to help develop new and existing therapies to better treat their effects. Such research can also be influential in identifying the causes of illness in these specific populations, and in testing the effectiveness of available treatments and methods of care. It is therefore vital that research of this type be conducted safely and ethically, and with due regard for the interests and needs of research subjects.

It is clear from the examples portrayed in Chapter 2 that many of the victims of past research abuses were people who would fall within the definition of participants lacking the capacity to consent on their own behalf. It is therefore crucial that their interests are properly recognised and protected, and that their vulnerability to exploitation is not abused. Yet, whilst it is clear that the most stringent mechanisms must be in put in place to provide this protection, it is also evident that their participation in research is hugely important, and that such measures should not stifle research.

The need to conduct ethically sound research involving people with mental incapacity is endorsed by international guidance and instruments such as the Declaration of Helsinki (para 24), and Art 15 of the Additional Protocol to the Convention on Human Rights and Biomedicine. Broadly speaking, the majority of the guidance recommends that adults who lack the capacity to consent should only be included in research if: it cannot be conducted using persons who are able to consent; it has the potential to benefit the group; the person offers no objection; and authorisation is given by an appropriate legal representative. Further safeguards are included in the Clinical Trials Directive, the Clinical Trials Regulations and the Mental Capacity Act 2005, all of which regulate different types of research involving people who lack the capacity to consent.

From this is it evident that research involving those who are not able to give informed consent is subject to significant constraints, and as a consequence the highest level of ethical scrutiny should be expected. Until recently, the burden of authorising research involving adults unable to consent for themselves was born entirely by RECs applying principles contained in non-statutory ethical guidance. However, although the ethics remain unchanged, there are now strict legislative requirements governing the inclusion of such persons in research in the United Kingdom and Europe. CTIMPs in the United Kingdom are now regulated by the Clinical Trials Directive and the Clinical Trials Regulations. Research that does not involve investigational medicinal products is governed by the Mental Capacity Act 2005 in England and Wales, and by the Adults with Incapacity (Scotland) Act 2000 in Scotland. The rules imposed by the legislation largely mirror the sound ethical principles by which NHS RECs have always conducted their reviews. However, because of the complexities associated with the legislation, the ethical review of research involving adults who lack capacity may only be conducted by specially trained and designated 'flagged' NHS RECs. At present this applies to both health and social care research, although it is expected that the Social Care Research Ethics Committee (SCREC), which is expected to become operational in 2009, will be recognised by the Secretary of State for this purpose.

Beginning with the Mental Capacity Act 2005 this discussion will examine the relevant legislative provisions governing this area of research. It will outline the distinctions and similarities between them to explain how they operate, and assess the impact they have on the regulation of research involving adults who are not able to give consent.

Mental Capacity Act 2005

The Mental Capacity Act 2005 (MCA 2005) applies to England and Wales, whilst in Scotland the Adults with Incapacity (Scotland) Act 2000 covers matters relating to medical treatment and research involving incapacitated adults in Scotland. However, in Northern Ireland there is no specific legislation that applies to research involving adults who lack capacity to give consent. In this jurisdiction researchers should seek and comply with ethical guidance that relates specifically to the protections required to safeguard the interests of the participant. The common law of consent will also apply. Essentially, this will involve determining whether or not a participant is capable of giving consent, and, if not, then assent should be sought from a relative or carer. Any dissent from participants themselves should be respected. Since this approach was adopted by RECs throughout the United Kingdom, including Northern Ireland, prior to the introduction of the MCA 2005, there is no reason to believe that the interests of the participant will not be adequately protected in these circumstances. Responsibility for the review of research involving adults unable to give consent has been bestowed upon a single designated REC in Northern Ireland.

The MCA 2005 is a wide-ranging statute that imposes statutory regulation on decisions affecting medical care, welfare and financial matters generally, and accordingly covers much more than healthcare research alone. Sections 30–34 are the key provisions with regard to the conduct of research in incapacitated adults and impose detailed responsibilities on both researchers and RECs. The Act enjoyed a long, tortuous and somewhat contentious route to the statue books, which included an influential report in 1995 by the Law Commission (Law Commission, 1995) followed by a Government Green Paper in 1997 (Lord Chancellor's Department, 1997) and a policy statement two years later (Lord Chancellor's Department, 1999). The draft Bill, then entitled 'Mental Incapacity', was finally presented to Parliament in 2003. The Bill then became the subject of a Joint Scrutiny Committee Report (House of Lords and House of Commons, 2003) whereby cross-party members of the House of Lords and the House of Commons recommended revisions to the Bill. Included amongst these recommendations was the controversial suggestion that provision should be made to facilitate research involving people who lack capacity to consent:

> Some of our respondents were strongly opposed to allowing medical research on those lacking the capacity to give consent. After careful consideration, we concluded that the Bill should allow it in limited circumstances under strict controls administered through medical ethics committees.
>
> (House of Lords and House of Commons, 2003: 7)

Overall, the Report of the Joint Scrutiny Committee met with a very favourable response from the Government of the day, especially with regard to making provision for the conduct of research:

> We agree with the Committee's conclusion that properly regulated research involving people who lack capacity is important, and that without research involving those with incapacitating illnesses the development of appropriate treatments may not be possible.
>
> (UK Government, 2004: recommendation 81)

The recommendation to include provisions covering research involving adults who are not able to give consent due to mental incapacity was duly endorsed with the words 'we accept that the Mental Capacity Bill should include provision for strictly controlled research to fill the gap that exists in the current law' (recommendation 85). Subsequently, the revised Mental Capacity Bill received its first reading in June 2004, and eventually became law on 7 April 2005.

The MCA 2005 *does not* apply to CTIMPs. Instead, it pertains to 'intrusive' research involving adults who lack the capacity to consent in England and Wales. Intrusive research is defined in s 30(2) of the Act as research 'of a kind that would be unlawful if it was carried out (a) on or in relation to a person who had capacity to consent to it, but (b) without his consent'. It should be observed that research that would not ordinarily require consent is excluded from the definition and therefore does not fall under the auspices of the Act.

In practice this research is not limited to healthcare or biomedical-type research and may also encompass social care, sociological, psychological and any other type of research that might be categorised as 'intrusive'. This applies whether the research is conducted within the National Health Service, the private sector or elsewhere. The defining features of whether and when a research project will fall under the auspices of the Act relate to the characteristics of the research participant and the nature of the research. More specifically, it is necessary to ascertain that the proposed participant lacks the capacity to consent and, this being the case, the research must aim 'to provide knowledge about the cause of, or treatment or care of people with, the same impairing condition – or similar condition' (Department for Constitutional Affairs, 2007: 207). Alternatively, the research must hold out the possibility of benefitting the participant, and the benefit 'must be in proportion to any burden caused by taking part' (Department for Constitutional Affairs, 2007: 207). Under the MCA 2005 it is illegal to conduct such research unless the Act and its Code of Practice are complied with (s 42(4)).

The Act is relevant to all adults over the age of 16, and contains at its core the presumption that all adults have the mental capacity to decide for themselves (s 1(2)). This is a rebuttable presumption that can be overturned following a formal assessment of the person's ability in relation to each decision she has to make. Section 2(1) of the Act states that a person lacks capacity in relation to a matter:

> . . . if at the material time he is unable to make a decision for himself in relation to the matter because of an impairment of, or disturbance in the functioning of, the mind or brain.

Chapter 4 of the MCA 2005 Code of Practice, and similar guidance that accompanies the Adults with Incapacity (Scotland) Act 2000, sets out how the assessment must be performed and what factors must be considered in the determination of whether or not a person lacks decision-making capacity. Section 2(3) of the Act states that the assessment of whether a person has capacity must *not* be based upon factors such as her physical appearance, age or assumptions about her behaviour or the condition from which she suffers. Instead, according to s 3(1), a person will lack the capacity to give consent if she is not able to understand and retain the information provided in order to weigh it in the balance and make a decision, or if she is not able to communicate her decision. This test reflects the common law test for capacity in *Re C (Adult: Refusal of Medical Treatment)* (1994) and *Re MB (Adult: Medical Treatment)* (1997).

In making the assessment it should be appreciated that incapacity may result from conditions as diverse as severe mental illness, unconsciousness or an inability to communicate following stroke or other brain trauma, and may therefore be temporary, permanent or fluctuating. Therefore, a person's underlying medical condition may dictate that her ability to consent varies from day to day, for example where she is suffering from progressive dementia. In recognition of this fact, researchers must not assume that the outcome of an initial assessment will sustain across time. For this reason, researchers who wish to conduct investigations involving people who may be vulnerable to fluctuating or deteriorating capacity over time must repeat the consent process at each research encounter to ensure that an initial valid consent can still be relied upon. If its continued validity is questionable then a further assessment of capacity must be undertaken. It is also sometimes the case that repeated experience of a given situation, such as a specific research intervention, will enhance a person's understanding and enable her to participate more fully in the consent process. Hence, the converse also applies and a researcher should not assume that an initial finding of incapacity will persist over time.

The level of capacity required is related to the gravity of the decision to be made. In practice, therefore, a finding that a person lacks the mental capacity to consent to participate in research does not mean that she lacks capacity in relation to all decisions, and vice versa. Similarly, the level of understanding required to give a valid informed consent to research is necessarily higher than that required to authorise treatment that would be in the person's best interests. As this is clearly an iterative process, capacity will need to be assessed each time the researcher engages with the participant to determine whether or not the participant's consent can be obtained.

The Act makes it incumbent upon the researcher not only to assess whether or not the participant has the capacity to give an informed consent but also to actively assist any person who apparently lacks capacity to decide for herself to engage with the decision-making process, and thereby enhance her autonomy. In practice, this will probably involve repeated meetings and explanations as to what is involved, as well as the provision of information in a form that is understandable to the participant. Easily readable prose, pictorial representations and the use of televisual media are favoured methods of achieving this.

If the participant is shown to lack the capacity to consent then s 32 of the Act requires that the researcher consults with specified persons before determining whether the person may be included in the research. This 'consultee' should be someone who is involved in the incapacitated person's care, interested in her welfare and willing to help, but under Chapter 11, para 23 of the Code of Practice, the consultee 'must not be a professional or paid care worker'. If no such person is available the researcher must follow guidance published by the Secretary of State or by the National Assembly in Wales, and nominate a person independent of the project as a consultee. All consultees must be provided with information about the study, and the researcher must seek their views as to what the incapacitated person's views would be concerning her participation and, whether she ought to be included. If the consultee believes that the person should not participate or, at a later stage, should be withdrawn, these views should normally be complied with. In addition, the researcher must take account of any previous wishes or views the participant may have expressed, as well as those of carers or other significant people, and any objections, wishes or feelings of the participant must be respected.

Before any research involving people who lack mental capacity commences in England or Wales, the researcher must obtain the approval of the relevant 'appropriate body'. This is defined, under the Mental Capacity Act 2005 (Appropriate Body) (England) Regulations 2006, SI 2006/2810, in England, as an REC recognised by the Secretary of State for the purpose of advising on 'matters which include, the ethics of intrusive research in relation to people who lack capacity to consent to it'. In Wales the appropriate body is an REC similarly recognised by the Welsh Assembly Government. The Act applies primarily to research commencing after 1 October 2007, and most researchers applying to RECs will be required under the Act to make a s 30 application relating to intrusive research to be conducted involving one or more adults lacking the capacity to consent. On reviewing such an application, the REC must satisfy itself that it agrees that the research is safe, relates to the person's condition and cannot be done as effectively using people who have mental capacity. The research must also be seen potentially to produce a benefit to the person that outweighs any risk or burden to the participant. Alternatively, if the project is designed to derive new scientific knowledge, it must be shown to pose only minimal risk to the incapacitated participants and should be carried out with minimal intrusion or interference with their rights.

Research participants may lose capacity to consent after a research project has started, in which case the researcher should make an application for approval for the continuation of the study under the Mental Capacity Act 2005 (Loss of Capacity during Research Project) (England) Regulations 2007, SI 2007/679, in England, and the Mental Capacity Act 2005 (Loss of Capacity during Research Project) Regulations 2007, SI 2007/837, in Wales. Under s 34 of the MCA 2005 these apply specifically to studies involving data or material that were approved and started before 1 October 2007, where the participant consented to participate before 30 March 2008, but subsequently lost capacity. In these circumstances the research may be allowed to continue lawfully so long as approval is obtained from the 'appropriate body' or REC. Practical arrangements for obtaining both s 30 and s 34 approval are detailed in guidance issued by the National Patient Safety Agency (NPSA) and the NRES (NRES, 2007).

All researchers are required to have regard for the Mental Capacity Act Code of Practice under s 42(4) of the Act, and it is incumbent on both researchers and the 'appropriate body' that approves the research to ensure that the research meets the Act's requirements in full. Accordingly, an REC that reviews applications pertaining to research involving adults who lack decision-making capacity adopts significant statutory responsibilities under the Act. For example, under para 11.11 of the Code of Practice, the REC will be legally required to ascertain either that the impairing condition under investigation affects the person who lacks capacity, or the treatment of that condition. Where the research is not likely to benefit the individual participant the REC must also ascertain, amongst other things, that the risks are minimal, that nothing 'unduly invasive' will be done to the participant, and that the person's freedom of action and privacy will not be interfered with. It will also need to be satisfied that the researcher is cognisant of her responsibilities in relation to the assessment of capacity and appropriate consultation, and is competent to undertake them.

In Scotland, the arrangements for the review of research involving adults who are unable to consent for themselves are broadly similar to those in England and Wales. The Adults with Incapacity (Scotland) Act 2000 requires that researchers must first obtain the approval of the designated 'Ethics Committee'. This REC is constituted under Regulations made under the Act by the relevant Scottish Ministers to review applications made under s 51(6) of the 2000 Act. There is, however, one fundamental distinction to be drawn between the MCA 2005 and the Adults with Incapacity (Scotland) Act 2000, which is that the Scottish legislation also applies to clinical trials of medicinal products. This has some practical implications for the administration of ethical review, such that where the research is to be conducted in Scotland, but the chief investigator is based elsewhere, any flagged REC is permitted to conduct the review. If, however, the research is to be conducted in Scotland, and the chief investigator is also based in Scotland, then the ethical review may only be conducted by a flagged and recognised Scottish REC. At the time of writing there is only one such REC. It should also be noted that the Clinical Trials Regulations also apply in Scotland. The terminology used differs from that used in England and Wales so that it complies with the Adults with Incapacity (Scotland) Act 2000, but for all practical purposes the effect is the same. More specifically, the terms 'guardian' or 'welfare attorney' are substituted for 'legal representative', and the 'nearest relative' is also included and defined as a person appropriate to consent. Where there is any conflict between the two regulatory regimes the Clinical Trials Regulations will prevail. That being the case, the next section will consider the regulation of clinical trials of investigational medicinal products involving adults who do not have capacity to give consent, throughout the United Kingdom.

Clinical trials of medicinal products that involve adults who lack capacity

In the United Kingdom, clinical trials of investigational medicinal products conducted on adults who lack the ability to consent are governed by the Clinical

Trials Regulations, which transposed the Clinical Trials Directive into domestic law. Schedule 1, Part 5 to the Regulations sets out the principles that underpin research conducted in this vulnerable group. All the general principles and conditions contained in the Clinical Trials Regulations apply to research involving incapacitated adults, but Sch 1, Part 5 contains additional requirements specific to this group. Like those that apply to research on children in Sch 1, Part 4, the regulations require that the interests of the participant 'always prevail over those of science and society' (Sch 1, Part 5, para 15) and that fear, discomfort and pain have been minimised in the design of the trial, as have all foreseeable risks associated with 'the disease and the cognitive abilities of the patient' (Sch 1, Part 5, para 13). Similarly, Sch 1, Part 5, para 14 demands that the 'risk threshold and degree of distress' present in the trial have been specially designed and that they are 'constantly monitored'.

These measures are identical to those covering research involving minors, and generally reflect the provisions contained in the Clinical Trials Directive. They equate to factors routinely considered by RECs in the review of all research, and more especially in relation to projects concerning the participation of vulnerable persons. However, there are some points at which the UK Regulations seem to diverge from the source legislation. Perhaps the most significant of these is based upon para 3 of the preamble to the Clinical Trials Directive which, in relation to adults unable to give consent, states that:

> Normally these persons should be included in clinical trials *only* when there are grounds for expecting that the administering of the medicinal product would be of direct benefit to the patient, thereby outweighing the risks.
>
> (emphasis added)

This is reproduced in slightly different form in Sch 1, Part 5, para 9 of the Clinical Trials Regulations, which provides that the incapacitated person may only be included in a clinical trial if '[T]here are grounds for expecting that administering the medicinal product to be tested in the trial will produce a benefit to the subject outweighing the risks or produce no risk at all'. Despite the subtle differences between the two, where the Directive requires *direct* benefit to the participant that outweighs any risk, the Regulations insist simply on producing *a* benefit and suggest that this be achieved at no risk at all if possible. This is clearly a highly restrictive requirement. Most clinical trials are conducted for the purpose of benefiting the group generally rather than the individual patient, rendering the requirement to benefit the individual participant both unusual and onerous. In addition, under reg 2(1) of the Regulations, Phase 1 trials are defined as:

> a clinical trial to study the pharmacology of an investigational medicinal product when administered to humans, where the sponsor and investigator have no knowledge of any evidence that the product has effects likely to be beneficial to the subjects of the trial.

This means that in practice Phase 1 trials involving incapacitated adults are prohibited, since they cannot be expected to offer a benefit and will encompass risks that by their very nature are likely to outweigh any benefit. Arguably, and depending on the interpretation of the use of the word 'normally' in para 3 of the preamble to the Directive, the UK Regulations are overly restrictive, as it seems possible that this prohibition was not necessarily intended. However, in the absence of definitive case law this cannot be certain.

Similarly, para 4 of preamble to the Directive contains further restrictions, particularly on the involvement of persons incapable of giving their consent due to conditions such as dementia or psychiatric illness. Their inclusion is permissible only when:

> . . . there are grounds for assuming that the direct benefit to the patient outweighs the risks. Moreover, in such cases the written consent of the patient's legal representative, given in cooperation with the treating doctor, is necessary before participation in any such trial.

The implication here is that the treating clinician should agree with the decision of the legal representative to allow the patient to participate in the study, or at least not object. By contrast, the UK Regulations are silent on this point other than designating 'the doctor primarily responsible for the medical treatment provided to that adult', as the legal representative of the incapax, where there is no other such person and that doctor is not connected with the conduct of the clinical trial (Sch 1, Part 1, para 2(a)(ii)(aa)). Furthermore, a consent given by the proposed adult participant's legal representative is taken to represent the 'presumed will' of the adult under Sch 1, Part 5 para 1 of the Regulations, and any dissent, 'explicit wish' to refuse participation or be withdrawn expressed by a participant 'capable of forming an opinion and assessing the information', need only be 'considered by the investigator' (Sch 1, Part 5, para 7). Schedule 1, Part 1, para 1(4) does stipulate that the provisions in Part 5 apply only where an incapacitated subject 'did not, prior to the onset of incapacity, give or refuse to give informed consent to taking part in the clinical trial'. Similarly, Sch 1, Part 1 para 1(5)(b) prohibits the inclusion of a person who refused to give consent to taking part in the specific clinical trial prior to losing capacity, which introduces a degree of respect, albeit limited, for the autonomy of the participant. However, ethical good practice would demand that an expression of dissent or objection should always be respected and acted upon wherever possible, save in circumstances where to do so may disadvantage the participant. Although subjective, ethically the views of a person who was known to be reticent about clinical trials generally prior to becoming incapacitated may therefore legitimately be regarded as informative and indicative of a desire not to be included, which ought to be respected. RECs may therefore find their traditional approach to such matters at odds with a researcher's understanding and application of the Regulations.

Only type 2 or 3 recognised RECs that are also flagged for the purpose of reviewing research with incapacitated adults are empowered to review applications relating to CTIMPs involving adults unable to give consent. They may conduct their review only after obtaining advice on the 'clinical, ethical and psychosocial problems' associated with the specific disease concerned, or pertaining to the specific patient population. Usually, these RECs will have a member with the requisite expertise, but, where they do not, reg 15(7) of the Clinical Trials Regulations stipulates that such advice should be sought from an independent expert. The inherent tensions between ethical considerations and the regulatory provisions in the UK Regulations place a heavy burden on those charged with this task. This is complicated further by some difficult legislative conundrums.

The first of these concerns Art 3(1) of the Directive. The article states that 'Member States shall, in so far as they have not already done so, adopt detailed rules to protect from abuse individuals who are incapable of giving their informed consent' and, in its preamble, that 'the notion of legal representative refers back to existing national law'. At the time of its adoption the Adults with Incapacity (Scotland) Act 2000 was in force, but there was no provision in England and Wales for the giving of legal consent to treatment or research on behalf of an adult who was devoid of decision-making capacity. The inclusion of research in the MCA 2005 was at least in part designed to rectify this anomaly and facilitate a system that would permit the kind of legal authorisation demanded by Art 3(1). This has been achieved, in part, by the provision in s 32 that permits a researcher to seek advice from a carer or other 'consultee' on what the participant's wishes and feelings would be in relation to taking part in research, but the Act also explicitly excludes research involving CTIMPs, which are instead governed by the Clinical Trials Regulations. Here, under Sch 1, Part 5, para 4, the legal representative of the incapacitated potential participant must have 'given his *informed consent* to the subject taking part in the trial' rather than merely being consulted about the wishes and feelings (emphasis added). Whilst the effect of these approaches may be comparable, there is a qualitative legal difference between giving a favourable opinion in a consultation and giving an informed consent, not least because the Regulations dictate that informed consent is based on an interview with the investigator and evidenced in writing, dated and signed.

In addition, unlike the MCA 2005, the Regulations include no guidance on the assessment of capacity and there is no accompanying Code of Practice to advise on practical interpretation. Flagged RECs charged with reviewing research involving incapacitated adults are necessarily invited to be aware of the distinctions between the two separate regimes, but in practice the interests of participants may be best served if they conflate the best features of each.

General conclusions

RECs are now charged with discharging statutory responsibilities with regard to clinical trials research involving both children and adults who lack capacity to give a valid consent. In addition, the MCA 2005 imposes statutory obligations concerning non-clinical trials research involving adults who are unable to consent to participation. RECs need to be aware of their responsibilities in relation to these statutory interventions and also, as a part of those responsibilities, to ensure that researchers are aware of and understand their own obligations.

There remains, however, a wealth of research that falls outside the ambit of these legal provisions but still, nevertheless, involves vulnerable populations. Non-clinical trials research involving children falls within this category, as does research with prison populations. In some circumstances, the infirm elderly, the dying, those suffering from chronic incurable diseases, and those who are in dependent social relationships, can, amongst others, be regarded as vulnerable when it comes to including them in research.

Prior to the recent legislative interventions discussed in detail above, the role of protecting the interests of these most vulnerable research participants fell squarely on the shoulders of RECs. In reviewing a research proposal to conduct research involving any of these groups, aside from the general ethical considerations concerning the veracity and originality of the project and its potential to generate new knowledge, an REC would also focus specifically on a number of relevant areas. First, could the same research be conducted using participants who do have capacity to consent? In other words, would it be possible to obtain equivalent data using an alternative research population? Secondly, is the potential harm to the participants proportional to the potential benefit to the group to which they belong as a whole? Thirdly, is the potential harm to the individual subject and the possible benefits to society more broadly, appropriately balanced?

Alongside these considerations a number of practical mechanisms would be applied to try to minimise the ethical risk to the individual participant. For example, it may be regarded as ethical to recruit people into a study who are unable to consent because of trauma, such as individuals admitted through emergency because of head injury, provided measures are included to ensure that their consent is sought immediately capacity is regained. Furthermore, if such a study involved taking samples which could be safely and easily stored prior to further investigation until such time as consent might be obtained, then the analysis of the samples should be delayed until either consent can be given or withheld, or until it becomes clear that it will never be possible to obtain consent. In addition, where the incapacitated person has carers, relatives or friends who might be consulted about the possible views of the potential participant and whether or not they would be likely to agree or refuse to participate, such consultations should be conducted and, where possible, the assent of that third party obtained. Intuitively, in some circumstances this approach seems like the most appropriate way to proceed in relation to research that is in itself considered ethical. However, RECs must now consider whether such an approach will be compliant with the legislative regimes that now prevail. Evidence suggests that the complexities of the different statutory regimes are resulting in confusion and misinterpretation amongst RECs (Dixon-Woods and Angell, 2009).

RECs exist to protect the interests of those who participate in research, which implies that at some level anybody who is involved in research as a participant may be vulnerable. However, the main ethical and legal consideration when recruiting persons who are considered vulnerable for whatever reason is how to maximise and protect their autonomy. As has been explained in Chapter 5, autonomy is primarily protected, enhanced and maintained through the mechanism of informed consent. Yet where it is not possible to obtain a valid informed consent from an adult, additional legal protections are provided by the Clinical Trials Regulations and the MCA 2005. These safeguards are considered essential to enhance established ethical principles because, as Silva has suggested, to be vulnerable is to experience 'diminished autonomy due to physiological/psychological factors or status inequalities' (Silva, 1995: 15). In this regard it is undeniable that, given the right circumstances, we may all find ourselves vulnerable, perhaps because of illness, emotional upset or unfamiliarity of surroundings. Moreover, the experiences relayed in Chapter 2 tend to suggest both that researchers are exploitative, and that all research participants are vulnerable to exploitation. Of course, in reality this is far from the truth.

Although there are still some researchers who fail to comply with established ethical standards, the vast majority are unstintingly concerned for the welfare of those who participate in their research. Similarly, whilst some participants are undoubtedly vulnerable to abuse and exploitation, others are perfectly able to protect their own well-being, with or without the intervention of an REC. That said, although it may lead RECs to be overly paternalistic, it is still arguable that, too often, research is something that is done to or for the volunteer participants, rather than as a joint venture with them (Edmunds, 2007). Alternatively, it has been postulated that researchers and RECs should seek a genuine partnership with volunteers, respecting their views and autonomy to participate as they wish, even where it may seem exploitative (Dowdy, 2006). By working to maximise the autonomy of all research participants, however vulnerable, RECs may have an impact on this, but their primary consideration must always be for the dignity, safety, welfare and rights of research participants.

Chapter 8

Research involving human tissues and body parts

Introduction

The claim that '[T]he way in which human tissue is obtained is not a morally neutral issue' (Jones, 2000: 148) lies at the centre of the discussion of the ethics and law relating to the use of human tissue in research. In recent years, several high-profile scandals in the United Kingdom have resulted from the unauthorised use of human tissues and body parts for research. A series of public inquiries followed the discovery of incidents of organs and tissues being harvested and retained without adequate consent, and even without the knowledge of those most intimately involved. The Bristol Inquiry (Kennedy, 2000) examined events that occurred at the Bristol Royal Infirmary, where the hearts of babies and children, many of whom had died during or following open heart surgery, were retained for research purposes. In 2001, *The Royal Liverpool Children's Inquiry Report* was published (Redfern, 2001), which revealed details of the acquisition of a large collection of children's tissues and organs. Some of the details were gruesome reading:

> . . . the organs from children's bodies were systematically and routinely extracted, frequently without the consent, and sometimes against the expressed wishes of their grieving parents. Some were examined to ascertain the cause of death and then stored. Many were simply retained, often for no apparent purpose other than the accumulation of a collection.
>
> (Biggs, 2002: 93)

These shocking events were followed by the *Isaacs Report* (HM Inspector of Anatomy, 2003), which concerned the removal and retention of the deceased's brain tissue, despite the previous wishes of the deceased and his wife to the contrary.

Many of these incidents occurred after coroners' post-mortem examinations had been conducted, with around 90 per cent of the hearts retained at Bristol coming from infants and children whose deaths were investigated by the coroner. Further investigations revealed that these practices were widespread, commonplace and routine in hospitals throughout the United Kingdom. For example, in

Scotland an independent review of the retention of organs was commissioned in 2000 to make recommendations and report to the Scottish Government (McLean, 2003). Like its counterparts in England and Wales, it discovered that the retrieval and storage of organs and tissues without consent was habitual, and largely regarded as acceptable by the medical professionals involved. This was evident in a census carried out by the Chief Medical Officer, which found that in hospital trusts and medical schools in England, over 100,000 organs and body parts had been conserved, including the bodies of stillborn children and fetuses (Chief Medical Officer, 2001).

The reasons behind this were many and various. David Price argued that:

> In some instances individuals' and/or relatives' wishes were simply ignored (as in the case of Mr and Mrs Isaacs), in others there was confusion generated by ambiguity as to the scope of terms such as 'tissue' used in 'consent' forms and other information provided, and sometimes only cursory information was given or approaches made to relatives, ostensibly out of a lack of knowledge or a paternalistic desire to spare relatives further suffering. The law even needed to be amended to permit cremation of body parts, see Cremation (Amendment) Regulations 2000 (SI 2000/58) amending the Cremation Regulations 1930 S.R. & O. 1930/1016.
>
> (Price, 2005: 798–799)

Whatever the reasons, the scandal culminated in the development of an entirely new legislative and regulatory regime centred around the Human Tissue Act 2004 (HTA 2004) in England and Wales, and the Human Tissue (Scotland) Act 2006, under which research involving human tissues is now governed. However, it should be noted that if the research involves clinical trials of investigational medicinal products (CTIMPs) as well as human tissues, the Medicines for Human Use (Clinical Trials) Regulations 2004, SI 2004/1031 ('Clinical Trials Regulations') will apply, rather than the specific provisions of the HTA 2004.

The scientific uses to which the human body and its component parts may be put are numerous and diverse (Brazier, 2006). Human tissue can be utilised for treatment in blood transfusions, organ transplantation and gamete donation, to name but a few. Indeed, blood products have been utilised, largely successfully for around 100 years (Machin, 2004), and the development of reproductive technologies using gametes can be traced back to the 1950s (Lee and Morgan, 2001). Furthermore, it has become routine for whole organs to be donated and transplanted (Price, 2000) and used as the means of research (Price, 2003). More recently, human tissue has been used to garner information depicting the very essence of humanity – the human genome. Our genetic make-up can now be identified, catalogued and studied through the use of a vast number of biobanks comprised of biological material and data. Research has been fundamental to the development of all of these innovations.

The use of human tissue in research raises profound ethical questions that revolve around issues of consent and individual autonomy, and have significant implications for confidentiality and privacy. As such, they build upon the subjects of Chapters 5 and 6 of this book, but also raise concerns about our understandings of self-identity and self-determination. The anxieties revealed in earlier chapters concerning the balance to be struck between the rights of the individual and the greater public good are frequently evident in this discussion. How, for example, are our own needs and desires to be weighed against a broader civic duty to others who may benefit from data that could be deduced from research involving tissues and materials gathered from our bodies? These are precisely the issues raised in the controversies mentioned above and, as will be seen, the attempt to address them through legislation often proved no less vexed.

Leading on from this brief overview of the contextual background to the issues, this chapter will examine the relationship between the law and ethics in the context of human tissue research. In an attempt to provide a logical structure to the analysis, it will look first at the Act's approach to different types of tissue generally, and in relation to research, and then consider issues relating to who may give consent, and in what circumstances. This will include an assessment of various controversies associated with the use of human tissues in research, in order to explain the central role that research ethics committees (RECs) can play in ensuring that the abuses of the past are not repeated.

Law and ethics

When introducing the 'landmark' Human Tissue Bill (Gibson, 2004), which became the HTA 2004, to the House of Commons, Rosie Winterton MP observed that:

> The origins of the legislation lie in the distress, grief and anger felt by families in Bristol and Liverpool when they discovered that the organs of their deceased loved ones had been retained without consent . . . The aim of the legislation is to ensure that it will not happen again.
>
> (Winterton, 2004)

Due to the emotive nature of its inception, there was almost universal support for the Bill and its provisions. However, its passage through Parliament was delayed following a protracted consultation period, which generated concerns from the research community. In addition, because the Bill was largely unopposed politically, it received relatively little parliamentary scrutiny at the drafting stages, which resulted in the need for many amendments during the debate stages. Ultimately, following a staggered implementation period, the HTA 2004 introduced a new regulatory regime governing all uses of human tissue, and set up the Human Tissue Authority, which is charged with overseeing the licensing arrangements with regard to the storage of material that comes under the auspices of the Act.

The HTA 2004 applies in England, Wales and Northern Ireland. It repealed and replaced the Human Tissue Act 1961, the Anatomy Act 1984 and the Human Organ Transplants Act 1989, as well as the equivalent legislation in Northern Ireland. In Scotland the Human Tissue (Scotland) Act 2006 is broadly equivalent to the HTA 2004, and effectively implements the same regime. Alongside these Acts the EU Tissues and Cells Directive (2004/23/EC) was implemented in April 2006, and transposed into UK law via the Human Tissue (Quality and Safety for Human Application) Regulations 2007, SI 2007/1523, on 5 July 2007. The Directive aims to create a Europe-wide framework that guarantees uniform standards in relation to the acquisition, storage, importation, exportation and distribution of tissues and cells. Its chief concern is with the safety and quality of cells and tissues that will be used for human therapeutic applications such as transplantation. It applies to both therapeutic and research-based uses of human tissue. However, prior to the introduction of the 2007 Regulations, the Directive was implemented through the HTA 2004, which operates on virtually identical ethical and legal principles in relation to research. Therefore, the HTA 2004 will be the main focus of this discussion.

The HTA 2004 is based on ethical best practice, and consequently locates consent at the centre of most research activities involving human tissue. However, since good clinical practice requirements and the need to obtain REC approval for research involving biological tissues and data pervade research practices involving human tissue, it could be argued that the Act should have only limited practical impact on the conduct of such research. Whilst this is true, it is also important to note that these requirements are now effectively placed on a legal footing, strengthening the obligation to adhere to them. This is reinforced where human tissues are combined with clinical trials of medicinal products, since the requirements of International Conference on Harmonisation (ICH) Good Clinical Practice (GCP) Guidelines on the performance of clinical trials ('ICH GCP') are also clearly incorporated into Sch 1 to the Clinical Trials Regulations.

The HTA 2004 was designed to provide a coherent set of rules to govern the removal, storage and use of human tissues and body parts for any reason, including transplantation (Brazier and Fovargue, 2006). This attempt to streamline the legislative framework by locating the regulation of all uses of human tissue within a single Act is at once its strength and its weakness. By including all activities associated with the use of human tissue in a single piece of legislation, the HTA 2004 is complex and complicated in its construction, and has led to confusion and uncertainty over its application (Brazier, 2005). In addition, it contains much that is outside the scope of a discussion of research involving human tissue, which can be perplexing for RECs.

For example, the Act contains numerous new, and sometimes unhelpful, definitions, and the many exclusions and exemptions it introduces tend to make its application difficult to understand in practice. In addition, although the Act is ostensibly all inclusive with regard to the use of human tissue, certain types of tissue fall outside of its remit. In fact, the Act applies only to what is termed 'Relevant material', which is defined in s 53(1) as 'material other than gametes, which consists of or includes human cells'. This broad definition includes blood, sputum, urine and faeces, as well as whole organs and other body parts, but excludes plasma and serum. Section 54 explicitly excludes human hair, nail and other material created outside of the body, such as cell lines, from the definition (s 54(7)). Where these are to be involved in research, or for other purposes, their use is governed by established common law principles relating to consent, rather than by the new legislative framework. Human embryos and gametes are also excluded from the provisions of the HTA 2004 because research on these is specifically legislated for in the Human Fertilisation and Embryology Act 2008.

It is a characteristic feature of the HTA 2004 that it distinguishes between human tissue obtained from living and dead donors. The removal, storage and use of tissue obtained from dead donors are regulated by the Act. The removal or retrieval of tissues and organs from living donors continues to be governed by the common law. However, the storage and use for research purposes fall under the auspices of the new Act. The Act describes particular consent arrangements that must be adhered to in relation to all categories of what it defines as 'relevant material', when these are to be used for 'scheduled purposes'.

'Scheduled purposes' are defined in Part 1 of Sch 1 to the HTA. They include 'research in connection with disorders, or the functioning of the human body', but there is also a list of other activities, most of which are not specifically relevant to this book, but are included here for interest. The list includes:

- anatomical examination;
- determination of cause of death;
- establishing after a person's death the efficacy of any treatment or drugs administered to that person;
- obtaining scientific or medical information that may be relevant to others, including future others, i.e. genetic data;
- public display;
- research in connection with disorders, or the functioning of the human body;
- transplantation of any bodily material;
- clinical audit;
- education or training, including training in research techniques;
- performance assessment, for example the testing of medical devices;
- public health monitoring;
- quality assurance.

From this it is apparent that the HTA 2004 covers most types of tissue, and most purposes for which it might be used. However, it is notable that consent is not required for the use of tissue taken from existing holdings such as archives where these were established prior to the implementation of the Act. Otherwise, it does encompass all classes of donor, specifically living adults and children, and cadaverous donation by both adults and children. In all cases, so-called 'appropriate consent' must be obtained. The licensing requirements in s 16 of the Act require a licence to be obtained for storage of relevant materials in connection with any of the activities listed in Sch 1. As a result, there is no requirement to obtain a licence to conduct research, but a licence must be held if relevant material is to be retained for research purposes.

In addition, the Human Tissue Act (Ethical Approval, Exceptions from Licensing and Supply of Information about Transplants) Regulations 2006, SI 2006/1260 permit the storage of relevant material if specific REC approval has been given. The Regulations also define the types of REC that are allowed to give approval for research that is exempt from the consent requirements in the HTA. These are RECs established or recognised under the Clinical Trials Regulations, or any other committee established, or person appointed, to advise on matters which include the ethics of research investigations on relevant material that has come from a human body, and is recognised as such by the Secretary of State or equivalent in Wales, Scotland and Northern Ireland. NHS RECs are included in this, as well as some Phase 1 RECs and other non-NHS RECs. University RECs are not generally included in this group.

Researchers must apply for REC approval if they wish to store or use tissue from living or deceased persons for research without a licence from the Human Tissue Authority, or where they seek to store or use anonymised tissue from living donors without consent. Anonymisation is taken to mean that the researcher is unable to identify the tissue donor. REC approval is also needed where a researcher seeks to analyse or use the results from the DNA analysis of material from a living donor without consent, or from a dead donor, except where the donor died 100 years or more prior to 1 September 2006. For the deceased donor the consent is described as 'qualifying consent', which can be given by any person in a qualifying relationship to the donor without having regard to the hierarchical ranking relating to 'appropriate consent' (see below). These very particular rules apply to DNA analysis under the HTA 2004 because the Act creates the specific new criminal offence of holding human material with the intention of analysing the DNA without consent. This offence is regarded extremely seriously, and consequently the Act specifically includes hair, nail and gametes from living persons in this provision despite the fact that they otherwise fall outside the scope of the definition of 'relevant material' contained in the Act.

REC approval is also specifically required where the research involves the storage or use of tissue obtained from adults who are unable to consent for themselves. In these cases the provisions of s 30 of the Mental Capacity Act 2005 apply unless the research also involves the clinical trial of a medicinal product, in which case the Clinical Trials Regulations come into play. In both cases it must be demonstrable that the research could not be performed using tissues from people who could consent for themselves, or by using anonymised tissues.

Aside from these very specialist concerns, and as might be expected given the genesis of the Act, the requirement to obtain 'appropriate consent' forms the central thrust of the Act. However, the Act itself does not include a specific definition of what is meant by 'appropriate consent', except that it is a consent obtained from an 'appropriate person' and will be required in relation to any and all specified uses of human tissue, including research. Who will be regarded as an 'appropriate person' for these purposes varies depending on whether the tissue donor is living or dead, whether the donor is an adult or a minor child and, in some circumstances, the particular use to which the tissue will be put. It was explained in Chapter 5 that very little statutory guidance exists in relation to how to obtain a valid consent and what consent means. However, the Human Tissue Authority offers some, albeit limited, advice on the process of obtaining consent in paras 67–109 of its first Code of Practice – *Consent* (Human Tissue Authority, 2006: 16–22). The following discussion takes this guidance into account in examining issues around who can give an appropriate consent in specific circumstances. It will begin with an overview of the specific consent requirements under the HTA 2004 for living and deceased donors, including some general principles detailed in the Code of Practice, followed by an examination of the situations where research is permitted without consent.

HTA 2004 consent requirements

Where adult living donors who have full mental capacity are invited to donate tissues for research purposes, the HTA 2004 requires that they give consent on their own behalf in compliance with established ethical and common law principles. If the adult person does not have mental capacity, and is therefore unable to give a legally valid consent to the use of her tissue in medical research, her involvement must be authorised under either the Mental Capacity Act 2005 or, if the research involves a CTIMP, under the Clinical Trials Regulations. The consent provisions under these instruments operate in the same way as was discussed in Chapter 7. It should be noted that the regulations permit research on incapacitated adults in the absence of consent only if it is in the best interests of the incapacitated adult, and has been approved by an REC recognised for the purpose. This suggests that the research use of human tissue may be limited to investigations that may be expected to result in benefit to others similarly incapacitated. How broadly best interests can be construed in this regard is a matter of judgment for the individual RECs concerned, which will weigh up the potential benefits of the research against any possible harm to the potential participants in the usual way.

If the proposed research involves obtaining tissue from a living child, defined in the HTA 2004 as a minor below the age of 18, similar arrangements to those outlined in Chapter 7 apply. More specifically, if the child is not capable of making a decision, consent must be given by a person with parental responsibility, as would be the case with medical treatment under s 2(3) of the HTA. Where a living child is deemed competent to consent on her own behalf under the common law (*Gillick v West Norfolk and Wisbech Area Health Authority* (1985)) she must give her consent before tissue can be lawfully used for research or other purposes. It is regarded as good practice to involve persons with parental responsibility in the process where possible (Human Tissue Authority, 2006: para 43). This seems appropriate in the circumstances, particularly since the HTA 2004 was introduced following research abuses involving children. Less usual perhaps is the situation where the child is regarded as competent but has chosen not to make a decision or is unwilling to decide. In these circumstances the Act permits consent to be given by a person with parental responsibility. Since RECs, as discussed in Chapter 7, prefer that a child assent before she is recruited into a research project this legal provision may conflict with some ethical approaches. In addition, the HTA 2004 and the Code of Practice are silent with regard to a child who actively dissents, or objects to her tissue being taken for inclusion in research. It is not difficult to envisage a situation where a child is unwilling to consent because she prefers not to participate, rather than merely avoiding engaging in the consent process. Although there is still a complete absence of case law on these issues it would be possible for any dispute arising from such a situation to be referred to a court, which would then be required to make a judgment according to the best interests of the child.

The consent arrangements for using human tissue obtained from the deceased, whether adult or child, are more complex. Appropriate consent to use tissue obtained from a deceased adult can be provided by the actual person concerned in advance of her death. Alternatively, it can be given by a person nominated by the donor prior to her death, to act as her representative. But if the deceased has not made any such provision, appropriate consent can also be given by a person who is in, what is termed in the Act as, a 'qualifying relationship'. Several categories of person are eligible to make such decisions, and these are ranked according to a statutory hierarchy. In order of priority, qualifying relatives are:

- spouse or partner (including civil partner);
- parent or child;
- brother or sister;
- grandparent or grandchild;
- child of a brother or sister;
- stepfather or stepmother;
- half-brother or half-sister;
- friend of long standing.

Section 54(9) states that a person is another person's partner if the two live as partners in an enduring family relationship.

The consent should be obtained from the highest-ranked person available, but the agreement of a single person who was in a qualifying relationship immediately prior to the person's death will be sufficient to make the use of the tissue lawful. However, the Code of Practice explains that where a person is unwilling or unable to deal with the issue of consent, for example if she is a minor, lacks mental capacity, or cannot be located in time, then 'the next person in the hierarchy would become the appropriate person to give consent' (Human Tissue Authority, 2006: para 57). It should be noted that if the deceased person has previously specifically refused consent to her tissues being taken or used for scheduled purposes, including research, this cannot be overridden.

Where tissue is to be obtained from a deceased child, the Act allows appropriate consent to be given by the child if she was competent to do so prior to her death. Despite this, the Code of Practice is sensitive to the issues that may be raised in these circumstances and advises that the situation should be discussed with the child's family before proceeding. Alternatively, if the child was not competent, or if no consent was obtained from the child, explicit consent must be obtained from the person with parental responsibility or, where there is no such person, somebody who stands in a qualifying relationship to the child.

Where the relevant material is derived from a person who died more than 100 years before the Act came into force, s 1(6) provides that there is no need to obtain consent. This is a useful provision for those who deal with archive material, and with regard to research involving museum collections and archeological specimens. It is not without controversy, however, since some cultures regard materials derived from their ancestors as sacred.

General principles to be applied to the process of consent

Regardless of who is required to give consent, the Human Tissue Authority Code of Practice explains (para 68) that obtaining consent should be regarded as a process, rather than a single act represented by the signing of a consent form. Consent should always be based on a sound understanding of 'the nature and purpose of what is proposed', including 'how the tissue will be used and any possible implications of its use'. Furthermore, the Code is insistent that 'if the person concerned is not a patient, and is volunteering samples purely for research, the general principles of providing adequate information should still apply' (para 77).

Notwithstanding the equivocal nature of informed consent at common law, the Code of Practice advises that 'valid consent can only be given if proper communication has taken place' (para 68). This operates specifically, but not exclusively, in the context of those for whom English is not a first language and is followed by the instruction that information should be provided in different dialects and formats, such as video or audio tape. Persons giving consent should also be 'told of any "material" or "significant" risks inherent in the way the sample will be obtained, and how the tissue will be used' (para 77), especially if identifiable tissue is to be used for research (para 79). Furthermore, 'full and clear information should be provided' to a nominated representative, or a person in a qualifying relationship who is considering giving consent for the use of tissue from a deceased person. In addition, 'it should be borne in mind that some people will want more detail than others' (para 81). Any consent obtained must relate specifically to all aspects of what will be done with the tissue. For example, if the tissue will be retained, stored and manipulated for research purposes, the donor, or the appropriate person from whom consent will be obtained, must be informed of each of these activities and give her explicit consent.

Such requirements were previously recommended by RECs in many contexts in order to facilitate the consent process and to try to ensure that those giving consent act voluntarily and autonomously, but this is the first statutory-based acknowledgement of their significance. As such the bar has been raised in terms of what is required for properly informed consent to the procedures involving obtaining, storing and using human tissue for research. Assuming that the Code of Practice is widely adhered to, anyone who flouts its requirements would in this context be operating outside of a practice accepted as proper, and therefore potentially liable in negligence (*Bolam* (1957)). The HTA 2004, therefore, appears to have implemented a more ethical and legally robust framework with regard to consent than has the common law generally.

Nevertheless, controversy surrounds these provisions in practice, and some researchers have argued that broad consent is adequate for some types of research involving human tissue. The issues have been discussed most often with regard to biobank research, where investigators frequently obtain consent to include tissue and related data in a bank, and simultaneously inform donors that their samples and data may be used for future projects without gaining their explicit consent to participate in subsequent studies. In support of this approach it is argued that individual autonomy is maintained because the donor participants are informed that there will be future uses and could elect not to participate (Hansson, 2006). In addition, the research enterprise would be hampered if explicit consent were required. This broad, or generic, consent approach has been widely adopted by researchers, is legally permissible in several jurisdictions, and is generally supported by NHS RECs, provided that subsequent uses of the materials and data in the bank are subjected to ethical scrutiny. However, for some commentators the practice is regarded as 'diluting ethics' (Hofmann, 2009).

The dilution of ethical principles, it is argued, occurs because of several co-existent misapprehensions. First, the notion that information relating to samples donated to the bank can be adequately protected through coding and anonymisation techniques is contested. Anonymisation, as has been suggested in Chapter 6, is frequently imperfect with regard to rendering information permanently unidentifiable. In relation to biobanks, where coding techniques may be needed to ensure that donors can be traced if necessary, and particularly those that hold genetic materials and data, the claim to anonymity is all the more spurious. Secondly, the use of broad consent effectively prevents the participant donors from withdrawing from the biobank, even if its contents are used for purposes with which the donors disagree. A key implication of futuristic broad consent is that those involved will have no knowledge of what the data is subsequently used for, which denies them the opportunity to withdraw from research about which they might object, and therefore severely limits their autonomy (Hofmann, 2009: 126). It is arguable that the requirement of ethical review of proposed later uses of data and materials will protect the interests of the participants. Yet this is easily refuted by simply considering the potential for a public interest defence. If, for example, a government agency sought access to the database or biobank on public interest grounds, it would almost certainly have the support of law and no REC would have the authority to prevent it. Related concerns also apply to the permitted uses of tissue without consent under the HTA 2004.

Using tissues without consent

Although the HTA 2004 makes consent pivotal to the removal, retention and use of human tissue, Part 2 of Sch 1 to the Act contains some significant exceptions to the general rule that consent is necessary. Included in these exemptions are the use of tissue taken from living people for education or training that relates to human health, public health monitoring, quality assurance and performance assessment, and clinical audit. As Price notes, the inclusion of clinical audit on this list is particularly interesting given the problematic distinction between the two that is often experienced by RECs (Price, 2005: 801). It is also not necessary to obtain explicit consent in relation to coroners' cases investigating the cause of death, where the tissue was held in storage prior to the introduction of the HTA 2004, in cases of extreme public health emergency, and where the tissue is left over following consensual surgery or diagnostic procedures.

Important issues relating to civil liberties are raised by the exemption from the consent requirements in situations of public health emergency, as permitted under s 7(4) of the HTA 2004. Effectively this is another example of a situation where the utilitarian public interest defence can be drawn upon if the public interest is deemed to outweigh the rights of the individual. It enables the Secretary of State to make regulations that dispense with the need for consent from living or deceased persons in extreme situations, such as bioterrorism, or pandemic in order to facilitate the investigation and research of organisms or diseases that jeopardise public health. In such extraordinary circumstances research would be permitted by order of the Secretary of State not just without consent, but even against the objections of those whose tissue was sought. It is questionable whether such interventions would be lawful under the Human Rights Act 1998. However, human rights do not generally apply after death, and it seems likely that, at least in situations of public health emergency, the utilitarian need to achieve the greatest good for the greatest number would provide justification.

The exclusion of surplus tissues resulting from diagnostic or surgical techniques from the HTA 2004 regime also raises important concerns. As originally conceived, the Act would have insisted upon specific consent for the use of tissue that would ordinarily be discarded following consented therapeutic and diagnostic procedures. However, following an outcry from the Wellcome Trust, amongst many others, claiming that invaluable research data and materials would be lost if explicit consent to their use was required, the Human Tissue Bill was revised. Consequently, surplus tissues and samples (including bodily fluids) that remain after surgery or diagnosis involving living donors, can be stored and used for research without the need to obtain specific written consent from the donor (Dyer, 2004). This includes, for example, the anonymous archive of tonsils, which is expected to generate information about the incidence of new variant Creutzfeldt-Jakob disease ('CJD'). Instead of explicit consent in such cases the research must be approved by a recognised REC, which will also need to ascertain that the material is sufficiently anonymised that researchers will not be able to identify its origins.

Like the biobank research, this provision has caused a great deal of controversy, both before and after its implementation. On one side of the debate, commentators like PJ van Diest argue that the value of the possible research outweighs any potential harm to donors, so long as tissue is anonymised, sufficient material remains available for the patient's needs, any reuse is non-commercial, and an appropriate ethical review has been conducted. In these circumstances, it is believed that the communitarian principle of helping others is more important than the right to self-determination, especially if those concerned have been informed of this potential research use when the sample is taken (van Diest, 2002). In a similar vein, John Harris has opined that the reasonable person would, and should, favour putting her body, and its parts, to uses which can potentially benefit others, rather than simply having them disposed of (Harris, 2002). Conversely, Julian Savulescu argues that people may be harmed by information discovered about them through this process. Therefore, consent is necessary because 'when we involve people in our projects without their consent we use them as a means to our own ends' (Savulescu, 2002: 650). Aside from the obvious claim for autonomy, this argument is founded upon the idea that when people consent they measure, and voluntarily accept, any risk posed by the potential breach of confidentiality or in respect of any information that might be acquired through their participation.

Nevertheless, long before the introduction of the HTA 2004 it had become customary for samples of tissues to be preserved and retained once the original purpose behind their retrieval had been fulfilled. This practice has facilitated a great deal of research in the past, and the contention by pathologists and researchers that requiring explicit consent would be detrimental to clinical research was clearly persuasive. Consequently, despite the controversies involving the storage of human tissues without consent that led to the introduction of the Act in the first place, it was revised in line with these arguments. Therefore, under s 1(7)–(9) it is now permissible to use such tissue for research without consent, providing it is anonymised and ethical approval is given by an appropriate REC. Some possible ramifications resulting from this have been suggested above, but outside the United Kingdom legal challenges have already been witnessed, albeit on rather different grounds.

One example of what can happen when research is performed using tissues acquired from a living person who was not fully aware of the facts surrounding their removal and use, occurred in the US case of *Moore v Regents of the University of California* in the late 1980s. John Moore suffered from a condition known as hairy cell leukaemia, and had his spleen removed as part of his treatment. The clinician caring for him, Dr Golde, discovered, whilst investigating the excised splenic tissues, that they exhibited some distinctive properties that might make them beneficial in the treatment of others. He therefore generated a cell line from the spleen and subsequently sold it to a pharmaceutical company for $15 million. On discovering this, Mr Moore brought a case claiming that he had a right to some of the profits acquired from the use of his tissues, and also that the doctors were in breach of the fiduciary duty to obtain informed consent in relation to the procedures performed on him. He lost the case with regard to the proprietary interest, the court holding that there was no precedent for such a right, and therefore it would be inappropriate for the law to recognise one. However, the court did accept that the duty to take informed consent from Mr Moore may have been breached. What this case seems to point out is that consent, above all else, is a key concern when it comes to using human tissue for research purposes. One would expect that the relatives involved in the Bristol, Alder Hey and similar debacles would agree.

To date, the law has not been called upon to adjudicate this specific issue in the United Kingdom. However, a case may be brought at some stage to ascertain the precise status of human tissue in such circumstances. At present there exists a general presumption that the human body and its parts are not equivalent to property that can be owned, which makes it difficult to categorise the vast numbers of samples and specimens that are dealt with by healthcare organisations every day. Who, for example, can claim rights over them, and who is responsible for their storage and disposal once treatment and diagnosis is complete? In the past there has been some speculation that bodily specimens and samples may be regarded as having been abandoned by the patients from whom they were obtained (Nuffield Council, 1995). This is significant because in law, abandonment of property generally means that the person to whom it might have belonged can have no claim further over it, and those who acquire it may treat it as their own, to keep or dispose of. Such an approach is problematic in many different respects, especially since the body and its parts are not generally regarded as property. In practice, bodies and their component parts are usually regarded as being in the possession of the institution, be that a hospital, undertaker or similar, after death or following excision, but the fact that they cannot be owned means that they cannot be stolen. However, the courts have accepted that when such material is altered by the application of human skill, body parts may become property for the purposes of the criminal law (*R v Kelly* (1998)).

This classification of human tissue is relevant in the context of situations that the HTA 2004 deems to be exempt from the consent requirements. For example, tissue may be used without consent if it has been imported or is derived from a body that has been imported. The emphasis behind this clearly rests upon obvious practical and logistical limitations. How, for example, would it be possible to police a requirement to obtain explicit consent from tissue donors overseas? Yet this exclusion highlights concerns regarding the quality of tissues, and the potential for abuses of the consent process in its country of origin. For materials imported from the European Union the Tissues and Cells Directive (2004/23/EC) should assist in the area of quality control and to some extent the maintenance of ethical standards with regard to consent. The Human Tissue Authority published its Eighth Code of Practice in May 2007 to advise on issues related to the use of imported tissue (Human Tissue Authority, May 2007), and the National Research Ethics Service (NRES) recommends that importers of tissue for research seek evidence that the collection of the tissue met with ethical and legal standards in the country of origin. Little or no monitoring is possible with regard to tissues obtained from beyond the United Kingdom, however, and the legal protection may not be as stringent as in the United Kingdom. The high-profile controversy relating to tissues acquired from the body of the late BBC broadcaster Alistair Cooke is a case in point.

Alistair Cooke was a renowned journalist and commentator who worked for the BBC in New York and died of cancer in March 2004 at the age of 95. After he died sections of his bones were removed without consent and used for dental and orthopaedic transplants. Some were imported from the United States and used to treat patients in the United Kingdom. This occurred as a result of the activities of a criminal gang, operating under the instructions of a former dentist who had been prevented from practising because of drug abuse. This man paid undertakers to permit his 'cutters' to remove the bones and other tissues from people who had recently died and then supply the tissues to organisations that processed them for medical use. The illegal practice was alleged to have earned the gang up to $5 million (Bone, 2008).

Regulation under the Food and Drug Administration in the United States had been designed to prevent tissue being removed from elderly people and from those who died from cancer. In Cooke's case this was particularly important because cancer had infiltrated his bones. However, the regulation failed to prevent the criminal intentions of the gang involved in this case. It is known that Cooke's tissues were exported from the United States to the United Kingdom and used for treatment of an estimated 40 patients, some of whom suffered harm as a result. Additionally, one patient is known to have contracted hepatitis B from infected tissue harvested by the same gang. It is also possible that similar tissues were used in research. Aside from the harm caused to recipients of infected tissues, the relatives of those whose loved ones' bodies were harvested suffered great emotional distress and turmoil in respect of their religious beliefs. The case demonstrates the dangers involved in the unregulated harvesting and marketing of human tissue. It exemplifies many of the reasons why explicit consent is so important in the protection of all who are involved in removal and use of human tissue, and raises concerns about the absence of the need for explicit consent in relation to the use of imported tissues.

The Act also makes provision for the use of human tissue without consent in order to obtain medical information that is or may be relevant to a person other than the donor. This applies specifically in the context of obtaining genetic information that may be required to diagnose or treat a third party, usually a family member. Section 7(1) permits this where the living person from whom stored material is derived cannot be traced after reasonable efforts have been made to find her. However, the tissue may only be used after an application has been made to the Human Tissue Authority, and it has exercised its power to 'deem consent' in these circumstances. Section 7(2) allows the tissue to be used if, in similar circumstances, a tissue donor has been traced but fails to respond to give or withhold consent despite the making of reasonable attempts to obtain a response. The approval of the Human Tissue Authority must also be obtained to authorise this and it must be established that there is no reason to believe that the donor has in fact died, become incapacitated or had previously refused consent. Although these provisions do not apply specifically to the use of tissue for research, there is an implied obligation for researchers to ensure that appropriate records are made and kept, since the retained tissue may have been obtained for research purposes. RECs may therefore need to be aware of these requirements and the role played by the Human Tissue Authority in this process.

Human Tissue Authority

The establishment of the Human Tissue Authority forms a central part of the HTA 2004. The Authority is an independent statutory body that has responsibility for the licensing of all activities covered by the Act, including the storage and use of human bodies and human tissues for research, and other scheduled purposes, including tissue banking. The HTA 2004 is also designated as the 'competent authority' under the Tissues and Cells Directive, which means that it has responsibility for implementing the licensing regime associated with the Directive. Organisations that store human tissue for research purposes after the implementation of the Act on 1 September 2006 must be licensed by the Human Tissue Authority for the specific uses they will make of human tissue. RECs must therefore ascertain that researchers involved in using human tissue in their projects are aware of their licensing responsibilities in relation to the Human Tissue Authority.

Alongside its licensing and monitoring functions the Human Tissue Authority also has responsibility to issue a series of codes of practice. These cover areas of specific interest to practitioners and researchers, including consent, anatomical examination, post mortem examination, and donation of organs, tissues and cells for transplantation. All the codes are published subject to parliamentary approval.

Conclusions

This chapter has focused on the legal implications of research involving human tissue following the implementation of the HTA 2004, even though it has been claimed that 'the events in Bristol and Alder Hey that *led* to the Act were nothing whatsoever to do with research approved by an ethics committee, or indeed any sort of research' (Warlow, 2005: 25; emphasis in original). In opposition to this claim it seems self-evident that the collections of tissues, organs and other body parts that were the subject of the scandals which preceded the introduction of the Act were ostensibly retained for research purposes, albeit spurious research, purposes. It is true that no ethics committees were involved, since no proper research protocols were developed or available for scrutiny. Instead, the tissues and body parts in question were mostly routinely, and unethically, acquired and retained as a potential research resource. The impact of these regrettable events would almost certainly have been avoided, or at least diminished, if those concerned had been subjected to effective regulation.

Having said that, the introduction of the HTA 2004, and the new regulatory regime that accompanies it, could be regarded as doing little more than placing good ethical practice on a statutory footing. Given that clinicians and researchers ought to have been aware of their ethical obligations even prior to its enactment, the Act may not change much in practice. However, although in many ways the Act simply represents a statutory recognition of the ethical imperatives associated with the removal, retention and use of human tissue in treatment, diagnosis and research, it actually does more than this.

One important advance is in the now statutory requirement to obtain written consent in two particular circumstances. The first is where it is intended to store tissue for future use, and the second concerns the use of tissue and whole bodies in anatomical examinations or where a corpse is to be displayed in public. The compulsion to obtain written consent is virtually unique in English law, where a signature on a consent form is usually simply regarded as evidence of agreement. In the context of research more widely, written evidence of consent accompanied by the provision of extensive information and safeguards against coercion are regarded as ethical best practice, and reflect the voluntary nature of participation in research. Its inclusion in the Act appears to signal a similar commitment, but also seems incongruous in conjunction with the areas where consent can be waived.

Nevertheless, the setting-up of the Human Tissue Authority to issue licences and oversee licensed activities certainly appears to make it less likely that the abuses of the past will be repeated. The production of extensive codes of practice in relation to activities relating to the use of human tissue is to be welcomed. Furthermore, for the most part the HTA 2004 endorses and supports the ethical principles that RECs uphold during the process of ethical review. Where research uses human tissue in conjunction with the development of medicinal products the Act reinforces the requirement for ethical approval contained in the European Clinical Trials Directive (2001/20/EC) and the UK Clinical Trials Regulations 2004.

In addition, the Act introduces several new criminal offences. Examples that might affect research practices include the imposition of criminal penalties for failing to observe the terms of a licence, and for conducting licensed activities in the absence of a valid licence. Criminal penalties can also be imposed for the holding of human tissue with the intention of analysing DNA without consent. Section 5 makes it an offence to store and use tissue for scheduled purposes without the necessary appropriate consent, and s 8 penalises the use of donated material for a purpose other than that for which the appropriate consent was obtained. Conviction under these provisions can result in a term of imprisonment of up to three years, or a fine, or both. In appropriate circumstances, however, practitioners and researchers accused of these offences can claim in their defence that they reasonably believed that appropriate consent had been given, or was not required. It is to be hoped, indeed expected, that these penalties will act merely as a deterrent and rarely, if ever, be imposed. Certainly, the current general awareness of the issues coupled with the codes of practice published by the Human Tissue Authority ought to militate against the need for such convictions.

There remain some areas where the application of the Act itself remains problematical. Specifically, these are the areas of activity that the HTA 2004 permits without explicit consent, such as in relation to leftover tissue following diagnosis or treatment. As the foregoing discussion suggests, the exemption from the requirement to obtain consent in such circumstances resulted from the outcry generated by researchers during the passage of the Bill through Parliament. Some of the objections raised were clearly difficult for politicians to resist. It was claimed, for example, that requiring explicit consent for research using leftover tissue would be financially unviable for the NHS. Accordingly, it was estimated that if the NHS was to spend even one minute obtaining consent for the use of all the excess or leftover tissues each year it would need an additional 1,339 full-time staff (Furness and Sullivan, 2004). Whilst this is in some respects persuasive, it needs to be assessed within the wider context.

Underpinning this claim is the assumption that the practice of storing and using such materials for research without consent is straightforward. Yet, experience shows that this is not the case. Further, just because a practice is commonplace or routine does not mean that it is right, as events at Alder Hey and Bristol clearly demonstrate. Similarly, just because it would be costly to obtain explicit consent does not mean that it is the wrong thing to do. In an environment where legislation was considered necessary to safeguard and respect the rights of individuals, it seems inappropriate to revise the proposed law to comply with the wishes of the very groups from which those whose actions forced the legal change in the first place, emanated. Arguing from this position David Price has stated that the revisions to the Bill 'unnecessarily dilute the philosophical coherence of this crucial piece of legislation' (Price, 2005: 800).

With this in mind some RECs may experience disquiet at the tension between the law and ethics in this regard. The mere fact that the HTA 2004 permits the research use of leftover tissues without consent does not make the practice ethical, particularly when one considers the political climate within which the Act was revised. The arguments put forward by Salvulescu (2002) and others in relation to the use of leftover tissue epitomise these conflicts and convincingly demonstrate the divide between commentators as well as the inherent contradictions between law and ethics. The same can also be said with regard to generic, or broad, consent for ongoing biobank research. As Hofmann (2009) implies, non-objection does not signify consent, particularly where those concerned are unaware of the details of what is involved.

The uncertainties surrounding the ethical use of human tissues in research go to the very heart of the process of ethical review. Balancing the dignity, rights, safety and welfare of potential and actual participant in human tissue research against the needs of society and science are never more graphic than here. They question, as Kapp retorts, whether 'you want a piece of me' and what you will do with it if I let you have it (Kapp, 2006). The excesses uncovered in the UK organ retention scandals provide clear insights into what can happen when bodily tissues from deceased persons, children and adults are used for research in the absence of consent. It should never be forgotten that for many, human tissue cannot easily be separated from the person to whom it was once attached, and that sections of bodies from living or dead donors are wholly representative of the person to whom they once belonged. Consequently, that person has a right to be treated respectfully, in life and in death. RECs are charged with protecting the interests of all classes of research participant, and generally perform their duty with alacrity. However, their professionalism may be tested to the limit if required to probe the boundary between law and ethics in the context of human tissue research.

Chapter 9

Conclusions – threads, themes and thorny issues

> The dominant theme in research ethics, whether in health and medicine or social science, remains the balance between the values of scientific freedom and the protection of the essential dignity of the individual research participant, particularly the vulnerable participant.
>
> (Chalmers, 2006: 100)

This quote from Chalmers concisely illustrates the central themes of this book and exposes the controversial threads that have run through it. How, precisely, can the values of science and scientific freedom be balanced against the protection of the individual research participant? What is meant by their 'essential dignity' and exactly who is vulnerable? Several of the preceding chapters have posed these questions and explored ways in which they might be addressed, but the thorny issues remain.

This concluding chapter will revisit some of these thorny issues to try to shed some further light on their critical influence on research ethics and the process of ethical review. It begins with a brief exploration of the nature of vulnerability – which will use several different scenarios to indicate the complexities of balancing the protection of the individual against the promise of scientific advancement – and lead into a discussion about research misconduct. The nature of research misconduct and fraud will then be examined to question whether the work of research ethics committees (RECs) can help to alleviate the problems and protect participants from the associated harms. From there it will conclude with some general comments about how best to distribute the risks and benefits of research across society and whether this would be better achieved by recognising that all have a moral duty to participate.

The vulnerable participant

Vulnerability may be the result of the inherent characteristics of a person, or the situation within which she finds herself, or a combination of both. It is arguable that people who are recruited to participate in healthcare research are vulnerable simply because they have become research subjects, but that would not be the whole story. What, for example, is the nature of their vulnerability, and what exactly are they vulnerable to? Further analysis is needed to answer these questions.

Before commencing this discussion it is important to note that despite the potential for every individual to be regarded as vulnerable, many are not. Some of the potentially most vulnerable participants decline invitations to be involved in research, and others who accept do so with total awareness and understanding of the implications. Vulnerability should not be assumed. The nature of vulnerability is largely socially constructed, but is also associated with a limited 'ability to make personal life choices, to make personal decisions, to maintain independence and to self determine' (Moore and Miller, 1999). It is the impact of these characteristics on people recruited to participate in research that RECs seek to minimise. However, RECs and their members can become so accustomed to the rhetoric and responsibility associated with safeguarding the interests of research participants that it is easy to become paternalistic and regard every possible participant as vulnerable. This is clearly not the case.

Potential or actual research participants may be vulnerable at different stages of the research process, and for a variety of different reasons (Weijer, 1999). A potential research participant may be invited to be involved in the study because of her specific attributes. She may have been identified as suitable to participate because she has a particular medical condition or belongs to a group that exhibits specific social features. The person may have disabilities or live in a particular environment, such as a nursing home or a prison. Such qualities suggest the potential for vulnerabilities to arise. For example, researchers may gain access to such people through the staff who work with them. But those who live in confined communities are often also in dependent relationships with the staff, and may therefore feel obliged to comply with a request to participate in research. Vulnerability could occur at the point of recruitment, hence the role of the REC is to try to ensure that the agreement to participate is given voluntarily and is uncoerced.

Other factors may also influence the decision of a potential participant to join a study. For example, it is argued that offering inducements or financial incentives to potential participants affects their ability to act autonomously, especially if they are already in an economically vulnerable position (Bentley and Thacker, 2004). The autonomy of the individual in such circumstances may be compromised (Dunn and Gordon, 2005), which is a major concern for RECs focused on the protection of individual research participants. Alongside this, however, is the possibility that the integrity of the research project may be damaged if participants are recruited predominantly from specific constituencies rather than representing the characteristics of the wider population. The Royal College of Physicians (RCP) argues that payments are acceptable provided adequate safeguards are in place (RCP, 2007: 76). Whilst the RCP acknowledges that it is incumbent upon RECs to check that the level of financial reward is appropriate to the circumstances, it may be difficult to determine what is meant by appropriate. With respect to Phase I volunteer studies, for example, an REC can try to ensure that any financial reward does not interfere with the value of other benefits or payments received by the participants so that they are not disadvantaged; but can it really prevent participants entering these studies purely for the money?

This kind of controversy arose in March 2006 when six volunteers participating in a Phase I study based at Northwick Park Hospital experienced extreme and unexpected events. They all became critically ill and required treatment in the intensive therapy unit of the hospital. The quality of the consent given to participate in the study was questioned. The volunteers received £2,000 each to participate in the trial of a monoclonal antibody known as TGN1412. All claimed that their motivation for taking part had been the money. In addition, despite the detailed information they were given in writing and through communication with staff at the research centre, they reported being unaware that serious side-effects could happen in this type of study. These were fit and healthy young men, who would not generally be considered vulnerable, yet despite the best efforts of the REC involved in approving the study they were allegedly oblivious to the risks they ran. Some have criticised the value of the research ethics review in the light of this incident, arguing that the process and procedures involved can detract from the impetus behind them (Goodyear, 2006). Yet regardless of how it is articulated the nature of risk is not, it seems, always appreciated. Mason and Laurie have asserted that 'a risk has ceased to be minimal where there is a risk that makes one stop and think' (Mason and Laurie, 2006: 687), but clearly other factors may disrupt the ability to stop and think. Furthermore, shortly after the TGN1412 debacle Mansell reported an unexpected rise in the numbers of volunteers contacting Phase I research units (Mansell, 2006). It seems that for some a financial incentive will outweigh a risk to physical well-being (Levine, 2005).

For others the voluntary nature of participation and protection of their well-being is apparently compromised for different reasons. Military personnel may not generally be associated with vulnerability. However, some of the greatest controversies in the recent past have occurred in this environment and epitomise another aspect of vulnerability – the power imbalance. In this context soldiers may be regarded as equivalent to the captive communities described above because of their employment status and the culture of subordination between ranks. The recruitment of army 'volunteers' into experiments at Porton Down between 1939 and 1989 has been the subject of much debate over the years, and exemplifies some of these concerns (Ministry of Defence, 2006). Similar controversy surrounds the use of pyridostigmine bromide and botulism toxoid vaccination in the first Gulf War in 1990. The injection of the substances was described as an experimental treatment but only limited provision was made to obtain informed consent because the injection was administered at a time of war and it was hoped that the troops would benefit from the application (Annas, 1992; BMA, 2004: 505). Aside from the difficulty of weighing the risk against the benefit in a case like this, the Gulf War example points out yet another recurring theme in this book – the utilitarian principle of the greatest good for the greatest number. Cases such as these epitomise what is perhaps the most thorny issue for RECs – how to calculate and weigh a speculative risk against a speculative benefit.

A further challenge for RECs is the identification of research misconduct and fraud. The discussion of the chequered history of research ethics in Chapter 2 demonstrated the close association between vulnerability in research participants, and the perpetration of abuses by researchers. Consequently, whilst it is self-evident that vulnerability can attach to particular research participants, it is also the case that the traits of the researcher may expose participants to situations that cause them to be vulnerable to exploitation. At what point does the power imbalance between the researcher and the researched tip over to allow vulnerability to lead to abuse? Frank Wells and Michael Farthing state in the preface to the fourth edition of their book *Fraud and Misconduct in Biomedical Research* (2008) that they had hoped that its subject matter would no longer be of relevance today. One would imagine that those who formulated the Nuremberg Code and the original Declaration of Helsinki might feel the same. Unfortunately, research misconduct continues to occur.

Research misconduct can take many forms. It can be deliberate or, where the behaviour of the researcher simply falls below accepted professional and ethical standards, unintentional. It relates to the performance of the research itself, the recruitment process, the generation of data or the dissemination of results. Examples of each of these have been witnessed in recent years and their occurrence is known to be widespread (Smith, 1991; Ranstain, 2001). Whatever form misconduct takes it is detrimental to the outcomes of the research. By implication this means that research participants have potentially been subjected to the risk of harm without that risk being balanced against the possibility of achieving results that will be beneficial for science and society, which is not ethical. It is misconduct to perform research involving human participants without first submitting the research proposal for ethical scrutiny. Most publishers would today decline to publish any paper that presented the results of human participant research but failed to provide evidence of ethical scrutiny. The main role of RECs in relation to research fraud and misconduct is therefore a preventative one. Intuitively, the requirement to subject research proposals to ethical review suggests that ethical standards should be complied with and maintained through the research process. Yet, this assumption may not always be as robust as it first appears. Without more, simply presenting a protocol for ethical review does not guarantee that the protocol will be followed in practice, or that the results will be genuinely presented. Most RECs do not fulfil a monitoring function, and neither are they expected to in the NHS.

Further, it is debated whether RECs should assess the scientific worth of projects submitted to them. An REC considering a highly specialist research protocol is unlikely to have members with sufficient expertise adequately to consider its scientific merit. In many ways this is appropriate, but it is also problematic. If the REC does not assess the science, how can it ascertain that the study is ethical? The debate about the role of the REC in relation to this aspect of the review has already been touched upon in earlier chapters. It is apparent that tensions exist between the requirements of the Medicines for Human Use (Clinical Trials)

Regulations 2004, SI 2004/1031 ('Clinical Trials Regulations') and the govern-ance arrangements for NHS RECs. More specifically, in relation to clinical trials of investigational medicinal products (CTIMPs) RECs are required, *inter alia*, to consider the design and relevance of clinical trials, the intended benefits, arrange-ments for recruitment and the suitability of the investigator and supporting staff. Yet under the *Research Governance Framework* (DoH, 2005), responsibility for this is explicitly removed from the remit of NHS RECs and delegated to the research sponsor. *Governance Arrangements for Research Ethics Committees* (GAfREC), however, advises (para 9.13) on the need to be 'reassured about the scientific design of the study' (DoH, 2001). An REC may be reassured by the delegated review, but would this necessarily prevent research misconduct?

Imagine a hypothetical situation where a doctor submitted a research proposal to an REC seeking ethical approval for a clinical trial funded by a reputable funding body. The REC did not conduct a scientific review or scrutinise in detail the qualifications of the researcher. Instead, it relied upon an apparently favour-able independent scientific review and the assurances of the sponsor that the researcher was appropriately qualified. A favourable ethical opinion was given and the study commenced. The doctor failed to comply with the research proto-col, and conducted a study that was entirely different to the one documented in the REC application. The participant patients were exposed to procedures that were not described in the approved information sheets, and in the course of the study several of them came to physical harm. In the ensuing investigation it was discovered that the scientific review was fabricated by the researcher herself and had also been used in the application for funding.

At first sight this may seem like an extreme situation that could never happen in practice. After all, 'trust lies at the heart of the practice of medicine. Patients must be able to trust their doctors with their lives and . . . medical research must always be conducted with scrupulous honesty and integrity' (Barrett, 2008: 271). But this quote has been deliberately taken out of context to illustrate how counter-intuitive it is to suspect that a medical practitioner could engage in such practices. In fact, those words formed part of the statement made by the Professional Conduct Committee of the General Medical Council (GMC), which struck a doctor off the medical register because he had been found guilty of research misconduct. So what would become of the hypothetical research doctor depicted above?

Regulation 49 of the Clinical Trials Regulations makes it an offence to submit false or misleading information relating to a CTIMP to an REC, so the researcher would clearly be liable under that provision. She would almost certainly also face disciplinary action by the GMC, which would probably result in her name being struck from the register so that she would no longer be licensed to practice medi-cine. In addition, a range of criminal charges could be brought. She could, for example, be charged with fraud in relation to obtaining the funding for the study based on a fabricated application. However, unless the sums involved were huge, it is unlikely that a fraud charge would be pursued in practice. Instead, she could be charged under the law of theft with obtaining money by deception. Depending on the precise circumstances, if she had managed to secure a new job on the basis of this fraudulent project she could also be guilty of deception offences under ss 15 and 16 of the Theft Act 1968. She clearly deliberately set out to deceive both the REC and the funding body, and was dishonest in the process, which would satisfy the element of criminal intention, and the facts demonstrate that monies were obtained, so it is possible that a conviction may be secured.

The researcher also caused harm to several participants, having first induced them to enter the trial under false pretences. There is extensive case law pertaining to the criminal implications of this kind of conduct. For example, in *R v Tabaussum* (2000) Tabaussum persuaded several women to submit to breast examinations by claiming to be medically qualified. He was in fact not a doctor. The court held that there was no consent since the women had only agreed on the basis of their belief that he was medically qualified. He was convicted of indecent assault. However, in *R v Richardson* the accused was known to her 'victims' as their dentist and had treated them for many years. Her alleged crime was that she continued to do so even after she had been struck off the dental register and suspended from practising. At first instance the court held that this amounted to an assault, but the decision was overturned in the Court of Appeal. It is therefore feasible that the hypothetical researcher could escape conviction if she was well known to her participant 'victims'. However, in these circumstances one would not expect the court to be swayed by such arguments.

The hypothetical researcher has deliberately misled the participants in two ways. First, she has elicited a fraudulent consent from them by knowingly recruiting them into a bogus study. Therefore, she has conducted procedures involving the participants on the basis of fraudulent consent. Secondly, the study actually conducted was not the bogus study to which the participants thought they had consented. Consequently, not only has she probably committed criminal battery or trespass in relation to the deception involved in the consent process, but there is also the possibility of a range of criminal offences relating to non-fatal offences against the person. Had somebody died as a result of their participation in this project under these circumstances, charges of manslaughter by gross negligence would certainly be appropriate.

In addition to these legal sanctions, reg 29A of the Clinical Trials Regulations requires the notification of serious breaches of good clinical practice (GCP) or trial protocol to the Medicines and Healthcare Regulatory Agency (MHRA). In a case like this, such a notification by the sponsor or REC is likely to be purely academic since action will already have been taken. However, ordinarily, on receipt of such notification the MHRA can decide whether simply to acknowledge and record the notification, or to investigate further and potentially halt the study and commence legal proceedings.

The legal position of the REC would also be complex. The discussion of the potential liability of RECs and their members in Chapter 4 demonstrated that it is extremely unlikely that a REC would be implicated where participants have come to harm through the actions of a researcher. In a case like this it is evident that the researcher knowingly exposed the participants to harm, and she would therefore be primarily responsible. It is possible, though unlikely, that the REC may be found to be in breach of its obligations under the Clinical Trials Regulations, although, as previously explained, since responsibility for scientific review had been delegated the defence of due diligence would probably apply.

Fortunately, this example of extreme misconduct in research is only hypothetical, but instances of research misconduct and abuse do still occur in practice. Examples are rare, but always regrettable, and when they do occur the consequences can be very real. The fraudulent claim by William McBride that Debendox caused deformities in children is a case in point. Dr McBride had previously been the first physician to raise concerns about the safety of thalidomide. Hence, when he reported similar instances relating to Debendox the drug was withdrawn from the market. His misconduct was subsequently exposed when the New South Wales Medical Tribunal held an inquiry and revealed that the results he claimed were statistically significant were in fact fabricated (Ragg, 1993). Years after these events, Jane Barrett reported meeting a woman who had suffered years of needless torment as a consequence (Barrett, 2005). This woman had been prescribed Debendox whilst pregnant and then been taken off it when McBride's results were published. Her son had been born healthy, but she had always wondered whether some abnormality would surface due to her actions in taking the drug, to the extent that she had dreaded becoming a grandmother in case her son's offspring were affected through her fault. It seems that the details of McBride's fraudulent research had been widely publicised, but the subsequent details of its falsity had been disseminated less publically.

The evidence presented above indicates that the mere fact that researchers are required to submit their proposals to undergo a process of ethical review will not of itself prevent research misconduct from occurring. From this discussion it is clear that the role of RECs in the detection and prevention of misconduct is necessarily limited, but it is not negligible. Although scientific review is now largely outside the remit of NHS RECs, the slogan 'bad science is bad ethics' remains pertinent, and the approval of studies that are scientifically weak is more likely if RECs do no actively engage in the scientific review. In some circumstances this can be avoided. For instance, many university RECs include a technical review of research proposals in their ethical review process, believing that this approach will help to inculcate the ethos that ethics is fundamental to the design of research. In the NHS some RECs have a member who is actively involved in the research governance process and can therefore inform the REC of relevant issues.

One of the most relevant issues with regard to preventing and detecting misconduct and fraud in research concerns the financial arrangements involved in the process. Good research is expensive to perform and can be financially very rewarding, but the money involved can be the cause of serious conflicts of interest. The recent case concerning Andrew Wakefield's claims of a connection between the MMR vaccine and autism in children is a clear example. Dr Wakefield published his claims in a now widely discredited article in the *Lancet* (Wakefield, 1998). The scientific findings have subsequently been extensively challenged and generally refuted. The probity of Wakefield's research more generally has also been questioned in light of later revelations that he received a payment of £55,000 from the Legal Aid Board to provide advice on whether families had a case in relation to possible vaccine damage to their children (Mason and Laurie, 2006: 676). This conflict of interest is viewed as material to subsequent events and is the subject of a GMC professional misconduct hearing. Following the highly publicised affair many families became concerned about the safety of the MMR vaccine and decided not to have their children vaccinated. Recent reports indicate that in 2008 there were 1,348 confirmed cases of measles in England and Wales, compared with only 56 in 1998, and that two children have died of the disease (Deer, 2009).

RECs are entitled to be informed of the financial arrangements of studies. Indeed reg 15(5)(k) of the Clinical Trials Regulations provides that 'In preparing its opinion, the committee shall consider, in particular . . . the amounts, and, where appropriate, the arrangements, for rewarding or compensating investigators and subjects'. However, if this information is provided out of context and without the benefit of an overview of the environment within which the researcher is operating, how many studies she is involved with, what other commitments she has and how many support staff there are, for example, it may at best be not particularly informative, and, at worst, irrelevant. That said, RECs can glean much from the details of the protocol in this regard. In particular, the finer points about recruitment targets and whether or not the recruitment processes is competitive between different research centres, will be instructive. RECs should also ascertain that the payment will go into a practice account, or designated trust account, rather than into the researcher's personal bank account. To impose an additional layer of accountability, it is also good practice to include details of the financial arrangements of the study in the participants' information documents. Participants have a right to know how the researcher may benefit from their involvement and the inclusion of such information will help to avoid situations such as that which occurred in *Moore v Regents of the University of California* (1990), which was discussed in Chapter 8.

There are, however, some types of misconduct that are not easily identified regardless of how robust the systems for detecting them. This was evidenced in a rare study published in the *British Medical Journal* where journal editors were asked to review a manuscript that contained a number of significant errors. The results demonstrated that editors identified less than one-third of the mistakes and misdemeanours, despite being trained to do so (Schroter *et al*, 2004). In this regard activities like plagiarism, duplication of publications and falsification of data are notoriously difficult to detect, and fall well beyond the remit of most human participant RECs. Their prominence was acknowledged in the United Kingdom as long ago as 1997 when a group of editors of medical journals got together to form the Committee on Publication Ethics (COPE). Its website now boasts a membership of 4,375 and includes evidence of a vast number of instances of research publication misconduct. Amongst these are cases where authors have submitted the same article to different journals and with different titles, whilst certifying to each that it has not been submitted elsewhere. Others cases include the submission of originally jointly authored articles under sole authorship, and the more obvious examples of plagiarism and falsification of data.

These concerns are not easily resolved. It is, however, questionable whether the entire burden for detecting and policing this misconduct should fall to journal editors (Marusic and Marusic, 2006). It is not in doubt that the publication and dissemination of research findings plays a major role in the ethics of research and research integrity. In support of this, para 27 of the Declaration of Helsinki explains this most clearly:

> Both authors and publishers have ethical obligations. In publication of the results of research, the investigators are obliged to preserve the accuracy of the results. Negative as well as positive results should be published or otherwise publically available. Sources of funding, institutional affiliations and any possible conflicts of interest should be declared in the publication. Reports of experimentation not in accordance with the principles laid down in this Declaration should not be accepted for publication.

These ideals would go a long way towards reducing many examples of misconduct in research. However, the lack of resource and commitment to this ideal in the research governance arrangements in the NHS, and in particular with regard to the ethics of research and the work of RECs, is worrying. If research fraud and misconduct is to be eliminated, the current approach to ethical review, which separates scientific review and dissemination of results from the approvals process, may be appropriate as a matter of practicality, but does not represent 'joined-up thinking'. In particular, given the damage often caused by research fraud and misconduct the system of ethical review is failing in its duty if the overall aim of research ethics is to protect participants from harm. Since there are sound measures in place in many other countries to detect and counter research misconduct, the United Kingdom appears to have adopted a rather relaxed approach to these matters in recent years. With this in mind the launch of the UK Research Integrity Office (UKRIO) in 2005 was widely welcomed (White, 2005). Unfortunately, it seems unlikely to live up to its initial promise.

According to its own website, '[UKRIO] is an independent body which offers advice and guidance to universities and other research organisations, and also to individual researchers, about the conduct of research' (UKRIO, 2009). To this end it advises the NHS, universities and other research organisations primarily on issues relating to health and biomedical research, but also in other disciplines. Its aims, however, do not appear to be sufficiently robust to stand any chance of combating the kind of research misconduct that has been depicted here. More specifically, it declares its aims to be to:

- promote the good governance, management and conduct of research;
- share good practice on how to address misconduct in research; and
- give advice and guidance on specific cases.

It does not, as one might have expected, seek to investigate allegations of misconduct or to monitor researchers who are suspected of misconduct. Instead, it will merely advise and 'share good practice'. The promotion of 'good governance, management and conduct of research' is of course to be welcomed, but there would appear to already to be sufficient mechanisms in place for education and training to fulfil this role. And no amount of good advice and training will uncover deliberate, fraudulent misconduct or eradicate it.

Taking into account current levels of resources it is understandable that NHS RECs need to delegate responsibility for aspects of the review process to others. However, they can undertake a limited assessment of the scientific and publication credibility of a proposal by conducting a simple literature review. Although this depends on results having been published, and under the correct title and accurate authorship, it will discover whether similar studies have been undertaken previously, and enable the REC to question the originality of the proposal and what it will add to existing knowledge. In a similar vein, John Saunders suggests that it could be made a condition of REC approval that studies are registered on a central database (Saunders, 2008: 115). He is right to believe that such registration would help to discourage misconduct, but it would also cause other problems. For example, registration of CTIMPs or trials sponsored by the pharmaceutical industry could probably be achieved relatively easily, and is already being attempted through the initiation of the International Standard Randomised Controlled Trial Number (Evans *et al*, 2004). But this does not capture the majority of university-led and social science research, and the large volume of student research that makes up the majority of projects reviewed by NHS RECs. Some other mechanism would need to be developed if the entirety of healthcare research is to be made accountable in the same way, and the logistics of this are probably insurmountable.

Final conclusions

The discussion of resources and logistics in the preceding paragraphs seems like an apposite place to begin the final discussion. A central, but largely unspoken, premise of this book has been that there is value in conducting healthcare research. Scientific advances can only be developed through the conduct of systematic inquiry, and in the field of healthcare this process generally requires the involvement of human participants. It is the job of RECs to protect the interests of participants during that process. NHS RECs are specifically charged with protecting the dignity, rights, safety and welfare of both actual and potential research participants, and, as has been shown, this can be an involved and complicated business. It encompasses respect not just for the physical safety of the participants but also for the integrity of their personal data, their emotional and psychological autonomy and the preservation of their tissues and body parts. If they belong to a particularly vulnerable population, their protection is doubly important. Yet it is questionable how far this emphasis should extend.

Some commentators have postulated that the emphasis on the ethics of research, with its focus on the protection of the individual, so-called vulnerable participant, is flawed. Rosamund Rhodes, for example, has suggested that those who seek to benefit from the outcomes of research without participating as subjects ought to be regarded as 'free-riders'. Accordingly, their access to the fruits of research should be restricted to the benefit of those who have participated (Rhodes, 2005). Others, however, conclude that this is not necessary so long as research participants are properly rewarded for their engagement (Levine, 2005). The inference here is that those who participate will benefit from the process, financially or in some other way. In these circumstances, the research process will operate in the same way as many other markets. Those who produce the goods or services are paid for their time and involvement and others consume the products. What is lacking from these approaches is proper regard for the vulnerability of research participants created by the mere fact of their participation. These arguments seem to suggest that the nature of the perceived vulnerability of participants is misinformed, and the majority of research participants are no more vulnerable to abuse than is the average consumer. Leaving aside the fact that there is today a wealth of legislation and regulation to protect consumers from entering into misguided transactions that will render them financially disadvantaged, this seems counterintuitive. Healthcare research often relies upon the recruitment of people who are unwell, infirm or in some other way disadvantaged, and therefore inherently vulnerable. In addition, we know from the abuses of the past that those who participate in research can be subjected to abuses that they are powerless to defend against, which indicates that protection is required.

Instead of reassessing our approach to research ethics by redefining the nature of vulnerability, the value of research and its participants to society could be reframed. John Harris has constructed a compelling argument to the effect that we each have a moral duty to participate in research (Harris, 2005). On the apparent premise that scientific progress is an unqualified good, he suggests that in order to benefit from healthcare that is predicated on scientific research, participation in research ought to be an obligation. Adopting such an approach would mean that the benefits and burdens of research were distributed more fairly across society, which would be its own reward. Presumably, everybody would be equally vulnerable, so the nature of vulnerability would change. Enticing as Harris' argument is at the societal level, at the level of the individual it is still open to challenge. Some types of research are inherently more risky than others, and some participants more prone to adverse reactions (Shapshay, 2007).

Regardless of these debates, the central focus of this book has been the interaction between ethics and the law in the context of medical research and the process of ethical review. This final chapter has focused extensively on research misconduct and identified a number of shortcomings in relation to its detection and prevention. This exemplifies the entire theme of the book. In practice, research ethics and the ethical review of medical research was, until very recently, almost entirely divorced from the law. This is no longer the case. As has been seen, the law now pervades every aspect of the review process. With regard to clinical trials of medicinal products this is because there is now specific law that regulates the process in minute detail. With regard to research involving human tissues, or adults who lack the capacity to consent, the same applies. Where there is no explicit legislation, the National Research Ethics Service (NRES) has imposed the clinical trials regime anyway.

Despite this invasion of formality, REC members remain for the most part volunteers. They apply sound ethical reasoning to the applications put before them, and, although this is anecdotal, seem more often than not to reach a conclusion equivalent to the one they would have reached prior to the imposition of legal responsibility. The introduction of legal frameworks superimposed upon the process of ethical review has, however, introduced new terminology and different approaches, which some RECs seem to be grappling with (Dixon-Woods, 2009). Ultimately, it is the researchers' compliance with sound ethical principles and ideals that will improve the quality of research and the protection of its participants. Machiavelli is reported to have commented that ethics is something that you do when you are alone. RECs are charged with ensuring that researchers no longer have that luxury.

Bibliography

ACHRE, *The Human Radiation Experiments: Advisory Committee on Human Radiation Experiments*, 1996, United States: OUP.

Additional Protocol to the Convention on Human Rights and Biomedicine Concerning Biomedical Research, available at http://conventions.coe.int/

Albin, RL, 'Sham Surgery Controls: Intercerebral Grafting of Fetal Tissue for Parkinson's Disease and Proposed Criteria for Use of Sham Surgery Controls', *Journal of Medical Ethics*, 28, 2002, 322.

Annas, GJ, 'Changing the Consent Rules for Desert Storm', *New England Journal of Medicine*, 236, 1992, 770.

Baeyens, C, 'Implementation of the Clinical Trials Directive: Pitfalls and Benefits', *European Journal of Healthcare Law*, 9, 2002, 31.

Barrett, G, Cassell, JA, Peacock, JL, Coleman, MP, 'National survey of British public's views on use of identifiable data by National Cancer Registry', *British Medical Journal*, 332, 2006, 1068.

Barrett, J, 'Unexpected feedback', *British Medical Journal*, 331, 2005, 664.

Barrett, J, 'Conduct of an enquiry into alleged misconduct', in Wells, F, Farthing, F, *Fraud and Misconduct in Biomedical Research*, 4th edn, 2008, London: Royal Society of Medicine, 260–73.

Baylis, F, Downie, J, 'The limits of altruism and arbitrary age limits', *The American Journal of Bioethics*, 3:4, 2003, 19.

BBC News online, 'Drug trial rules 'should change', 25 July 2006, available at: http://news.bbc.co.uk/1/hi/health/5213264.stm (last accessed May 2009)

BBC News online, 'Facing up to my uncertain future', 7 December 2006, available at: http://news.bbc.co.uk/1/hi/health/6217728.stm (last accessed May 2009)

BBC News online, 'MMR Doctor Admits Ethics Failing', 11 April 2008, available at: http://news.bbc.co.uk/1/hi/health/7342618.stm (last accessed August 2008)

Beauchamp, TL, Childress, JF, *Principles of Biomedical Ethics*, 6th edn, 2004, Oxford: OUP.

Beecher, H, 'Ethics and Clinical Research', *New England Journal of Medicine*, 274, 1966, 1354.

Bentham, J, *Introduction to the Principles of Morals and Legislation* (1789).

Bentley, JP, Thacker, PG, 'The influence of risk and monetary payment on the research participation decision making process', *Journal of Medical Ethics*, 30, 2004, 293.

Beyleveld, D, 'Conceptualising privacy in relation to medical research values', in McLean, SAM (ed), *First Do No Harm*, 2006, Aldershot: Ashgate, 151–163.

Biggs, H, 'Forever and ever amen: Life and death in perpetuity', *Res Publica*, 8, 2002, 93.

Biggs, H, 'Human Tissue: New Law, Same Issues', *The Good Clinical Practice Journal*, 13(7), 2006, 25.

Biggs, H, 'Is consent enough? Issues in patient safety and data protection', *CR Focus*, 19(2), 2008, 23.

Bone, J, 'Alistair Cooke bodysnatch ring head gets up to 54 years in jail', *The Timesonline*, 27 June 2008, http://www.timesonline.co.uk/tol/news/world/us_and_americas/article 4227565.ece.

Bowsley, S, 'NHS on Trial over Secret Baby Tests', *The Guardian*, 9 May 2000.

Boyd, KM, Higgs, R, Pinching, AJ (eds), *The New Dictionary of Medical Ethics*, 1997, London: BMJ Publishing.

Brazier, M, 'Patient autonomy and consent to treatment: The role of law', *Legal Studies*, 7, 1987, 169.

Brazier, M, 'Liability of ethics committees and their members', *Professional Negligence*, 1990, 186.

Brazier, M, 'Where the law and ethics conflict?', *Research Ethics Review*, 1(3), 2005, 97.

Brazier, M, 'Human(s) (as) Medicine(s)', in McLean, SAM (ed), *First Do No Harm*, 2006, Aldershot: Ashgate, 188–202.

Brazier, M, Fovargue, S, 'A Brief Guide to the Human Tissue Act 2004', *Clinical Ethics*, 1, 2006, 26.

Bridgeman, J, 'Because we care? The medical treatment of children', in Sheldon, S, Thomson, M (eds), *Feminist Perspectives on Healthcare Law*, 1998, Cavendish: Aldershot, 97–114.

British Medical Association, *Confidentiality and Disclosure of Health Information*, 1999, London: BMA.

British Medical Association, *Consent, Rights and Choice in Healthcare for Children and Young People*, 2001, London: BMA.

British Medical Association, *Medical Ethics Today*, 2004, London: BMA.

British Medical Journal, editorial, 'Nuremberg Doctors Trial: the Nuremberg Code', *British Medical Journal*, 313, 1996, 1448.

British Psychological Society, *Conducting research with people not having the capacity to consent to their participation: A practical guide for researchers*, 2008, Leicester: British Psychological Society.

Burroughs, V, 'Racial and ethnic inclusiveness in clinical trials', in Santoro, MA, Gorrie, TA (eds), *Ethics and the Pharmaceutical Industry*, 2005, New York: CUP, 80–96.

Caldicott, F, *Report of the Review of Patient-Identifiable Information*, 1997, London: DoH.

Caldwell, PHY, Murphy, SB, Butow, PN, *et al*, 'Clinical Trials in Children', *Lancet*, 364, 2004, 803.

Campbell, A, Gillet, G, Jones, G, *Medical Ethics*, 3rd edn, 2001, Oxford: OUP.

Campbell, AV, 'The ethical challenges of Biobanks: Safeguarding altruism and trust', in McLean, SAM (ed), *First Do No Harm*, 2006, Aldershot: Ashgate, 203–214.

Case, P, 'Confidence matters: The rise and fall of informational autonomy in medical law', *Medical Law Review*, 11, 2003, 208.

Cave, E, Holm, H, 'New governance arrangements for research ethics committees: is facilitating research achieved at the cost of participants' interest?', *Journal of Medical Ethics*, 28, 2002, 318.

Cecil JS, Wetherington, GT, 'Court-ordered disclosure of academic research: a clash of values of science and law', *Special Issue of Law and Contemporary Problems*, 3, 59, Summer 1996.

Chalmers, D, 'International medical research regulation: from ethics to law', in McLean, SAM (ed), *First Do No Harm*, 2006, Aldershot: Ashgate, 81–100.

Chief Medical Officer, *Report of a Census of Organs and Tissues Retained by Pathology Services in England*, January 2001, London: DoH, available at: http://www.doh.gov. uk/organcensus/index.htm

CIOMS, *International Ethical Guidelines for Biomedical Research Involving Human Subjects*, 2002, available at: http://www.cioms.ch/frame_guidelines_nov_2002.htm

Clark, PA, 'Placebo Surgery for Parkinson's Disease: Do the Benefits Outweigh the Risks?', *Journal of Law, Medicine and Ethics*, 30, 2002, 58.

Clouser, KD, Gert, B, 'A critique of principlism', *Journal of Medicine and Philosophy*, 15, 1990, 219.

Conroy, S, Choonara, I, Impicciatore, P, *et al*, 'Survey of unlicensed and off-label drug use in paediatric wards in European countries', *British Medical Journal*, 322, 2000, 79.

Council for International Organisations of Medical Sciences, *International Ethical Guidelines for Biomedical Research Involving Human Subjects*, 2002.

Declaration of Geneva as amended at Stockholm, 1994 –

Deer, B, 'MMR doctor Andrew Wakefield fixed data on autism', *The Sunday Times*, 8 February 2009, available at: http://www.timesonline.co.uk/tol/life_and_style/health/ article5683671.ece

Department for Constitutional Affairs, *Mental Capacity Act 2005 Code of Practice*, 2007, London: TSO.

Department of Health, *Local Research Ethics Committees*, HSG(91)5, 1991, London: DoH.

Department of Health NHS Executive, *NHS Indemnity: Arrangements for Handling Clinical Negligence Claims Against NHS Staff*, HSG(96)48, 1996, London: DoH.

Department of Health, *Ethics Committee Review of Multi-Centre Research*, 1997, HSG(97)23, London: DoH.

Department of Health, *Governance Arrangements for NHS Research Ethics Committees (GAfREC)*, 2001, London: DoH.

Department of Health, *Governance Arrangements for Research Ethics Committees in Scotland*, 2001, London: DoH.

Department of Health, *Reference Guide to Consent for Examination and Treatment*, 2001, London: DoH.

Department of Health, *Confidentiality: NHS Code of Practice*, 2003, London: DoH.

Department of Health, *The Protection and Use of Patient Information*, 2004, London: DoH.

Department of Health, *Research in the NHS: Indemnity Arrangements*, 2005, Gateway reference: 5957.

Department of Health, *Research Governance Framework for Health and Social Care*, 2nd edn, 2005a, London: DoH,available at: www.dh.gov.uk.

Department of Health, *Patient Information Advisory Group (PIAG)*, January 2009, London: DoH, available at: http://www.advisorybodies.doh.gov.uk/piag/ (last accessed 1 June 2009)

Dickens, BM, 'What is a medical experiment?', *Canadian Medical Association Journal*, 1975, 113635.

Dixon-Woods, M, Angell, EL, 'Research involving adults who lack capacity: how have research ethics committees interpreted the requirements?', *Journal of Medical Ethics* (2009, forthcoming).

Douglas, TM, 'Ethics committees and the legality of research', *Journal of Medical Ethics*, 33, 2007, 732.

Dowdy, DW, 'Partnership as an ethical model for medical research in developing countries: the example of the "implementation trial"', *Journal of Medical Ethics*, 32, 2006, 357.

Doyal, L, 'Informed consent in medical research: Journals should not publish research to which patients have not given fully informed consent – with three exceptions', *British Medical Journal*, 314, 1997, 1107.

Dunn, LB, Gordon, NE, 'Improving informed consent and enhancing recruitment for research by understanding economic behavior', *Journal of American Medical Association*, 293, 2005, 609.

Dyer, C, 'Human Tissue Bill is modified because of research needs', *British Medical Journal*, 328, 2004, 1518.

Dyer, O, 'Psychiatrist is struck off for wide ranging dishonesty and lack of insight', *British Medical Journal*, 336, 2008, 738, also available at: http://www.bmj.com/cgi/content/full/336/7647/738–a.

Edmunds, LAA, 'Protecting the volunteer: a question of law versus ethics', *Res Ethics Rev*, 3(2), 2007, 54.

Edwards, R, 'The Baby Bones Scandal', *The Sunday Herald*, 17 June 2001, also available at: http://www.robedwards.com/2001/06/the_baby_bones_.html

Elliston, S, *The Best Interests of the Child in Healthcare*, 2007, London: Routledge-Cavendish.

ESRC, *Research Ethics Framework (REF)*, 2007, Swindon: ESRC.

Evans, HM, 'Should patients be allowed to veto their participation in clinical research?', *Journal of Medical Ethics*, 30, 2004, 198.

Evans, M, 'Porton Down guinea-pigs get apology', *The Times*, 18 January 2008, available at: http://www.timesonline.co.uk/tol/news/uk/article3206993.ece

Evans, T, Gulmezoglu, M, Pang, T, 'Registering clinical trials: a role for WHO', *Lancet*, 363, 2004, 1413.

Fadan, R, Beauchamp, T, *A History of Informed Consent*, 1986, Oxford: OUP.

Ferguson, P, 'Human "guinea pigs": why patients participate in clinical trials', in McLean, SAM (ed), *First Do No Harm*, 2006, Aldershot: Ashgate, 165–185.

Feigal, J, 'Ensuring safe and effective medical devices', *New England Journal of Medicine*, 348, 2003, 191.

Foster, C, 'Commentary: the ethics of clinical research without patients' consent', *British Medical Journal*, 312, 1996, 817.

Foster, C, *The Ethics of Medical Research on Humans*, 2001, Cambridge: CUP.

Fovargue, S, 'Consenting to bio-risk: Xenotransplantation and the law', *Legal Studies*, 25, 2005, 404.

Fovargue, S, Ost, S, 'A plea for precaution with public health: the xenotransplantation example', *Clinical Ethics* (2009, forthcoming).

Furness, P, Sullivan, R, 'The Human Tissue Bill', *British Medical Journal*, 328, 2004, 533.

Gardener, P, 'A virtue ethics approach to moral dilemmas in medicine', *Journal of Medical Ethics*, 29, 2003, 297.

General Medical Council, *Confidentiality. Protecting and Providing Information*, 2004, London: GMC.

General Medical Council, *0–18 Years: Guidance to All Doctors*, 2007, London: GMC.

General Medical Council, *Consent: Patients and Doctors Making Decisions Together*, 2008, London: GMC, also available at: http://www.gmc–uk.org/news/articles/Consent_guidance.pdf (last accessed May 2009)

Gibson I, MP, HC Deb, Vol 416, col 1012, 15 January 2004.

Gilligan, C, *In a Different Voice*, 1982, Cambridge, Massachusetts: Harvard University Press.

Gillon, R, *Philosophical Medical Ethics*, 1985, Chichester: Wiley.

Goncalves, E, 'Grave injustice – body snatching in the 1950's to aid nuclear research', *The Ecologist*, May 2001, available at: http://findarticles.com/p/articles/mi_m2465/is_4_31/ai_74583520/pg_2

Goodyear, M, 'Further lessons from Northwick Park', *British Medical Journal*, 333, 2006, 270.

Grady, C, 'Payment of clinical research subjects', *Journal of Clinical Investigation*, 115(7), 2005, 1681.

Greenhalgh, T, Taylor, R, 'Papers that go beyond numbers (qualitative research)', *British Medical Journal*, 315, 1997, 740.

Gudena, R, Luwemba, S, Williams, A, Jenkinson, LR, 'Data protection gone too far: Questionnaire survey of patients and visitors views about having their names displayed in hospital', *British Medical Journal*, 329, 2004, 1491.

Gunn, MJ, *et al*, 'Decision-making capacity', *Medical Law Review*, 7, 1999, 269.

Hammersley, M, 'Against the ethicists: on the evils of ethical regulation', *International Journal of Social Research Methodology*, 12(3), 2009, 211.

Hansson, MG, Dillner, J, Carlson, J, 'Should Donors be Allowed to Give Broad Consent to Future Biobank Research?', *Lancet Oncol*, 7, 2006, 266.

Hare, RM, *Moral Thinking*, 1981, Oxford: Clarendon Press.

Harris, J, 'Law and Regulation of Retained Organs: the Ethical Issues', *Legal Studies*, 22, 2002, 550.

Harris, J, 'Scientific research is a moral duty', *Journal of Medical Ethics*, 31, 2005, 242.

Health Service Journal Editorial Report, 'Cancer Experts call for Action on GMC's Confidentiality Rules', *Health Service Journal*, 2 November 2000, 4.

Herring, J, *Medical Law and Ethics*, 2nd edn, 2008, Oxford: OUP.

HM Inspector of Anatomy, *The Investigation of events that followed the death of Cyril Mark Isaacs*, May 2003, available at: http://www.doh.gov.uk/cmo/isaacsreport/

Hofmann, B, 'Broadening consent – and diluting ethics?', *Journal of Medical Ethics*, 35, 2009, 125.

House of Commons Select Committee on Health, *Fourth Report* (2005), available at: http://www.publications.parliament.uk/pa/cm200405/cmselect/cmhealth/42/4202.htm

House of Lords, House of Commons Joint Committee on the Draft Mental Incapacity Bill (2003), HL 189-1, HC 1083-1, London: TSO, also available online at: http://www.publications.parliament.uk/pa/jt200203/jtselect/jtdmi/189/189.pdf

Human Tissue Authority, *Code of Practice: Consent*, 2006, London: DoH, available at: http://www.hta.gov.uk/_db/_documents/2006-07-04_Approved_by_Parliament_-_Code_of_Practice_1_-_Consent.pdf

Human Tissue Authority, *Code of Practice: Import and export of human bodies, body parts and tissue*, 2007, London: DoH, available at: http://www.hta.gov.uk/_db/_documents/2007-05-10_Code_of_Practice_8_Import_and_export_of_human_bodies,_body_parts_and_tissue.pdf

Hunter, D, Pierscionek, B, 'Children, Gillick Competency and consent for Involvement in Research', *Journal of Medical Ethics*, 33, 2007, 659.

Iverson, A, Liddell, K, Fear, N, Hotopf, M, Wessely, S, 'Consent, confidentiality and the Data Protection Act', *British Medical Journal*, 332, 2006, 544.

Jackson, E, *Medical Law: Text, Cases and Materials*, 2006, Oxford: OUP.

Jones, DG, *Speaking for the Dead: Cadavers in Biology and Medicine*, 2000, Aldershot: Ashgate.

Jones, JH, *Bad Blood: The Tuskegee Syphilis Experiment*, 1993, New York: Free Press.

Jones, M, 'Informed consent and other fairy stories', *Medical Law Review*, 7, 1999, 135.

Kalra, D, Gertz, R, Singleton, P, Inskip, HM, 'Confidentiality of personal health information used for research', *British Medical Journal*, 333, 2006, 196.

Kapp, MB, 'Ethical and legal issues in research involving human subjects: do you want a piece of me?', *Journal of Clinical Pathology*, 59, 2006, 335.

Kaufman, JL, 'Protecting research subjects', *New England Journal of Medicine*, 346, 2002, 2093.

Kennedy, I, *Treat me Right: Essays in Medical Law and Ethics*, 1991, Oxford: OUP.

Kennedy, I, *Bristol Inquiry Interim Report: Removal and Retention of Human Material*, 2000, available at: http://www.bristol–inquiry.org.uk/interim_report/report.htm

Kennedy, I, The Bristol Royal Infirmary Inquiry, *Learning from Bristol: The Report of the Public Inquiry into Children's Heart Surgery at the Bristol Royal Infirmary 1984–1995*, 2001, London: TSO (Cm 5207II), available at: http://www.bristol–inquiry.org.uk/

Kent, A, 'Consent and Confidentiality in Genetics: Whose Information is it Anyway?', *Journal of Medical Ethics*, 29, 2003, 16.

Kmietowicz, Z, 'Registries Will Have to Apply for Right to Collect Patients' Data Without Consent', *British Medical Journal*, 322, 2001, 1199.

Kodish, E, *Ethics and Research with Children: a case based approach*, 2005, Oxford: OUP.

LaFleur, WR, Bohme, G, Shimazono, S (eds), *Dark Medicine: Rationalising Unethical Medical Research*, 2007, Bloomington: Indiana University Press.

Laurence, DR, 'Guide, guide thyself: law and order in clinical research', *Research Ethics Review*, 4(2), 2008, 69.

Law Commission, *Report No. 231 Mental Capacity. Item 9 of the Fourth Programme of Law Reform, Mentally Incapacitated Adults*, 1995, London: HMSO.

le Carre, J, *The Constant Gardener*, 2001, London: Hodder and Stoughton.

Lederer, S, *Subjected to Science: Human Experimentation in America before the Second World War*, 1995, Baltimore: Johns Hopkins University Press.

Lee, R, Morgan, D, *Human Fertilisation and Embryology: Regulating the Reproductive Revolution*, 2001, London: Blackstone.

Levine, R, 'Reflections on "Rethinking Research Ethics"', *American Journal of Bioethics*, 5(1), 2005, 1.

Lewis, JC, Tomkins, S, Sampson, JR, 'Ethical Approval for Research involving Geographically Dispersed Subjects: Unsuitability of the UK MREC/LREC System and Relevance of Uncommon Genetic Disorders', *Journal of Medical Ethics*, 27, 2001, 347.

Leyland, P, Woods, T, *Administrative Law*, 4th edn, 2002, Oxford: OUP.

Liamputtong, P, *Researching the Vulnerable: A Guide to Sensitive Research Methods*, 2007, London: Sage Publications.

Lincoln, YS, Guba, EG, *Naturalistic Inquiry*, 1985, London: Sage Publications.

London, AJ, 'Equipoise and International Human Subjects Research', *Bioethics*, 15, 2001, 312.

Lord Chancellor's Department, *Who Decides? Making Decisions on Behalf of Mentally Incapacitated Adults*, 1997, (Cm 3808), London: HMSO.

Lord Chancellor's Department, *Making Decisions*, 1999 (Cm 4465), London: HMSO.

Lowman, J, Palys, T, 'Ethics and Institutional Conflict of Interest: The Research Confidentiality Controversy at Simon Fraser University', *Sociological Practice: A Journal of Clinical and Applied Sociology*, 2(4), 2000, 245.

Lowman, J, Palys, T, 'Ethical and Legal Strategies for Protecting Confidential Research Information', *Canadian Journal of Law and Society/Revue canadienne droit et société*, 15(1), 2000, 39.

Machin, SJ, 'Contaminated Blood', *Medico-Legal Journal*, 72, 2004, 77.

Macintyre, A, *After Virtue*, 1984, University of Notre Dame Press.

Mansell, P, 'Healthy Motivation?', *Pharmatimes*, July/August 2006, 54, available at: http://www.pharmatimes.com/Magazine/july06/54_56.pdf

Manson, N, O'Neill, O, *Rethinking Informed Consent in Bioethics*, 2007, Cambridge: CUP.

Marusic, A, Marusic, M, 'Killing the messenger: should scientific journals be responsible for policing scientific fraud?', *Medical Journal of Australia*, 2006, 632.

Mason, JK, Laurie, GT, *Mason & McCall Smith's Law and Medical Ethics*, 7th edn, 2006, Oxford: OUP.

McHale, J, 'Waste, Ownership and Bodily Products', *Health Analysis*, 2000, 45.

McHale, J, 'The Human Tissue Act 2004: Innovative Legislation – Fundamentally Flawed or Missed Opportunity?', *Liverpool Law Review*, 26, 2005, 169.

McHale, J, Fox, M, *Health Care Law: Text and Materials*, 2nd edn, 2007, London: Sweet & Maxwell.

McLean, SAM, *The Report of the Independent Review Group on Retention of Organs at Post-Mortem* ('the McLean Report'), 2003, available at: http://www.sehd.scot.nhs.uk/scotorgrev/Final%20Report/ropm–01.htm

McLean, SAM, Williamson, L, *Xenotransplantation: Law and Ethics*, 2005, Aldershot: Ashgate.

Medical Research Council, *Responsibility in Investigations on Human Subjects*, 1962 (Cmnd 2382), reproduced in the *British Journal of Anaesthesia*, 39, 1967, 283.

Medical Research Council, *Personal Information in Medical Research*, 2000, London: MRC.

Medical Research Council, *Medical Research Involving Children*, 2004, London: MRC.

MHRA (2003), available at: http://www.mhra.gov.uk/Aboutus/Whoweare/Ourmissionand values/index.htm

MHRA, *Medicines and Medical Devices Regulation: What you need to know*, 2008, London: MHRA, available at: http//www.mhra.gov.uk/Aboutus/index.htm

Mill, JS, *On Liberty* (1859).

Miller, FG, 'Research ethics and misguided moral intuition', *Journal of Law, Medicine and Ethics*, 32, 2004, 111.

Ministry of Defence, 'MOD publishes Porton Down Volunteers Historical Survey', 14 July 2006, available at: http://www.mod.uk/DefenceInternet/DefenceNews/Defence PolicyAndBusiness/ModPublishesPortonDownVolunteersHistoricalSurvey.htm

Miola, J, 'On the Materiality of Risk: Paper Tigers and Panaceas', *Medical Law Review*, 17, 2009, 76.

Montgomery, J, 'Power/knowledge/consent: Medical Decision-making', *Modern Law Review*, 51, 1988, 245.

Moore, LW, Miller, M, 'Initiating research with doubly vulnerable populations', *Journal of Advanced Nursing*, 30(5), 1999, 1034.

Morin, K, *et al*, 'Managing conflicts of interest in the conduct of clinical trials', *Journal of the American Medical Association*, 287(1), 2002, 78.

Mulhall, A, De Louvois, J, Hurley, R, 'Chloramphenicol Toxicity in Neonates: Its Incidence and Prevention', *British Medical Journal (Clin Red Ed)*, 287, 1983, 1424.

Munson, R, *Intervention and Reflection,* 4th edn, 1992, Belmont: Wadsworth Publishing.

Nicholson, RJ, 'Final act in the Case of Evelyn Thomas', *Bulletin of Medical Ethics*, 75, 1992, 3.

Nicholson, R, 'Another threat to research in the United Kingdom', *British Medical Journal*, 328, 2004, 1212.

NRES Homepage, http://www.nres.npsa.nhs.uk/aboutus/what–are–recs/ (last accessed February 2009)

NRES, *Defining Research*, 2007a, London: DoH, available at: http://www.nres.npsa.nhs.uk/rec–community/guidance#researchoraudit.

NRES, *Information Sheets and Consent Forms: Guidance for Researchers and Reviewers (version 3.2)*, May 2007, London: NPSA, available at: http://www.nres.npsa.nhs.uk/rec–community/guidance/#PIS (last accessed May 2009)

NRES, *Research Involving Adults Unable to Consent for Themselves (version 2)*, September 2007, London: NPSA.

NRES, *Medicines for Human Use (Clinical Trials Regulations) 2004: Informed Consent in Clinical Trials (version 3)*, May 2008, London: NPSA, available at: http://www.nres.npsa.nhs.uk/rec–community/guidance/ (last accessed May 2009)

NRES, *Approval for Medical Devices Research: guidance for researchers, manufacturers, research ethics committees and NHS R & D offices (version 2)*, 2008, London: DoH.

NRES, *Standard Operating Procedures for Research Ethics Committees (version 3.5)*, May 2008, London: DoH, available at: http://www.nres.npsa.nhs.uk/news-and-publications/publications/standard-operating-procedures/#Documents

NRES, *Standard Operating Procedures for Research Ethics Committees (version 4.0)*, April 2009, London: DoH, available at: http://www.nres.npsa.nhs.uk/news-and-publications/publications/standard–operating–procedures/#Documents

Nuffield Council on Bioethics, *Human Tissue: Legal and Ethical Issues*, 1995, London: Nuffield Council.

Nuremberg Principles 1947, *British Medical Council*, 313, 1996, 1448.

O'Donovan, K, Gilbar, R, 'The Loved Ones: Families, Intimates and Patient Autonomy', *Legal Studies*, 23, 2003, 353.

O'Neill, O, 'Some Limits on Informed Consent', *Journal of Medical Ethics*, 29, 2003, 4.

O'Riordan, T, Cameron, J, *Interpreting the Precautionary Principle*, 1994, London: Earthscan.

Pappworth, M, *Human Guinea Pigs*, 1967, London: Routledge and Kegan Paul.

Pattinson, S, *Medical Law and Ethics*, 2006, London: Sweet & Maxwell.

Pattinson, S, 'Consent and Informational Responsibility', *Journal of Medical Ethics*, 35, 2009, 176.

Patton, MQ, *Qualitative Evaluation and Research Methods*, 2nd edn, 1990, London: Sage Publications.

Pegg, MS, 'Some Research Ethics Committees Believe in Facilitating Ethical Research', *British Medical Journal*, 333, 2006, 398.

Perna, MA, ' "Fair's fair argument" and voluntarism in clinical research: But, is it fair', *Journal of Medical Ethics*, 32, 2006, 478.

PIAG, *Response to GMC Revised Confidentiality Guidance Consultation*, November 2008, DoH, available at: http://www.advisorybodies.doh.gov.uk/piag/piagresponse–gmc–confidentialtiy.pdf (last accessed 1 June 2009)

Pope, C, Mays, N, 'Opening the black box: an encounter in the corridors of health services research', *British Medical Journal*, 306, 1993, 315.

Price, D, *Legal and Ethical Aspects of Organ Transplantation*, 2000, Cambridge: CUP.

Price, D, 'From Cosmos and Damien to Van Velsen: The Human Tissue Saga Continues', *Medical Law Review*, 11, 2003, 1.

Price, D, 'The Human Tissue Act 2004', *Modern Law Review*, 68(5), 2005, 798.

Proctor, R, *Radical Hygiene – Medicine under the Nazis*, 1988, Cambridge: Harvard University Press.

Rabbitt-Roff, S, 'A Long Time Coming', *New Scientist*, 6 February 1999, available at: http://www.newscientist.com/article/mg16121726.200-a-long-time-coming.html

Ragg, M, 'McBride guilty of scientific fraud', *Lancet*, 341, 1991, 550.

Randerson, J, 'Ethical Red Tape is Stifling Us, say Medical Researchers', *The Guardian*, 4 August 2006, 8.

Ranstain, J, Bayse, M, George, SL, *et al*, 'Fraud in Medical Research: an international survey of biostatisticians', *Controlled Trials*, 21, 2000, 415.

Redfern, M, Keeling, J, Powell, E, *The Royal Liverpool Children's Inquiry Report*, (Session 2000-1 HC 2001, London, TSO, available at: http://www.rlcinquiry.org.uk/download/index/htm

Rhodes, R, 'Rethinking Research Ethics', *American Journal of Bioethics*, 5(1), 2005, 7.

Rosenheim, ML, 'Supervision of the ethics of clinical investigations in institutions', *British Medical Journal*, 3, 1967, 429.

Rothmann, DG, 'Ethical and social issues in the development of new drugs and vaccines', *Bulletin of the New York Academy of Medicine*, 63, 1987, 557.

Royal College of Paediatrics and Child Health: Ethics Advisory Committee, 'Guidelines for the Ethical Conduct of Research Involving Children', *Archive of Diseases of Childhood*, 82, 2000, 177.

Royal College of Physicians, *Research Involving Patients*, 1990, London: Royal College of Physicians.

Royal College of Physicians, *Guidelines on the Practice of Ethics Committees in Medical Research with Humans*, 4th edn, 2007, London: Royal College of Physicians.

Royal College of Psychiatrists, *Guidelines for researchers and for research ethics committees on psychiatric research involving human subjects*, 2001, London: Royal College of Psychiatrists.

Royal College of Surgeons, *Facial Transplantation: Working Party Report*, 2004, London: Royal College of Surgeons, 19.

Roy-Toole, C, 'Illegality in the research protocol: the duty of research ethics committees under the 2001 Clinical Trials Directive', *Research Ethics Review*, 4(3), 2008, 111.

Rudolph, M, *et al*, 'A search for the evidence supporting community paediatric practice', *Archives of Disease Childhood*, 80, 1999, 257.

Salvulescu, J, 'Against: No consent should be needed for using leftover body material for scientific purposes', *British Medical Journal*, 325, 2002, 648.

Sample, I, 'Porton Down veterans had raised death rates after chemical warfare tests', *Guardian.co.uk*, 25 March 2009, available at: www.guardian.co.uk/science/2009/mar/25/porton-down-chemical-weapons-warfare-mortality

Santoro, MA, 'The ethics of clinical research conducted in private enterprises', in Santoro, MA, Gorrie, TA (eds), *Ethics and the Pharmaceutical Industry*, 2005, New York: CUP, 9–20.

Saunders, J, 'The role of research ethics committees', in Wells, F, Farthing, M, *Fraud and Misconduct in Biomedical Research*, 4th edn, 2008, London: Royal Society of Medicine, 108–118.

Schmidt, U, *Medical Films, Ethics and Euthanasia in Nazi Germany*, 2002, Husum: Matthiesen Verlag.

Schroter, S, Black, N, Evans, S, 'Effects of training on quality of peer review: randomised controlled trial', *British Medical Journal*, 328, 2004, 673.

Shamoo, AE, Resnik, DB, *Responsible Conduct of Research*, 2003, London: OUP.

Shapshay, S, Pimple, KD, 'Participation in Biomedical Research is an Imperfect Moral Duty: A Response to John Harris', *Journal of Medical Ethics*, 33, 2007, 414.

Shultz, MM, 'From informed consent to patient choice: a new protected interest', *Yale Law Journal*, 92, 1985, 219.

Silva, MC, *Ethical Guidelines in the Conduct, Dissemination, and Implementation of Nursing Research*, 1995, Washington DC: American Nurses Publishing.

Singh, I, 'Capacity and Competence in Children as Research Participants', *European Molecular Biology Organization Journal*, 8, 2007, 35.

Smith, J, 'Preventing Fraud', *British Medical Journal*, 302, 1991, 362.

Smith, R, 'Audit and Research', *British Medical Journal*, 305, 1992, 905.

Smyth, RL, 'Research with Children', *British Medical Journal*, 322, 2001, 1444.

Taylor, CM, Saunders, J, Davies, H, 'Research Ethics Committees and legal opinion', *Research Ethics Review*, 4(4), 2008, 165.

Taylor, M, 'Elderly couple die after gas cut off', *The Guardian*, 23 December 2003.

Thomson, JJ, 'The Trolley problem', *Yale Law Journal*, 94, 1985, 1395.

Tobias, JS, Souhami, RL, 'Fully Informed Consent can be Needlessly Cruel', *British Medical Journal*, 307, 1993, 119.

Turnberg, L, 'Common Sense and Common Consent in Communicable Disease Surveillance', *Journal of Medical Ethics*, 29, 2003, 27.

UK Biobank, available at http://www.ukbiobank.ac.uk/faqs/confidentiality.php and http://www.ukbiobank.ac.uk/faqs/results.php (last accessed June 2009)

UK Government Response to the Scrutiny Committee's Report on the Draft Mental Incapacity Bill, February 2004 (Cm 6121), also available online at: http://www.dca.gov.uk/pubs/reports/mental-incapacity.htm#part2

UKRIO, http://www.ukrio.org.uk/home/ (last accessed May 2009)

van Diest, PJ, 'For: No Consent Should be Needed for Using Leftover Body Material for Scientific Purposes', *British Medical Journal*, 325, 2002, 648.

Vollmann, J, Winau, R, 'Informed consent in human experimentation before the Nuremberg Code', *British Medical Journal*, 313, 1996, 1445.

Wade, D, 'Ethics, audit and all shades of grey', *British Medical Journal*, 330, 2005, 468.

Wakefield, A, 'Ileal-lymphoid-nodular hyperplasia, non-specific colitis, and pervasive development disorder in children', *Lancet*, 351, 1998, 637.

Walker, C, 'Police chiefs in Huntley row', *The Times*, 25 February 2004.

Walker, C, 'Police at fault for Soham says watchdog', *The Times*, 5 March 2004.

Walmsley, J, 'Normalisation, emancipator research and inclusive research in learning disability', *Disability and Society*, 16(2), 2001, 187.

Warlow, C, 'Should research ethics committees be observing the law or working by ethical principles?', *Research Ethics Review*, 1(1) 2005, 23.

Wedler, D, Shah, S, 'Should Children Decide Whether they are Enrolled in Non-Beneficial Research?', *American Journal of Bioethics*, 3, 2003, 1.

Weijer, C, 'Selecting subjects for clinical research: one sphere of justice', *Journal of Medical Ethics*, 25, 1999, 31.

Wells, F, Farthing, M, *Fraud and Misconduct in Biomedical Research*, 4th edn, 2008, London: Royal Society of Medicine.

White, W, 'UK agency to combat research misconduct', *British Medical Journal*, 330, 2005, 616.

Winterton, R, HC Deb, Vol 416, col 984, 15 January 2004.

World Medical Association, *Declaration of Geneva and International Code of Medical Ethics*, 2006, available at: http://www.wma.net/e/policy/c8.htm

World Medical Association, Declaration of Helsinki, *Ethical Principles for Medical Research Involving Human Subjects*, Sixth version adopted at the 52nd WMA, Edinburgh 2000, 2000, available at: http://www.wma.net/e/policy/b3.htm

World Medical Association, Declaration of Helsinki, *Ethical Principles for Medical Research Involving Human Subjects*, Ninth version adopted at the 59th WMA, Seoul 2008, 2008, available at: http://www.wma.net/e/policy/b3.htm

Index

Lightning Source UK Ltd.
Milton Keynes UK

171824UK00002B/11/P